To

Karen Janelle, Aaron Dean and Jordan Elisha

May their heartfelt investments in this book and in me return to them in many ways, and be passed along through them to others.

TRANSFORMING LEADERSHIP

New Skills for an Extraordinary Future

BY

TERRY D. ANDERSON

University College of The Fraser Valley

Abbotsford, British Columbia, Canada

Published by Human Resource Development Press, Inc.
22 Amherst Road
Amherst, Massachusetts 01002
1-800-822-2801
1-413-253-3488 (inside Massachusetts)

ISBN 0-87425-181-8

First Printing, June, 1992

Cover Design by Old Mill Graphics

Production Services by Susan Kotzin

Editorial Services by Terri Slocombe and Lisa Wood

Transforming Leadership

Transforming Leadership is for those people who have moved beyond HRD buzzwords and slogans. This book provides the individual manager, consultant, counselor, human resource executive, leadership team, and company a clear insight into the distinct elements that cultivate leadership. Through a straightforward, integrated method, the individual self-evaluates his or her leadership skills, then commences to enhance them by implementing specific actions. For anyone eager and serious about developing leadership, this book is an absolute must.

William C. Bean
Managing Partner, William C. Bean and Associates

Table of Contents

Preface

*"Institutionalizing a leadership-
centered culture is the ultimate
act of leadership."*

John Kotter
Harvard Business Review
May–June, 1990

Leadership development is an exciting but complex topic. But developing the competencies needed to be an effective leader is in a sense like going to the dentist or to the doctor. You have to find out what problems you have first. This is anxiety arousing. No one strongly desires to be examined unless they are serious about prevention and health, or at least wanting to avoid more serious disease. After you do a diagnosis of what strengths, problems and skill deficits you have, then you have to undergo a series of "treatments" in which ultimately you yourself must act as the doctor. You can find a mentor, engage in training programs, enroll in courses or take higher degrees, but ultimately your performance and the judge of your level of competency must reside within. This book will assist you to develop this "expert within" vantage point so that as you grow you will be able to say with confidence, like a professional should, "I know what I am doing."

When I began the task of writing *Transforming Leadership*, I was over-whelmed by the wealth of information, conflicting views, divergent theories and lack of integration surrounding our notion of what it is to be a leader. But I was also intrigued by the challenge of trying to integrate some nuggets and gems in this vast array of knowledge into some kind of workable whole. I felt it would be worthwhile to attempt to construct a model which could encompass a wider range of theory and practice but which would be applicable to the daily lives of leaders. I believe this integrated and com-prehensive approach to understanding leadership development is called for at this most difficult time when there is such a critical need for leaders to deal with problems and challenges which are ever complex and fast-changing. It is important that they gain an overarching view of leadership and a wider range of skills in response to more increasingly confounding changes and demands. These demands include: a more diverse workforce, global marketing competition, a faster pace of change, depersonalization due to technological change, and for many, increasing anxiety as we face the next ten to twenty years.

In their "Call for Executive Appreciation," Srivastva and Cooperrider (1990)* have expressed deep concern about the need for discernment of a positive direction for the decades ahead:

> ...the meaning of everything is under assault in this chaotic world. Many organizations have literally lost their way, and for this reason, virtually all are in some kind of process of deep search for a renewed sense of purpose—or soon will be. The modernist world is experiencing no temporary upset. When viewed from the eye of the postmodern hurricane, where the shared sentiments and affective ties between people have been tossed apart in an upheaval of the greatest historic magnitude, there is little question that the concerns raised by the authors of this book are among the most important in all of management thought.

The broad "mission" of this book is that individual readers would find opportunity and challenge to self-examine, gain a renewed sense of purpose, clarify their foundational beliefs, and gain a broad spectrum of knowledge and skills. In light of this stated purpose this book seeks to present a positive and hopeful approach: an integrative and innovative self-assessment curriculum—one which I hope can accomplish several objectives:

1. To act as a tool for the assessment of training requirements in order to pinpoint a manager's (or potential manager's) need to gain critical knowledge and skills in order to become a better leader of individuals, groups and organizations.

2. To function as an integrated knowledge and theory base which an executive, manager or supervisor can use as a planning guide for

---

* S. Srivastva and D. Cooperrider, *Appreciative Management and Leadership: The Power of Positive Thought and Action in Organizations*. (San Francisco: Josey-Bass, 1990), 2-3.

internalizing key knowledge "chunks" in areas that are self-assessed as scanty.

3. To provide a meta-theoretical base for the development of leaders who will, as they become more adept, be better enabled to develop others through training, coaching and mentoring activities.

4. To provide concentrated focus points for needed and specific "micro" skills training until competency is attained in the areas which have been determined to be necessary for an individual's effective leadership functioning.

5. To introduce new "awareness" and "versatility" skills which are needed to adapt to fast-changing and demanding environments—role, style and skill shifting skills.

6. To have this book serve to prepare leaders to deliver the *Leading Manager* program modules (presently under development), whether the paper-based version or the interactive video instructional (IVI) version of the program (which is planned for completion in 1993).

7. To point the reader toward innovative resources which can act as catalysts to facilitate further individual, group or organization development. Some of these resources are by many other authors, and some by me. Various works available through my publishing company, Consulting Resource Group International, Inc., are listed at the end of this book. I call your attention to the comprehensive personnel system, PeopleSystems Software, which is being released early in 1992.

To my knowledge, no other single leadership development book has provided such an overarching model for leadership development nor provided an accompanying training program able to target specifically and simultaneously the means for creating the strongest impact on personal, group and organizational effectiveness.

The need for such a book has become increasingly clear on two fronts—followers need leaders/managers who are concerned about effective strategic management and also about the human side of enterprise. They hunger for managers who inspire cooperation and creativity in reaching shared goals and dealing with planned and unexpected change. This rare combination of qualities and aptitudes encourages followers to be optimistic and to perform more effectively.

This book is not a book written out of alarm. Nor do I have any intent to cause anxiety for anyone by forecasting difficulty or doom. Rather, it is written to assist people to develop into more fully qualified leaders. It will also assist them in their preparation for further clarification and achievement of their sense of purpose in the overall scheme of life. It is a book that anticipates our best response to the exciting challenges we face as we move toward the end of this century.

Who Should Read this Book?

This book is intended for a *very diverse readership* audience. The generic knowledge and skills focus, and rich composite of competencies are needed by a wide range of professional leaders. The reader should expect to find examples of various concepts and skills from a wide range of working environments including business, education, health, social services, criminal justice and government. This broad focus was also intentional. There are many books written for leaders in various occupations but few books which contain knowledge and skills which can be applied from several disciplines. This book will provide a "bigger picture" of leadership competencies to anyone who is in a position of leadership, or who aspires to be.

In addition, *Transforming Leadership* has been designed with a special emphasis for **those who intend to lead leaders**: by those in consulting, training, coaching or mentoring roles. More specifically, this book is designed especially for **internal and external consultants, educators and trainers**, who are often in key positions of influence with senior people in organizations. In an ideal sense, good educators, consultants and trainers are the leaders of existing and future leaders. Yet most of the leaders who are already in key positions need further training and development, more support and greater encouragement. This book can help those who aspire toward senior leadership positions to develop their talents.

Perhaps more than anyone else, internal consultants and trainers are already in positions as potential "change agents" who can pass along the knowledge, skills and tools to senior people, who can in turn (through mentoring, training, counseling and coaching) pass them along to others under their influence. Some of these people who have been mentored will, of course, eventually move into more senior positions.

Transforming Leadership provides the content, structure and process for the development of those who want to be effective in preparing others to lead more effectively, whether they are managing, consulting, mentoring, training, counseling or coaching others' development.

The Japanese have utilized mentors to practice this kind of succession planning and leadership development for centuries. In North America, formalized mentoring programs are becoming established in large corporations like AT & T, Exxon, Kodak, Pacific Bell, Lytton Guidance and Control Systems, Motorola, Esso Resources, Allegheny Ludlum Steel Corporation, Varian Associates and many others. William Gray, Ph.D., and Marilynne Miles Gray, M.S., principals of The Mentoring Institute of British Columbia, have conducted formalized mentor training programs for the companies mentioned above utilizing the Mentoring Style Indicator, co-authored by Dr. Gray and me. Dr. Gray has also written the Afterword to this book in an effort to help establish the relationship between leadership skills development and effective mentoring. I see mentoring as an eventual consequence and outgrowth of an effective leadership development program.

However, **those who are newer to their external or internal consulting and training** professions are often lacking in key skills which they must have to be effective. For this reason they may need to develop in certain areas themselves prior to attempting certain projects. This book will act as a personal and professional development planning guide for these younger professionals, or for those who aspire to be. It can therefore function as a challenging orientation for those who plan to enter the fields of consulting or training.

Transforming Leadership is also aimed at **managers who have had successes in their leadership endeavors** but who want to "hone" their awareness and skills, or develop new skills which they lack. Many of this group of managers have had some training already in interpersonal skills, decision making, problem management, change management, or various other skills, but lack training in other critical leadership areas such as group and team development, meeting effectiveness, organizational needs and problems assessment, culture building or organizational effectiveness. This book will be a catalyst which can begin the filling in of some of these gaps.

It is also for those who are **new to the management or leadership arena**, have been timid in their leadership, are fearful due to lack of experience, and even for those who have not seen much success in their leadership endeavors. It is often from lack of knowledge, lack of skill, lack of wisdom (which comes primarily from direct experience), lack of opportunity, or because of fear that many leaders fail to have the kind of impact they would really like to have.

Transforming Leadership is appropriate reading for those who are in any positions of leadership in small, medium and large companies, or in agencies and institutions. It is for managers and supervisors who aspire to be managers. It is for educators, business people, social services professionals, therapists, counselors, health care professionals and others who also deal with the development of people and performance in systems (in organizations and groups).

Transforming Leadership could also be used by **undergraduate and graduate students** as a comprehensive introduction to the theory and practice of leadership in any course which has this introductory focus as its goal. For example, business degree programs such as B. Comm., M.B.A., Entrepreneurship, and Organizational Behavior, could benefit from a self-assessment and planning program such as this; and in other change agent programs such as M.A. programs in Human Resource Development, Organization Development, Counseling, Social Work and Criminal Justice. The book could be used as an adjunct to existing texts, and to update many university programs which are still functioning without any kind of overall theory and skills model or competency based training program. There is an important move afoot in many programs to provide *both* a liberal arts education and competency-based educational opportunites prior to graduation with a baccalaureate degree.

In addition to those in business and helping fields, managers in education, health, government and non-profit organization sectors could also benefit greatly from completing the self-assessment and planning activities as a matter of course while reading this book.

Lastly, *Transforming Leadership* is for **those who inevitably lead in the family unit** who wish to use these same knowledge and skills to stimulate and encourage the development of their spouses, their children and themselves. Even though the book focuses primarily on leadership in management-type positions, I have tried to write it in such a way that those who are also parents will find the book to be accessible. The reason for this is because they too are leaders on the grandest scale. Parents can potentially make more impact on our culture and our world than perhaps any other people.

A Desire for Integration and Comprehensiveness

The book grew out of my students', my colleagues', and my own search for an integrative model for developing self, others, and organizations which could be accessible and readily applicable. Attempting to integrate and apply several fields of knowledge normally taught in separate disciplines can be difficult and confusing, especially for people who have received little professional training or formal education. Unfortunately, most people seem neither to have the time nor the opportunity to "put it all together."

Therefore, this book is my effort at integrating several fields of knowledge and practice into one model which is transformable (like a set of "Legos," or modular units), so that later you can design your own unique version of it to suit your needs for different situations.

Incomplete understanding of leadership, what it is, and how it works has resulted in confusion, rigidity or vagueness in the minds of executives and managers as they have attempted to lead people and organizations toward higher achievement and effectiveness. As Bennis (1985)[*] has indicated:

> *Never have so many labored so long to say so little. Multiple interpretations of leadership exist, each providing a sliver of insight but each remaining an incomplete and wholly inadequate explanation. Most of these definitions don't agree with each other, and many of them would seem quite remote to the leaders whose skills are being dissected. Definitions reflect fads, fashions, political tides and academic trends. They don't always reflect reality and sometimes they just represent nonsense. It's as if what Braque once said about art is also true of leadership: The only thing that matters in art is the part that cannot be explained.*

If some of the definitions of leadership are confusing and contradictory, so much more overwhelming are the diverse theories and practices. Hopefully, this book will assist you to sort through some of this confusion and inspire you to apprehend within yourself some of the "art [of leadership]...that cannot be explained."

---

[*] W. Bennis and B. Nanus, *Leaders, Strategies for Taking Charge.* (New York: Harper and Row, 1985), 4.

Phrases like "managing strategic change," "the challenge of change," and "developing change agent skills..." are becoming a part of a new language which has been emerging in the human resource development field for the past decade.

A shift toward a more interdisciplinary approach is already occurring in the fields of communication, counseling and leadership. It is essential that professionals who educate others to work in human service, health, education, business, industry, the military and government organizations shift to broader and more integrative educational models if personal, interpersonal, organizational and social problems are to be more potently managed and better prevented. In order for this paradigm shift to be accelerated, a program similar to that is planned and under development. It is titled, *The Leading Manager*, and could be successfully implemented with all of the above groups of professionals.

The Leading Manager Program

To accompany this book, there are under development training modules for the *Leading Manager* program. These modules, in their generic forms will provide structure for the final forms, which can be custom-designed for each unique training environment. These paper-based training materials will eventually be developed into Interactive Video Instruction (IVI) programs which can be tailored to meet the needs of individual organizations.

This book, as a guide, provides the knowledge and the format for the training needs assessment (which can be self-administered or assessed by others), and the *Leading Manager* program modules provide the practice, feedback and training designs to move the learning process ahead significantly.

Prior to entering any one of the four levels of training, a one day self-assessment program is envisioned. This could occur on-site with existing managers who would receive his or her own training plan, or could occur off-site at an educational institution, training facility or even at a hotel. The self-assessment instrument, *The Leadership Skills Inventory* (LSI) (also currently under development), could also be administered to self or to others to more quickly determine the extent to which they perceive the manager or supervisor as exhibiting important knowledge, skills and abilities. It is envisioned that the *Leadership Practices Inventory*, developed by Barry Posner and Jim Kouzes, will also be used in the up-front self-assessment aspect of the *Leading Manager* program.

This entry level seminar will introduce the comprehensive skills development model for *Transforming Leadership* and will guide the manager or supervisor to assess the extent to which he or she really needs to experience the various modules of what will eventually be a personalized multi-media training program. This will spare people from having to go through training modules for which there is no need and maximize the effectiveness of training time and dollars.

This self-assessment program could also be administered by Interactive Video Instruction (IVI) and if a whole work group were to complete the assessment a group training plan could be tailored to fit that specific group of people.

After this initial assessment using the assessment and planning process in the book, *The Leadership Skills Inventory*, or the IVI assessment and planning program, The *Leading Manager* program will be implemented at one of the following of three levels:

The first level: is self-administered, self-planned and self-managed and uses this book as a self-assessment and professional development planning guide. The manager who utilizes the program at this level may already be experienced and adept at performing most skills, and will take advantage of the book to polish and further integrate his or her understanding and development. The IVI version of the knowledge and skills development sections of the program could also be highly appropriate for this first level of administration (when available).

The second level: is administered by a Consultant, Trainer and/or Mentor who would work with a leader on an individual and mutually agreed contractual basis (and optionally in conjunction with the IVI program) to assist in targeting for and accomplishing specific leadership knowledge and skills development goals, and to achieve specific organizational objectives. Individuals taking the program at this level would likely already be functioning as managers, but are in need of further skill and knowledge development in order to become more competent as leaders.

The third level: is designed as a group training program which can be conducted "in-house" in your organization, or during off-site training sessions. These sessions will be facilitated by qualified trainers who will provide you with live practice and feedback opportunities. The second and third levels are enriched by the use of the *Leading Manager* program practice modules and practice on IVI in specific skills areas.

The Experience of Humility

Of course, there's no doubt that this is a presumptuous book. And I would like to offer some insight into why I have chosen to write it when there are many who would criticize its breadth of scope and seemingly (to some) grandiose ideals. This book is perhaps more serious than many books currently in print. It challenges managers to examine and prepare themselves very deeply and personally in a wide range of areas of personal and professional life. To illustrate my concern, let me present an insightful personal letter I received from Robert Marx, Ph.D., Professor at the University of Massachusetts School of Management. His letter was in response to my first draft of the manuscript for this book. He so generously, but critically, wrote:

Dear Terry,

I have spent a lot of time with your marvelous book and marked all over it. I am in awe of your ability to get to the heart of leadership problems and bring together so many crucial resources that bear on these problems. I have tried to be critical (in the book editor sense) in a helpful way by asking questions that the managers who read this book may ask you.... I am asking the questions—Will a theory X, "hard line" type manager be motivated to stay with a book like this, and how can you help potential "converts" identify with your mission of assisting them to make a transforming impact on themselves, others and organizations?

My main concern about your book as a way of reaching the hard core, number-crunching managers (they need your book perhaps more than most?) is that there is not much "stroking" of their predicament—they often went to business school or the school of hard knocks and learned a way of doing business that placed second in priority the values, people, listening, etc. (keys to transforming leadership); and now the game has changed and they are scared, just like a true humanist, poet or spiritual person who doesn't trust floppy disks and other such technology.

Somewhere in your writing I feel you could tap into the needs and fears of these people by telling them that they are OK; that planning, pricing and other things they do well are a critical part of leadership, but that adding the transforming leadership part to those strengths will make it all work much better.

I think these managers want to know that sometimes there are employees who will not respond to any of these ideas and they may have to be disciplined or even fired. Once you tell them that transforming leadership won't always work I think you will get a lot fewer, "Yes, but's....." Your book seems preachy at times, and you will have to get around that or it could turn some people off.

My guess is that when you use these ideas in person with your clients, your warmth and charisma are important parts of the equation. When writing it, you have less opportunity to convey these messages.

Please let me know your reactions to these comments.

Bob

My first reaction to his letter was discouragement. I suspect that nearly all those who have done graduate work have experienced a kind sinking feeling when they receive such critical feedback about a work which they have written in their own blood. But I knew Bob was right. I also knew he was encouraging me, in a positive but critical manner.

I share his letter in the hope you will appreciate that despite the lofty aims of this book I am as much a struggling fellow voyager in the leadership arena as you are, and do not presume to be above anyone in worth or wisdom. As a post-secondary educator for 20 years, and an entrepreneur for the past 11 years, I personally and daily experience how difficult it is to implement what I have written in this book!

Acknowledgments

My deepest gratitude is toward my wife Karen, and our sons Aaron and Jordan, who have sacrificed dearly in their sharing of my vision that this book and the ideas in it will eventually make a positive difference in this wondrous world which is becoming so fraught with complexity and negativity. They have sacrificed time with me so that I could complete the work of this book. They knew this was a book about love, about the development of people, about our futures. They supported me in good faith with their energy, encouragement, and in providing ideas for some examples throughout the book. They also supported me through their confidence that I could finish the work when at times I wanted to abandon the project.

I also appreciate Darryl Plecas who has been a model of a transforming leader in many ways. He has had a positive and transforming impact on the individuals and organizations he has had contact with. He also was the source of great encouragement to me when many times I wondered if the work of writing the many necessary revisions of this book was worth the trouble. As a close colleague and friend, he provided a number of fun times, incredible laughter, and stress release when times got tough. His tenacious mental abilities also inspired me to stretch for more understanding and a larger gestalt as I did more and more research into the field of leadership.

I acknowledge and appreciate Gerard Egan of Loyola University of Chicago, who over twelve years ago was the original inspiration for me to write *Transforming Leadership*. In 1978, when I organized his visit to University College of Fraser Valley to give his first "People in Systems" workshop in Canada, I saw a vision for this book. I also thank him for originally agreeing to be on my doctoral committee for the Transforming Leadership project because this was a validation I needed at that time: to get started with the confidence of a leader in the field who I respected. I remember asking him what it was like to write a book: He replied, "It is the most difficult and rewarding of work."

I want to thank Everett Robinson for his faith in my ability as a creative thinker and writer. If he hadn't encouraged me to write some earlier works I may never have attempted this book. I also thank him for his incredible patience and assistance in inspiring me to develop "whole brain" thinking, especially in the left side of my brain. As a friend, Everett has inspired me to stay on track with my highest spiritual ideals and goals, one of which was to complete this book.

I appreciate Jim Kouzes who encouraged me to trust myself and complete this rather unconventional book in the way that I believed would meet real needs. I was tempted, because of this being my first published book, to write a rather conventional textbook on leadership. The success of his work, *The Leadership Challenge* (co-authored with Barry Posner), led me to believe that there is a place for books which point toward self-examination, a spiritual orientation, human values, human development and idealism.

I am grateful to Bob Marx of the University of Massachusetts, for being willing to take Gerry Egan's place on my doctoral committee when it became necessary for health reasons for Gerry to withdraw from his commitment in 1987. I appreciate his pouring over the manuscript for this book a number of times and giving me caring but critical feedback and even collegial mentoring regarding philosophy, practical meaning, structure, content and additional editorial issues. His understanding of the transformative "softer" aspects of leadership and the harder side of management helped to balance this book's presentation of ideas, and helped to round out my own perspective.

I am appreciative of Allen Ivey at the University of Massachusetts, who also served on my doctoral committee, and who has had a transforming impact on my thinking about helping others to develop. He challenged me through his work to more deeply understand and apply developmental theory: The "Style-shifting" concepts and methodologies included in this book are partly a result of our many "dialectic" encounters over the phone and in person during the past decade.

I also have a deep feeling of gratitude for hundreds of students in interpersonal communication courses at the University College of Fraser Valley, in leadership courses at Trinity Western University and in counseling courses at the University of British Columbia who have given me feedback about the clarity, practicality or difficulty they had with various parts of this book over a period of several years. I believe they were honest with me, and thanks to them I learned to throw out over one-third of what I normally would have tried to cover in one book, and to include some of what I may have never thought of on my own.

I warmly and appreciatively acknowledge Ted James who has kindly and patiently assisted me to develop more professional writing skills, and who through his editorial comments has sharpened the focus of this book and the organization of its contents.

Finally, on this day before Christmas, I find myself most deeply appreciating and acknowledging the Spirit of my Christian heritage, the power of which I experience and know to be the driving force behind my writing this book.

Terry Anderson
Abbotsford, British Columbia, Canada
December 24, 1991

Foreword

by Gerard Egan
January, 1992
Chicago, Illinois

Transforming Leadership is an attempt to present a new synthesis of much of the knowledge, skills, and tools which managers and leaders need in these turbulent times. It is a unique book in that the reader has an opportunity to complete self-appraisals in a wide range of leadership-related skill areas. These appraisals can then be used to formulate a specific skills training agenda. While Mintzberg (1989) vividly portrayed the somewhat chaotic nature of moment-to-moment management, Anderson's book presents a fresh understanding of the complexity of moment-to-moment leadership—the kind which can have a transformative impact on individuals, groups, and organizations. *Transforming Leadership* reviews previous theories, introduces an overarching model to integrate them, identifies the critical skills sets required for leadership success, and provides role, style, and skill "shifting" guidelines for enhancing the situational effectiveness of leadership behavior.

There is a need for this book. Many have observed that many managers and executives in key positions have skill deficits in certain areas of their lives. These deficits prevent them from being all that they might. For instance, many find it difficult to strike a balance between attending to both the task and relationship aspects of their work, a problem Gabarro (1991) has identified as a formidable barrier to both management and leadership. Too many managers and leaders lack versatility in the ways in which they approach both people and situations. They find it difficult to identify and name what it is that they lack. Deficits in self-management, interpersonal communication, problem management, and consultative skills account for many of the problems leaders face in their day-to-day work.

The primary reason for this lack is that few people in management and leadership positions are given an opportunity to accurately pinpoint their strengths, weaknesses, and needs for training in critical skills areas. MBA programs, which one would hope could provide leaders with such self-assessment capabilities and skills development, are just beginning to include the three "C's" in their curricula: Communication, Counseling, and Consulting. Even fewer people in leadership positions have taken advantage of opportunities for university or non-university training which could help them face difficult leadership challenges. As an obvious example, we have all seen the tragic blind spot of well educated people in important positions with respect to their ability to listen to others. Chris Argyris (1986) has spent years in challenging what he once called the "skilled incompetence" of managers and leaders. The very communication skills in which they pride themselves often subvert the communication process itself. *Transforming Leadership* addresses issues such as these and provides a road map for ongoing leadership development.

Much of the literature on leadership has focused on the "big" things that need to be done to face the difficult challenges of moving into the 21st century. Far less has been written on how leaders can inwardly examine and prepare themselves for these challenges. Unlike most other books on the topic, *Transforming Leadership* suggests that leadership development begins at the center of leaders themselves; it is a self-conscious and intentional process. It involves the whole person of the leader as he or she interacts with and has an impact upon both individuals and social systems at all levels within companies and institutions.

When it comes to leadership, the position, strategy, and goodwill are not enough. Having "heart" as described by Posner and Kouzes (1987) is essential; clear beliefs, values, commitments, ethical and moral instincts, and the skills outlined above are the cornerstones of leadership behavior. "Know Thyself" is as good advice today as it was in ancient Greece.

Gareth Morgan (1988), in *Riding the Winds of Change* calls for a "competence mindset" in the preparation and development of managers. *Transforming Leadership* provides an overarching model for the development of basic, but critical skills and competencies and highlights how these must be tailored to different situations. Style, skill, and role shifting are concepts which challenge the reader to explore the kind of versatility that leads consistently to the kind of "results beyond the ordinary" (Egan, 1992), that constitute the essence of leadership.

Argyris, C. (1986). "Skilled Incompetence." *Harvard Business Review,* September-October, 74–79.

Egan, G. (1992). *Adding Value: A Blueprint for Taking Management and Leadership Seriously.* San Francisco: Jossey-Bass. In press.

Gabarro, J.J. (1991). "Retrospective Commentary." *Harvard Business Review,* November-December, 108–109.

Kouzes, J. and Posner, B. (1987). *The Leadership Challenge: How to Get Extraordinary Things Done in Organizations.* San Francisco: Jossey-Bass.

Mintzberg, H. (1989). *Mintzberg on Management.* New York: Free Press.

Morgan, G. (1988). *Riding the Waves of Change: Developing Managerial Competencies for a Turbulent World.* San Francisco: Jossey-Bass.

Chapter 1

▼

INTRODUCTION

Unlike physical assets,
competencies do not deteriorate:
As they are applied and shared, they grow.

Gary Hamel

The Challenge of Adapting to Change

We can respond to changing conditions in different ways. We can stalk the territory like wolves of destruction seeking new opportunities for gratifying selfish ends. We can wander aimlessly behind others, like sheep lost in a fog of indecision. Or we can soar as birds of creative change, rising above the clouds of mediocrity and inspiring others to achieve cooperative fulfillment.

Transforming leaders are those who have inwardly decided to grow into being more conscious, developed, skilled, sensitive and creative participants. They strive to make positive differences in organizations and in the lives of others wherever they go.

They climb the heavens, reaching beyond the ordinary, the predictable, the average; charting new territories and possibilities. They reach up for leadership from those who are wiser, and pull others "below" them upward to greater, unseen heights on the way. This is no mean feat, especially in a rapidly changing world where it seems that many people will belittle such lofty ideals.

Of course, the ability to adjust successfully to changing environmental circumstances has always presented people with a challenge. Today, however, not only is the sheer pace of change occurring at an ever more rapid rate but the characteristics of these changes are increasingly different as well. It's almost as though the nature of change itself appears to be changing.

Our response to change, therefore, may need to be qualitatively different too. When economic changes occur slowly or in localized areas, the existing systems and procedures can always be amended, altered, or adjusted to suit the new conditions. But when the change is wholesale and its extent is widespread, the prevailing mechanisms simply cannot adjust swiftly enough to make the necessary corrections. A spiral of declining productivity, efficiency, and morale begins to spin, pulling an organization or a whole industry into a vortex of failure. A recent example of this is that General Motors is facing a major crisis in 1992 and beyond. Before long, the problem is no longer the severity of the external threats but the inadequacy of the internal systems for dealing with those threats.

Under these circumstances, as Rosabeth Moss Kanter pointed out in *The Change Masters* (1983),[1] the only effective response is to embrace the need for internal change in order to meet the challenges being created by external change:

> *As America's economy slips further into the doldrums, innovation is beginning to be recognized as a national priority. But there is a clear and pressing need for more innovation, for we face social and economic changes of unprecedented magnitude and variety, which past practices cannot accommodate and which instead require innovative responses. (p. 19)*

Over the past decade, managers, executives and corporate decision-makers across North America have struggled to respond to this challenge in the face of severe international competition. Many have achieved considerable success by restructuring their organizations and improving their production lines and levels of service. They strove for "excellence" and produced some excellent results.

But the intensity with which managers have had to push toward excellence in order to stay afloat and compete has too often been at the expense of losing balance in their business and in their personal lives, damaging their physical health, marital and family harmony and even eroding their general outlook on life.

Hence, as we move further into the 1990s, we are confronting a kind of "excellence burnout" within a considerable number of people. In the 1980s, the pendulum swung so much in favor of external performance, account-

---

1   R. M. Kanter, *The Change Masters* (New York: Simon and Schuster, 1983).

ability and technological innovation, that many people are now experiencing a need for reassessment, for renewal, for a time of "unstressing," and for a turning "inward" to re-examine first principles.

"We got so caught up in our techniques, devices and programs that we forgot about the people—the people who produce the product or service and the people who consume it," suggested Tom Peters (1985)[2]. Perhaps in the same way, we have since become so caught up in the management of business that we have forgotten to train people in the art of being able to lead others. Instead we have fallen into the mistakes of over-managing and under-leading.

The Challenge of Integrating Diversity

More than half of North America's workforce now consists of minorities, immigrants, and women. White males will make up only about 15% of the increase in the workforce over the next 10 years. As summarized by Thomas (1990)[3]:

> Today the melting pot is the wrong metaphor even in business, for three good reasons. First, if it ever was possible to melt down Scotsmen and Dutchmen and Frenchmen into an indistinguishable broth, you can't do the same with blacks, Asians, and women. Their differences don't melt so easily. Second, most people are no longer willing to be melted down, not even for eight hours a day—and it's a seller's market for skills. Third, the thrust of today's nonhierarchical, flexible, collaborative management requires a ten- or twentyfold increase in our tolerance for individuality.

As our world is becoming increasingly what McLuhan called a global village, we must realize the incredible potential in valuing the diverse perspective and talent of each person, and learn to assist people of divergent values, beliefs and backgrounds to weave their efforts into a fabric of life and work styles which could ultimately benefit each individual and the community as a whole: the ultimate "multiple-win." In order to achieve this valuing of diversity people who have very distinct and seemingly "exclusive" belief systems (such as those who adhere to Islamic, Jewish and

---

2   T. J. Peters, *A Passion for Excellence: The Leadership Difference* (New York: Random House, 1985).

3   R. Thomas, "From Affirmative Action to Affirming Diversity," *Harvard Business Review.* (March-April, 1990), vol. 68, no. 2.

Christian faiths, for example) will need to develop awareness and skill in communicating respect and value to those who stand outside their belief positions. Likewise, those who espouse more universalistic belief systems (such as existential humanists, "new-agers," and Unitarians, for example) will need to develop awareness, appreciation and skill in communicating respect and value toward those whose perspective appears to them to be more linear and specifically tied more deeply to historical roots. As Srivastva Cooperrider (1990)[4] have elucidated:

> ...the deepest assumptions of society and science are shifting at the same fundamental level that they did at the time of the scientific revolution in the seventeenth century—then as the authors of this book submit, the postmodern twenty-first century will likely be as different from modern society as the modern was from medieval times. But since no new metaphysic will necessarily be locked in place, and since no preceding ones will be altogether negated, the questioning of value systems will surge to the fore: Value dynamics will be thrust center stage and the prime unit of relational exchange governing the creation or obliteration of social existence. Organizing, one might foretell, will no longer be confined to the metaphor of machine, but will instead be seen as a living value system—a multiperspective colloquy of valuing.

The Goal of Transforming Leadership

This book aims to redress some of the imbalance wrought in the stress of adapting to difficult changes and offer preparation for difficulties which will be encountered when attempting to integrate diversity. It seeks to provide you with a model you can use as a leader, or potential leader, to develop yourself, diverse types of people, and the families, groups, communities or organizations with whom you live and work. With the knowledge, skills and tools presented in this book, you will be better able to make a positive difference, in whatever roles you find yourself, as parent, spouse, teacher, social worker, worker, manager, supervisor, counselor, consultant or executive. It seeks to place on the table for your access some of the most useful knowledge, skills, and tools which are based on previous theory, research and practice from the fields of personal development, communication,

---

4   S. Srivastva and D. Cooperrider and Associates, *Appreciative Management and Leadership*, 6.

counseling, consulting, human development and organization development.

You probably have not encountered a model like this for your own development as a leader which charts the territory of leadership development and assists you to envision yourself passing through. It will be a challenge for you to see where you stand and to gain some highly specific knowledge, skills and tools which you can use to assist you to move ahead in your development. But that is a challenge worth embracing.

Your development can be achieved in a number of ways. It is possible to develop leadership capabilities through contact with key people who act as mentors (see the Afterword in this book). You can also enhance your likelihood for success as a leader through structured educational experiences and training programs. But the most crucial element in the process is your initial and ongoing, conscious decision to develop yourself as a person or manager who can lead. A person who becomes a leading manager or transforming parent decidedly intends to do so, understands the steps in becoming one, and sets out on a life-long course to build this goal into an expanding reality.

Therefore, it is my "mission" in writing this book to assist you to achieve a thorough self-assessment of your leadership, to develop a plan for comprehensive growth as a leader who manages people and organizations more effectively (whether you are a parent or a chief executive officer), and to learn to intentionally utilize key skills and tools which will assist you to make more effective leadership impact as a result of more innovative thought, more effective words and more empowering actions.

Transforming Leadership offers this sort of a structured opportunity for self-assessment and self-development. In doing so, it will assist you to accomplish five main objectives:

1. To identify gaps in your knowledge, education, training and experience.
2. To formulate a plan for your own short and long range personal and professional development as a leader.
3. To develop key areas of knowledge and skill which will round out your skills repertoire as a leader.
4. To target opportunities for you to begin applying desired knowledge and skills immediately in your personal life and work environments.

5. To use this book as an adjunct to an existing program in which you may be involved, or to initiate a new training program which could be designed for you individually.

Transforming Leadership acts as a catalyst to develop individuals who have the desire and potential to become agents of critical development in their organizations. Therefore, it my sincere hope that as a result of reading this book you will, over time, increasingly become a transformative leader of other people who will also better lead others because of your influence. But, to achieve this, people who seek to become leaders must first develop themselves from the inside out.

Your Development From the Inside Out

Successful leadership development, at its best, begins on the inside, develops its strength on the home front, finds an environment which is in harmony with its vision, beliefs and purpose, and grows in stature both at home and in the work place.

A General Definition of Leadership

To "lead" in this book means to exert a transforming and developmental impact on people, groups and organizations for the purpose of enhancing the quality of life and the effectiveness of your own and others' performances, whether at home, at work or in other environments.

Consequently, this book heads inward to explore what lies at the core of leadership behavior with the intention of having its impact ripple outward to effect planned changes in self, other individuals, work groups, and organizations, including community organizations and the family system.

Turning inward (while remaining outwardly mindful and active) is a preparatory step toward developing leadership ability, much in the same way as when Luke Skywalker in *Star Wars* had to learn to rely on a new inward directing of attention toward "The Force" when fighting "the good fight" against an invisible enemy.

The same principle of inward focus for improved outward performance can be seen in the accomplished musician who seeks to communicate subtleties of expression while playing a well-known classical or jazz piece of music.

Mother Theresa is another example of one who has consistently demonstrated tremendous inner intensity of concentration in the face of serving the hungry and diseased world she confronts on a daily basis. She could easily be considered a transforming leader.

I believe that the pace of change that we face at this time in world history will force us to turn inward to re-examine some of our fundamental assumptions about life in general, and more specifically about human interaction and organizational life. For many individuals, this turning inward will provoke a profound re-examination of their system of values and beliefs, their concept of "self" and their view of the world and the universe as a whole. As we are confronted with what existentialists call an increasing sense of "thrown-ness" into an accelerating and seemingly unclear future, the need for inner clarity and strength will be particularly felt by those in positions of leadership. They will feel the weight of responsibility for helping to develop others in their communities and organizations.

Personal assumptions about what is true and what isn't, between what has intrinsic value and what doesn't, and between what is good and what is bad will be re-examined with unusual intensity. In turn, commitments to belief positions will more than likely be made out of necessity rather than out of philosophical speculation. The desire is already strong among many community leaders to generate a "strengthening of what remains" as we move into this last decade of the twentieth century. They sense that what is "brewing" on the horizon may require unusual strength of character and wisdom. *Transforming Leadership* provides a structured opportunity for developing this important inner architecture of beliefs, values, ethics, priorities, plans and abilities.

But more than a strengthening is required. In order to deal with what is likely to come, we need to become transformable and transformed. We need to engender a positive transforming impact in our encounters with people, groups, and organizations in our own and other countries. Wisdom, flexibility, innovation, versatility, and creativity will all surely be key ingredients for success and will determine the quality of life in the decades to come.

While the personal development of one individual can spread and inspire personal development in others, the personal development of leaders can cause a wave of influence in groups and whole communities of people. This is because leaders are in such strategically important positions that they can, if they so choose, reach large numbers of people.

To deal with the urgent need to manage change effectively, we cannot simply hope that the qualities of leadership will naturally develop at random in a handful of people. Instead, we need to seek the intentional development of leadership abilities in as large a number of people as possible.

Vast numbers of managers, supervisors, principals, teachers, counselors, as well as parents and community officials, will need to become "charged" with a new sense of positive purpose because they are justifiably stressed and discouraged by a number of negative developments.

Ultimately, I believe that a transformation of the inner and deepest part of a person is what is required to release the strength and wisdom that will be needed to meet the challenges ahead of us. For me, such a transformation has occurred to an extent and is continuing as a result of a life-long spiritual search, which is intensely personal, but one which I would share with anyone. The search process I went through and the steps involved will be discussed in a new book I am writing titled, *Living on Purpose: Understanding Your Personal Search*.

It is important for me to emphasize that I also believe that *Transforming Leadership* can act as a kind of psychological and behavioral preparation for such an inner transformation, but by itself will not produce such a profound change as the one to which I refer. I believe that such a transformation in spirit must be desired and sought after by each individual after he or she believes it to be a real possibility. Therefore, I take the stance that developing knowledge and skills is a valid preparation for more profound inner development.

Organizational and Social Change Occurs on the Inside First

Development within individual leaders and followers must occur prior to positive social change. If we can harness a training technology which will assist people in their developmental process we will be of great help to many people both directly and indirectly. This is the task and the challenge of the transformative leader: to develop self, then other individuals, then groups and organizations.

This is the case whether the goals of development are focused on the spiritual, emotional, mental, interpersonal, group or organizational aspects of life. People either facilitate or retard the development of other people. Leaders can be developed to pass along their expertise to other leaders who can pass it along to followers who will become leaders, etc.

An example of a program which prepares such leaders is the Community and Organization Development program (CORD). In the mid-1970s Gerard Egan spearheaded this program at the Loyola University of Chicago. Graduates from such programs (and there are a number of these types of graduate schools developing, especially in North America) go out as consultants and managers into the marketplace to more knowledgeably and skillfully develop individuals, organizations and communities. By the time they have completed the CORD program, for example, they have been well introduced to a broad band of skills and a wide range of knowledge in how to develop people and organizations. But very few of the managers who need such knowledge and skills can go back for this kind of a graduate degree. *Transforming Leadership* acts as a catalyst to make such knowledge and skills available to a wider range of people.

An example from the corporate world includes the Eastman Kodak head office in Rochester, New York where they have instituted a formalized mentoring program: key managers are being trained to pass on their expertise and knowledge to their eventual successors. Although these and other programs are innovative and inspiring, *Transforming Leadership* provides a theoretical and practical introduction to a life-long personal and professional development process which, in an important way, goes beyond such training. Mentors must have a foundation of skills and knowledge in order to successfully "pass the torch" to those who are willing to continue running the race.

Training has to begin inside each individual's awareness with a self-assessment, then an assessment by others occurs in some kind of training and feedback process, then practice in a laboratory environment, then practice and feedback in an ongoing mentoring arrangement (ideally), then independent practice, then action takes place in a real work assignment. This kind of process creates challenging opportunities for people's development and advancement.

These steps resemble flight training for pilots: first they study the knowledge that is required of flying and instrumentation, then they fly in a simulator and receive feedback, then they go up with their instructor, then they fly solo, and finally they take on jobs and various other types of flight missions. How much more so should leaders have opportunity to receive adequate training! In a sense the world's leaders fly whole organizations, countries, and even fly the earth itself (in that it is possible for them to cause it to crash)!

Transforming Leadership provides the theoretical background and structure for such development to occur. The *Leading Manager* training program provides the process for the training goals to be realized.

The Critical Care Factor

Perhaps the greatest need of all is and will be for those in leadership positions to know and act from the Spirit of Love, to care deeply about others, self, life; and to understand the "mechanics" of caring, the know-how of caring, or even the skills of caring, if you will. Perhaps those leaders who demonstrate potent caring for others are the ones who are able to inspire respectful and powerful following responses in others. Without caring, leading is dead and managing is dry.

Authority Is Not Power

Authority is not enough for managers anymore, they need to harness and direct the most significant source of power for positive change which is within the large numbers of people who can be inspired to follow their visions and examples. By writing this book I have tried, at least in my own ways, to contribute to this important preparation of leaders. It is my hope that this book will stimulate and facilitate an increased personal clarity and development for leaders and potential leaders at the spiritual, intellectual, emotional, interpersonal and even physical levels. I also hope that leaders will be moved, touched or otherwise educated by what they read in this book and thereby will be more empowered to touch the lives of others more deeply, potently, effectively and in a more caring manner.

A Portrait of a Good, Undeveloped Manager

One clear example of the difficulty of being a good manager but a poor leader is that of Rodney Ruff (fictitious name). After having completed a B.S. in Mechanical Engineering and having worked as an engineer in a Fortune 500 company in North America for 5 years, Rod enrolled in a master of business administration program, graduated, worked for 5 years in personnel at one of the Fortune 500 companies and then moved into teaching management courses at a university.

At his first big job after graduating with the MBA, he did well managing the human resource function where everything was performance driven and production standards were concretely defined, and he even contributed to the clarity of their definition. He developed innovative systems for tracking employee performance-to-standards and coupled that with rewards or disciplinary action. His system saved the company well over a million dollars in one year. He got raving performance reviews from his superiors for the business results he achieved, and no one minded terribly that he was interpersonally ineffective.

However, he was having a difficult time with the less concrete informality of relating to students at his new job at the university, and seemed to be officially friendly but role-bound as "El Professor." He believed that he had to prepare his business students for the "real world" and tried not to emphasize the people side of things for fear of seeming too "soft" and "unrealistic." His students reported being bored with his classes and complained that he lacked any personal interest in their success or development. His teaching evaluations suffered to the point that his job was in jeopardy.

Rod's "official business" attitude spilled over into his marriage and his relationships with his children where he expected performance and accountability. They were distanced and hurt by this impersonal approach which was lacking in careful understanding of their feelings and views, to the point that his wife threatened to leave him if he did not change into a softer, more understanding, gentle and patient man.

The irony is that under the veneer of this business-oriented approach is a person who is very sensitive to others and deeply concerned for the welfare of others. Rod did not learn that as a manager who leads it is his responsibility to be effective at both the task and relationship aspects of his business and family management practices.

Rod learned about the general importance of interpersonal skills, but was not trained in business school to develop these skills to the point of competency. He even read books which described the importance of the people side of enterprise, and read a book which described the bottom line impact of human resource development, but he never learned and developed the new language and skills required to become able to shift effectively from task to relationship behaviors and back again. He had some knowledge but lacked working knowledge, skills and interpersonal development.

His performance in this "style shifting" from task to people and back again was inconsistent and jerky at best. Employees and students resented his overbearing impersonality and some even refused to perform better because of the way he delivered his messages to them with a matter of fact, but facetiously friendly manner: "My way or the highway." In my consultations with Rod regarding the results of an employee opinion survey which he agreed to allow me to conduct on his first job as Manager of Human Resources, he said that he couldn't see what everyone was so upset about— look at the results he was getting on the bottom line!

At his corporate job as Personnel Manager he complained that people didn't understand the pressure he was under and that he didn't have time to play "patsy" with people who were "whiners," including his wife and kids. Couldn't they understand that he was working so hard to achieve his standards for their own benefit as well as his? After all, they would all get raises or rewards if production went up enough!

Later, during a session I had with him, he conceded that he could perhaps improve "some" in this area of interpersonal effectiveness and agreed to take a competency based interpersonal skills course at a local college. Because he was concerned about the stability of his marriage relationship as well, he and his wife also came to me for six sessions of basic interpersonal skills training to improve the quality of their interactions, which were often one-way. During these sessions it was very difficult for him to admit that he was in fact grossly failing in this critical area of establishing a mutual decency and respect in relationships. He wasn't respecting others and wasn't earning the respect (or performance) of others. After the six sessions he was engaging in more effective two-way communication with his wife and gained a real sense of control and self-esteem from that experience, which motivated him to make it work on the job as well.

Rod's inner clarity regarding his beliefs about life, human nature and his sense of purpose prior to this were not very developed. He worked hard to attempt to write out his own statements of belief around life's key issues. This helped him to define himself in relation to others, in relation to ultimate values and beliefs, and in realizing that inner clarity of beliefs, purpose and goals is critical to his well being and longer-term success.

It's been over 5 years now, and he has integrated his new people skills with a new understanding of how to develop humane corporate and family culture: He is positively addicted to the new patterns because he is getting even better and more consistent production results at work, and has developed more satisfying relationships with his employees, his wife and children. What was on the verge of falling, rose to unexpected heights.

This is a success story. There are far more stories of "successful" business people who have turned away from the responsibility and challenge of making the people-connection work well. They often try to compensate for being undeveloped by overworking and over proving their value in their achievements or in the financial department. This book is about how to develop balance toward completion in your personal, interpersonal, corporate and professional life. It will assist you to capitalize on your abilities to manage well, while at the same time you will become more effective at making a leadership difference in the personal and corporate lives of others.

In a deeper sense, Rod moved from being a "Following Manager" (one who follows traditional expectations for bottom-line results) to becoming a "Leading Manager" (one who gets both people and better bottom-line results). Before, Rod followed his narrower engineering and business training and over depended on it at the expense of broader and deeper learning. As he developed, he became broadened inwardly, grew in heart and in wisdom about what the impact of leading and developing other people can have on longer term organizational effectiveness.

It Won't Work With Some People: The Free Will Factor and the Irregular Person Theory

Even if you were to learn all the knowledge, skills and wisdom there is it would obviously not work with everyone. Each person has a free will and a unique perspective on life at the moment. There are also some "irregular people" who are not going to respond to others' efforts to assist them to grow or change possibly because they are just quirky or strange "ducks." Some people are even, it would appear, consciously destructive to others and to organizations. This book will assist you to identify the developmental level of these "resistant" people, and their readiness to receive various leadership interventions from you or from others around them. It will also refer you to a systematic personnel process by which disciplinary action or dismissal can legally and fairly occur (Anderson and Zeiner, 1989).[5]

---

5   T. Anderson, and B. Zeiner, *Selecting and Developing Exceptional Employees with the Comprehensive Personnel System*. (Abbotsford, B.C. Canada: Consulting Resource Group International, Inc.: 1989).

Why Leaders Can't Lead

Lastly, there are some other key reasons why leaders have become discouraged, and many reasons why potentially good leaders are fearful to exercise real leadership, even when they are in positions where there is greater opportunity. There has even been a book written in part about "why leaders can't lead." Bennis (1976)[6] writes that leaders can't lead because:

1. They give in to the pressures of continuing the status quo.
2. They try to do too much too soon in order to impress others.
3. They allow others to put too many monkeys on their backs.
4. They fail to get others to see the value of true leadership, and settle instead for day-to-day management of operations.
5. They allow themselves to be crippled by bureaucratic machinery.
6. They fail to set clear cut, challenging but realistic goals so that real contributions can be made due to their innovative leadership.

Know-How and Competencies Are Required

The American Society for Training and Development and the United States Department of Labor conducted a two-year research project which delineated key areas of know-how and competency which can be translated into trainable "microskills." These were the skills identified as "Workplace Basics: The Skills Employers Want" (Carnevale, 1988). [7] The skills identified included reading, writing and arithmetic skills which we would expect, but beyond this were listed the critical "life" or people skills of interpersonal communication, problem solving, decision making, goal setting, motivation, negotiation and leadership. Transforming leadership theory asserts that all of these skills must be at the disposal of effective leaders, not just skills typically thought of as "leadership" skills.

But even this formidable list of skills has holes in it if we were to use it as a skills map for training leaders. And skills training itself can become robotic and stilted unless training programs are in and of themselves intense life experiences which are truly developmental and life-changing. This is far

---

6   W. Bennis, *The Unconscious Conspiracy — Why Leaders Can't Lead* (New York: AMACOM, 1976).

7   Anthony P. Carnevale et al., "Workplace Basics: The Skills Employers Want," *Training and Development Journal* (Oct. 1988).

more the case in training human skills than when training technical skills. Thus, it is necessary to train trainers, executives, managers and leaders to pass on critical skills in the context of their everyday settings, through communicating, coaching, counseling and in formalized mentoring programs—where contracts to learn meaningful skills are committed to by both parties. *Transforming Leadership* provides a structure and a vehicle for such a versatile leadership development program. There is also a set of assessment tools which can optionally be used with this book to train mentors to be more effective, and to match mentors and proteges in formalized mentoring programs (Gray and Anderson, 1990).[8] This book can also be used to train mentors to be more effective.

Let us now examine the importance of good management as a required climate or "stage" that must be set for the emergence of transforming leadership in individuals, groups and organizations.

Management: The Foundation of Leadership

Webster's New World Dictionary[9] definition of "manage" suggests that its root meaning is in the Latin word "manus" (hand); and it means to 1) control the movement of behavior, 2) have charge of, to direct; 3) succeed in accomplishing.

This definition is close to what is in the minds of many managers who have to deal with the constant concern of the bottom line. The day-to-day realities of even some top level managers are so concrete and often quantified that their attention is captured by the demands of realities which require decisions and action.

But we are entering a time when change and the ability to foresee and adapt to the future is already of critical importance. To get an in-depth look at these changes I recommend reading the book which goes beyond *Megatrends* in its specificity: *Supermanaging,* by Arnold Brown and Edith Weiner.[10] In this future all of the important things inherent in good management will continue to be a critical foundation for the success of

---

8   W. Gray and T. Anderson, *The Mentoring Style Indicator* (Vancouver, B.C., Canada: The International Centre for Mentoring, 1990).

9   D. Guralnik (ed.), *Webster's New World Dictionary* (New York: Simon and Schuster, 1984).

10 A. Brown and E. Weiner, *Supermanaging* (New York: New American Library, 1984).

businesses and other organizations. With the current emphasis on the development of leadership, we do not want to lose sight of the true value of the key management functions.

These important management functions are planning, deciding, organizing, controlling, accounting and researching. Without these six critical functions continuing to be performed well there will obviously be little or no opportunity for leadership innovation and intervention. The paradox of the above statement, and of management, is that it has to be positive and innovative leadership vision which designs, implements and sustains appropriate and effective management practices. For example, an effective people leader in an ill-managed organization will have to put out too many fires and flounder to the point of not being able to exercise any significant leadership impact. Successful organizations depend critically on both management and leadership capabilities and the demands of the future will require even better management and excellent leadership.

Therefore good leaders implement effective management practices which set the stage and provide the opportunities for transforming leadership to move and have its being. As in any endeavor, we cannot create until we have established a baseline of materials and options. Iacocca could not have created a transforming leadership impact had the stage not been set with some good management in place. Management is the more visible and concrete part of organizational life. It is the "left brain," analytical, result oriented, linear, sequential, logical, rational part of the picture. Leadership impacts the more nonrational, relational, creative, visionary, "right-brain" side of things. Management tends to be high-tech, leadership "high-touch." Transforming leadership is the integrated technology of "high-tech-touch" for individual, group and organizational development.

A graphic presentation of the process of an organization, managers and employees moving from a traditional management orientation to a transforming leadership orientation can be developmentally charted as seen on the next page.

Stage One: In the practice of management, it is necessary for MANAGERS to provide the goals, structures and policies for controlling and monitoring organizational life. Followers often have no say whatsoever in how the organization is to be structured or how objectives will be achieved. Even how jobs get done is controlled by standard operating procedures.

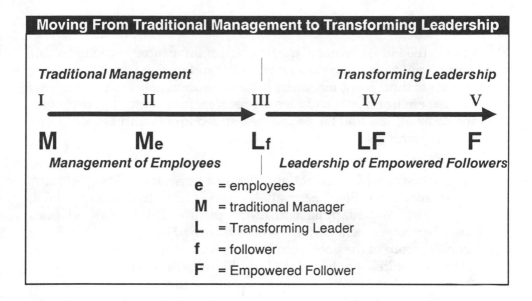

Moving From Traditional Management to Transforming Leadership

Traditional Management | *Transforming Leadership*

I   II   III   IV   V

M   Mₑ   Lf   LF   F

Management of Employees | *Leadership of Empowered Followers*

    e   = employees
    M   = traditional Manager
    L   = Transforming Leader
    f   = follower
    F   = Empowered Follower

Stage Two: Management must continue in stage two to manage and control the activities of their employees. In stage two of a developing organization the employees have little say in how things will be done or even what will be done.

Stage Three.   In stage three however, as the MANAGER assumes a transforming leadership stance, he or she becomes a leader with followers who begin, with supervision, counseling and coaching to participate in the planning and the implementation of goals, responsibilities and strategies for achieving organizational objectives.

Stage Four: In stage four, after some development has taken place in the followers, leaders move more into the background in a supportive and consultative role as followers become more capable of taking the lead in running their own work groups and achieving objectives on their own. In fact, it is at this stage that followers begin to make real contributions—empowerment is set into motion.

Stage Five: Eventually, in stage five, highly competent leading FOLLOWERS sit around the planning table to design departmental objectives and plans for change without the direct supervision of top management.

Leadership: The Creative Development of Management

Managers in the industrial era of the first half of this century used to be able to strategize, put a plan into place, fine tune it and manage its operation for long periods of time. Now, managers have to continuously scan the internal and external environments and identify reasons for change, opportunities for improvement, and find the people best suited to create and execute new policies and processes.

Transforming leadership represents the more abstract, philosophical and interpersonal aspects of organizational life. In a sense, it is the "right brain" side of organizational life: The spatial, abstract, intuitive, interpersonal, creative, sensing and adapting part of the picture. The human relations movement in management perhaps would have had Mr. Spock thrown out of the control room of the good ship Enterprise; and the scientific thrust in management would likely have told Luke Skywalker to stop kidding himself. They would have never let him in a control room or in a fighting craft in the first place, no matter how much he sensed or trusted in "The Force."

Webster's dictionary[11] definition of "lead" has its root meaning in Latin word laedan (to direct); and its meanings are:

- To direct, as by going before or along with, by physical contact, pulling a rope, to guide;
- To direct by influence;
- To be the head of (an expedition, orchestra, etc.);
- To be at the head of (to lead one's class);
- In first or front place;
- The role or example of a leader.

Although the dictionary definition of leadership captures some of the qualities of transforming leadership, there is an important difference. It is important that a transforming leader avoid even the appearance of being "above" other people in value. The transforming leader values people as the highest manifestation of intelligence and potential in all of nature, and views self as a servant and catalyst to bring forward those potentials rather than a "capitalist," manipulating others to achieve personal ends.

---

11 D. Guralnik (ed.), *Webster's New World Dictionary*.

The key functions of leadership when married to the key functions of management create a dynamic working relationship between the two orientations. Results vs. process, task vs. relationship, structure vs. flow, logic vs. intuition are no longer opposing forces but in transforming leadership integrated dynamics of the same creative force.

Therefore, transforming leadership trusts in all positive resources and functions which are available, and seeks to integrate them—both hard-headed and soft-hearted forces—because it is possible to develop and incorporate both at the same time in each person. Transforming leadership envisions the qualities and capabilities of both Mr. Spock and Luke Skywalker embodied in the same person. It is possible to develop a broader range of knowledge, skills, styles and roles from which to have a more positive and significant impact on self, others and organizations. This integration and development is an important thrust of this book.

Three Enlivening Areas of Knowledge and Skill

When I looked upon much of the field of knowledge in the three areas of communication (corporate and mutual interpersonal skills), counseling (personal and interpersonal problem management), and consulting (group, team and organizational development), I realized I had a difficult task ahead of me. I envisioned a model which could integrate and summarize key knowledge and skills areas into a framework, a kind of unfinished symphony which you can develop toward completion yourself as you gain insight and understanding of leadership from your own experiences and build an even larger model which can respond to your needs in your unique environments. This book will help you see how these three areas of knowledge and skill are necessary for effective leadership, and how they fit together into a workable model for your development and the development of others.

I have had many business, criminology, social services, and counseling students and experienced managers in my interpersonal communication, counseling and leadership classes over the past 16 years who have expressed a strong desire to understand, in some comprehensive way, what they needed to do to more fully develop as persons and as leaders. It wasn't until I began to speak of three key dimensions of leadership that they began to become visibly excited:

1. Interpersonal communication—for improved morale, relationship development and conflict resolution;
2. Counseling—for personal and interpersonal problem management; and,
3. Consulting—creatively innovating and systematically intervening in groups, work teams and organizations for planned change.

These three areas of knowledge and skill are the ones which are often sorely lacking in most of the education and training of those who are given leadership positions.

Now we can look at the relationship of management to transforming leadership. In the chart below you will see that management is conceived of as being the operational foundation of leadership, and the result of integrating them is the more effective achievement of organizational objectives:

Achievement of Organizational Objectives

Development of Individuals, Groups, and Organizations

Major Roles and Skills of Transforming Leadership

Communication, Counseling, Consulting

Foundation Skills of Effective Management

Planning, Deciding, Organizing, Controlling, Accounting And Researching

Transforming Leadership Provides a Model

A model is a framework of integrated knowledge and understanding which resembles reality enough to have some practical use. In the chapters to follow, this book provides you with a model for determining the strengths, styles, limitations, and plans for development of yourself, others, groups and organizations with which you live and work. Through gaining ability to practically apply human development and organization development principles and frameworks, you will become better able to visualize and specify what are major problems, potentials, and solutions in a wider range of situations. This increased clarity will enable you to better engage in breakthrough relating, thinking, planning and acting.

In the same way a carpenter can show the apprentice how to use various tools, and demonstrate the knowledge required to make beautiful furniture, this book can reveal and demonstrate some appropriate learning to you. I know from teaching my own two sons how to play music or tennis that knowledge has to develop into skills, and more importantly, skills can only be applied wisely after many repetitions and considerable experience with feedback from someone who is qualified to help evaluate present levels of performance.

It is this quality of wisdom, or appropriate application of knowledge, which is so hard to teach because it seems to come from the inside of a person after a time of searching, finding, some failing, and finally, some learning. And just when we think we "know" it, there is nearly always that humbling experience just around the next corner to remind us that there is more wisdom than our own, that we can learn much more, and that we can be renewed or deepened in our understanding again. Even the house most finely crafted requires wisdom to become transformed into a home where people can be relatively free to live and grow without fear of emotional pain or interpersonal strain. Of course companies and organizations are similar in this respect.

Structured Self-challenge

I would also like you to experience the expansion and freedom in your work and personal life which can come from adding a new set of skills and more knowledge to your repertoire. New knowledge and skills have revived my career with new zest a number of times. For example, during my career life I had no idea what was possible, and no one sought to assist me to make sense of the wider range of professional, career and life options I had. When I sought assistance with my own personal and professional development from professionals in the career and life planning fields I received little practical assistance, understanding or wisdom about how I could continue to develop. Interest inventories and personality tests gave me some perspective on my self; and, courses and workshops really helped to stimulate my development; but I could not find a book like this to help me to gain a broad enough perspective on personal and professional development so I could see what more of my options were.

A Map of the Leadership Terrain for Planning Your Development

When first introduced to the transforming leadership model, many managers experienced a great sense of relief that they could now map out the territory, assess what they had as knowledge and skills and identify what they needed to do to continue to grow. They could then move ahead more systematically to develop a wider range of skills and knowledge. They would better know which courses or professional development programs to select. This would assist them to become more confident and prepared to handle a wider range of people and situations or organizations.

Other professionals in the field who had various positions from front line workers to executive posts, invariably expressed that they had "holes" in their university training, gaps in their on-the-job training programs, or gaps in their life or work experiences which were felt but hard to specify. Some shared with me that if they could administer a program or organization well (they were efficient), then they had difficulty in leading it and the people in it to become something greater (effectiveness). Others said they had good interpersonal skills but they lacked in the "big picture" view of their organization or their job, and that they therefore found it difficult to make the more administrative or management type decisions.

During more than 16 years of working as a educator, consultant and trainer to managers in various organizations I have conducted an informal survey. I found less than one in ten professionals who claimed that their formal training or on-the-job training gave them a wide range of practical knowledge and skills. Most of them asserted that the skills of communication and problem management were critical life skills at home, and important professional skills at work. Most also agreed that they did not even get the opportunity in their formal studies to learn these practical, hard-hitting skills which could enable them to make relationships better, solve problems better, manage people better to get improved results, or minimally, to help their own children to develop as persons.

Some had a course or two during their formal training. Most experienced difficulty in putting into practice the theories they had learned in the classroom and only a few received formal mentoring or coaching. Most felt unprepared after their formal training, and still think that their preparations are incomplete.

Realistic Expectations: How Quickly Can You Develop?

Most people who aspire to be effective in leadership, and who realize the complexity of the task and the preparations which are needed, understand that development does not come primarily because of a course or a book. Usually people have to go through the following levels in developing competency and the ability to pass the "torch" to others:

1. Knowledge about concepts and skills that they are able to recall is developed relatively quickly. Some people can memorize and internalize the knowledge in this book in one or two readings. For others, it takes more exposure before it is internalized enough to be recalled.

2. Understanding and working knowledge (ability to try the skills on one's own without supervision) of the wide range of knowledge and skills in this book is possible within 4 to 6 months.

3. Competency (the ability to perform reliably well) is not easily attained, is learned through mentoring, training, coaching and through making unpleasant mistakes as well as having successes. These all pave the way to competency and this is achieved through years of application and feedback.

4. The development of dynamic creativity in the application of the knowledge and skills increases with many years of practice and experience, and with a commitment to excellence, both personal and corporate.

5. The development of the ability to mentor and train others toward empowerment can emerge after one has seen others do this effectively, experienced good training and mentoring, and received ongoing assistance in developing these most advanced of skills.

I will use an example very close to home to illustrate the four stages of development you will likely go through in becoming better able to integrate knowledge and skills into creative applications. I am a guitarist who has been studying and playing guitar on a part time basis for entertainment and relaxation for just over 30 years. During the first few weeks, it was relatively easy for me to learn my first few lessons about how to hold the guitar, play a few chords and read a few notes. I had some of the "basics" down and saw quite clearly that I had a very long way to go before I would actually "play" something well. This is the "introduction to knowledge and concepts" stage.

After this brief time of familiarization with the rudiments of guitar playing I began to apply things I had learned at my lessons when I arrived at home. I even applied these basic chords and notes to learn a few other tunes on my own. This is the "working knowledge" stage.

Over the next few years I developed quite a repertoire of songs and techniques and became able to play a number of different styles of music: Spiritual, rock, folk, jazz and classical. I played various pieces with some individual self-expression and creativity, which for me at that time in my musical development was quite an accomplishment. By age 25 I had become better than most of the other guitarists around the university I attended. This is the competency stage. I thought I was pretty good. But then something intensely inspiring and at once humbling occurred.

The Romeros, from Spain, "The Royal Family of the Guitar," gave a concert in the University Auditorium. There were three sons and a father, playing Vivaldi's "The Four Seasons," some of Bach's *Harpsichord* concertos and some flaménco improvisations which were so "fiery" I could hardly sit in my chair. As I listened to the unbelievable beauty and precision with which they played, I was at once overwhelmed with mixed feelings of inadequacy and inspiration. On the one hand I wanted to reach for the new level of excellence in true artistic expression which I had neither heard nor imagined before, but on the other hand I was filled with doubt and fear, that it would be futile for me to try to reach so high. I feared either that I would not be able to attain such a high level or that I would find the way to the creative and dynamic application stage so gruelling that I would eventually give up (so why start in the first place, I thought).

That one performance by the Romeros (who had spent their whole lives since about age 7 practicing at least six to eight hours per day) made me realize that neither my present level of musical nor personal development was actually as high as I had thought, and that I had a long way to go to reach my own potential.

This experience of seeing what was possible on the guitar when played by dedicated and gifted people forced a major life decision upon me: Do I choose mediocrity or active commitment to further development—even to the point of excellence? This decision, which was pressing upon me, involved not only my development as a musician, but all other areas of my life as well.

At that time in my life even though I grew up in a basically good home, had a good childhood and early adulthood I had not become my own person. I did not have a really great score on making my love relationships work. I didn't get along really well with some other students and co-workers, and my friends were few. My financial life was that of a depleted graduate student. Even though I nearly had two degrees, I had neither skills nor knowledge which were developed enough to be marketable and truly valuable to people. I realized that I had no clearly resolved beliefs about life, no clear purpose for my life, a confusing and vague world view of an existential humanistic Christian—a self-made doctrinal combo that even logically cannot be integrated! My values were neither solidified nor prioritized so that I could not act upon them with consistency and strength. I had no motivating dreams for my life in the long term and no firm goals beyond graduate school. I realized that I was mediocre, suffering from the "psychopathology of the average." Even though my grades were all "A's" and "B's", I felt as though I was getting a "D" in life.

This hurt deeply. In addition, I was already feeling stretched to the limit with my work load at school and at my part time jobs. How could I grow past the level I had reached? I didn't see much hope to break out and fly like any good bird should. I became depressed because I felt like one of Plato's people who were down in the cave watching the dancing shadows on the wall after having ascended into the upper world where the light of reality was so bright it was too overwhelming to bear.

However, over 20 years ago I did make a conscious decision to go out of the "cave" into the brighter light of the unknown. I refused to settle for "good enough," and decided to commit myself to develop as fully as possible in all areas of life (spiritual, intellectual, emotional, interpersonal and physical). A clear vision took shape for my life and I also later committed myself to assisting others who might want to reach for similar ends to attempt the same. Since that time, my life has been structured and shaped by this vision of encouraging and realizing my own and others' development, for the purpose of their helping others (particularly leaders and potential leaders) and organizations to develop.

My commitment to the development of organizations is a more recent interest during the past 11 years. This interest follows naturally from my sense of purpose to support, develop and encourage leaders because organizations are so intricately interwoven with the overall fabric of our lives, and so powerfully impact the development of people.

I do not want to give the impression that I personally have "arrived" to full development in any of the areas in which I charted for my own growth. However, I have been happily married for nearly two decades to a fine woman and friend, have two healthy sons with whom I am able to maintain good relationships, have very good work relationships with most of my colleagues and associates, have a stable and growing financial life and have growing opportunities to serve with greater impact in the fields of education, publishing, consulting, training and counseling.

Over the years, I have had the opportunity to have two private lessons with Pépe Romero, who is my favorite flaménco guitarist. This was a most significant experience. I still play the flaménco and classical guitar, but not as well as Pépe Romero. He has something I have not developed to the same extent. Natural talent? A gift? An unseen essence?

The Elusive Element

Why do some people, like Pépe, seem to "have it," without having to work for years to get "it." Why do some people say, "Oh, he and she are just natural leaders—others follow them and they accomplish great things together." I believe this question is very important. In this book I hope to reveal a search process to you which will result in your having some of the unexplainable parts of yourself and your life as a leader become more visible to you. Some of these ineffable qualities may be revealed by presenting the most recent research in leadership effectiveness. Some of the "magic" of leadership may be revealed in a person's deepest sense of purpose or "ultimate concern."

Perhaps this unseen essence of life, of leadership, is something as ideal or abstract as the Spirit of Truth, the hope of some greater wisdom, and the faith that which is unseen and difficult to understand can be honestly encountered, if not fully understood. This encounter with an unknown and uncharted presence or knowledge seems to first occur on the inside of ourselves when we earnestly seek wisdom to understand a previously difficult area of life or work. We sense it as a need or thirst for more understanding, or as pain which prods us to grow in certain areas, or perhaps even as a "tugging" on our heartstrings by a gentle and powerful but quiet Spirit who we too often ignore.

So as you read this book, I invite you to attempt to define for yourself what is this essence, this "art," this wisdom, this sense of wise appropriateness about life and leadership which some people seem to have more than others. How might you gain greater proximity to it?

Without presuming to be all-knowing in this area I have tried to write this book in such a way as you will find assistance and challenge in what to me is this exciting and important area of spiritual discovery, and gain some clarity about the nature of this essence which is so difficult to describe.

Some call it genius, others call it "guts," political savvy and stick-to-it-iveness, and others call it inspiration, charisma, revelation or vision. One challenge that is put to you in this book is for you to come to increasing clarity and resolution about your positions on or answers to life's most difficult questions: Who am I? What is my purpose? Is there an ultimate purpose for life and my life beyond my own self-created purpose? How can I know what is true, false, real, unreal? Who is my real self? Are there any criteria for discerning what is true or false? How do I know which criteria are true?

Your answers to all of these and other key questions will to a significant extent influence your beliefs about why it is important for you to lead, and what you think you can and perhaps should accomplish as a leader. To some extent we live our lives and lead from a base of inner structures of belief and assumption. We can choose what these structures will be once we are aware of what our present structures are, and what other options there are.

Your views on what you consider to be the nature of the "unseen" will control how you treat people, how you dream your dreams, how you speak and how you act. You will have opportunity to review this often confusing but also exciting area of your life in a structured manner in chapter four of this book.

Integrating a Developmental Perspective

Lastly, *Transforming Leadership* will give you a developmental perspective on yourself, others and organizations. By integrating developmental theory into the transforming leadership you will gain perspective on human development, which can assist you to become more realistic and patient.

An interesting study of the development of the lives of 60 men is in a book titled, *The Seasons of a Man's Life,* [12] chiefly authored by Daniel Levinson. I found the book a most stimulating reflection of my own life and the directions I have intentionally or unwittingly chosen. This is recommended reading for those who wish to get an even deeper sense of the process of adult development across the life span. Change takes time, transformation takes more time.

A key book for gaining an in-depth developmental perspective on some of the background skills which underlie *Transforming Leadership* is edited by Dale Larson and is titled, *Teaching Psychological Skills, Models for Giving Psychology Away.* [13]

A book about the changes which are about to take place which I have recently found to be illuminating is *the Human Resources Revolution,* [14] by Dennis Kravetz. This book traces the development of a number of companies and outlines cases of bottom-line successes as a result of implementing just some of the "progressive management practices" which I call transforming leadership.

Another book, by Frank Feather (1989) [15] outlines a futuristic look at the global trends which could restructure our world. As he states in the introduction:

> *The prospects are dazzling. The world has within its grasp the potential to change—and progress—like never before. The outcome is in our hands. We need to rewrite the course of our collective destiny—to re-invent the world*

---

12 D. Levinson et al., *The Seasons of a Man's Life* (New York: Knopf, 1978).

13 Dale Larson (ed.), *Teaching Psychological Skills, Models for Giving Psychology Away* (Monterey, California: Brooks/Cole Publishing Company, 1984).

14 D. Kravetz, *The Human Resources Revolution* (San Francisco: Jossey-Bass Publishers, 1988).

15 F. Feather, *G-Forces. Re-Inventing the World: The 35 Global Forces Restructuring Our Future* (Toronto: Summerhill Press Ltd., 1989), 1.

---

with a geostrategic agenda that will take us to an affluent and peaceful future. That this future is possible, and that humankind must pursue it, underlies everything in this book.

But as Honoré de Balzac wrote in his book, *Seraphita*: "Why build these cities glorious, when man unbuilded goes?" The remainder of this book is presented with the hope that you will be able to use *Transforming Leadership* to have greater positive leadership impact, and to encourage, mentor, train and inspire others to reach for their potentials as leaders, even if it takes longer than we expect or hope for problems to be successfully overcome. Along with the "geostrategic mindset" recommended by Feather, there is also needed a thoughtful, integrated "technology" for developing leaders who will be wise enough, skilled enough and kind enough to lead the way toward the future. This need for competency development is present in all leaders, regardless of their belief positions, or present level of development.

Chapter 2

THE NATURE OF LEADERSHIP

*During the 1980s, people and organizations pursued "excellence"
with great vigor and determination. And, while creating excellence
will probably continue as a mainstay during the 1990's, a new
quest has clearly emerged: the pursuit of integration and balance.
Individuals, families, organizations, and society in general
increasingly see the need for greater harmony among professional
career and personal relationships, worldly success and spiritual
fulfillment, economic prosperity and environmental protection,
accomplishment and peace of mind, tough-mindedness and
gentleness, immediate gratification and enduring joy, this
generation and future generations.*

Craig Hickman

THE GOALS OF THIS SECOND CHAPTER involve your gaining perspective on the nature of leadership, comparing traditional vs. transformational views on leadership, and understanding the Transforming Leadership Model:

1. Philosophies of Leadership
2. Definitions of Leadership
3. Theories of Leadership

Comparing Traditional and Modern Philosophies of Leadership

The nature of leadership is changing. There are so many ways to view it that it can be confusing and overwhelming. Rather than recommending any one approach, it is wise to do a survey of the many philosophies of leadership

---

in order to compare their fundamental assumptions and the consequences which flow from these assumptions. As a first step toward understanding and achieving a balanced approach to philosophies of leadership it is important for you to grasp the basic assumptions which have guided various leaders in the past, and consciously formulate more encompassing assumptions that can guide you as a leader into the future. This first step of achieving this balanced understanding can be achieved by looking at some definitions:

Webster's New World Dictionary (1984)[1] defines *philosophy* as: "A study of the *principles* underlying conduct and thought." It is valuable to compare the traditional with the more modern assumptions (principles) because we can then better see the value of them both. Gaining a basic understanding of leadership philosophies will assist you to formulate your own balanced and integrated philosophy of leadership.

The Operating Assumptions Behind Theories X, Y, Z, and R

The first philosophy of leadership which we will look into is outlined in Douglas McGregor's work (McGregor, 1960).[2] After studying a number of organizations, and the operating assumptions of those who were in positions of decision-making authority, he identified a set of beliefs which summarize this early view. He called this first view Theory X. Here it is called a *philosophy*, not a theory, because it is really a set of *beliefs* about the nature of work, and the nature of workers. McGregor based his work on the work of Maslow, and he, like Maslow, was interested in what motivated people toward greater personal development and improved performance. McGregor argued that traditional leader behavior was inappropriate since it was based on questionable assumptions about employees. These assumptions are outlined below:

Theory X Assumptions
1. Employees are inherently lazy and will avoid work unless forced to do it.

2. Employees have no ambition or desire for responsibility; instead they prefer to be directed and controlled.

---

1   D. Guralnik (ed.), *Webster's New World Dictionary of the American Language* (New York: Warner, 1984).

2   D. McGregor, *The Human Side of Enterprise* (New York: McGraw-Hill, 1960).

---

3. Employees have no motivation to achieve organizational objectives.
4. Employees are motivated only by physiological and safety needs.

These assumptions form the basis of a philosophy which can be very dehumanizing to others, and even to self as a leader. McGregor believed that Theory X assumptions were outdated, and that employees would perform better if treated with a very different set of assumptions he called Theory Y. This is the second philosophy, or set of operating assumptions, we will look into. Outlined below are the basic tenets of Theory Y:

Theory Y Assumptions
1. Employees find work as natural as play if organizational conditions are appropriate. People appear adverse to work only because their past work experiences have been unsatisfactory.
2. Employees can be motivated by higher-order needs such as ego, autonomy, and self-actualization.
3. Employees seek responsibility since it allows them to satisfy higher-order needs.

Autocratic philosophy is at the root of Theory X, with the leader initiating all the structure, and where the central focus is on production, not on people. In Theory Y, there is a more *democratic* philosophy where leaders "believe the best" about employees, and treat them more as people who work rather than as workers who also happen to be people.

Even today, McGregor's work stands as a breakthrough in identifying basic operating assumptions of leaders and the impact those assumptions can have on morale and organizational effectiveness. However, much development has taken place since McGregor's findings regarding basic assumptions or philosophies about leadership.

Theory Z Assumptions

In 1981, Ouchi[3] presented a clear set of operating assumptions which have impacted the functioning of a number of companies in the Fortune 500 cadre. These assumptions are:

---

3 W. Ouchi, *Theory Z: How American Business Can Meet the Japanese Challenge* (Reading, Mass.: Addison-Wesley, 1981).

1. Offer people long-term employment, a positive "family" of co-workers and leaders, and clear objectives; and they will stick around, do a good job, and have a sense of pride in the work done.
2. Offer people a piece of the pie when it comes to making decisions which will affect their work and they will understand and support the decisions more often and more wholeheartedly.
3. Expect people to take individual responsibility for their own performances as an important part of a bigger "team," and they will fulfill that expectation.
4. Evaluate people over the long-term rather than frequently because this gives them opportunity to develop based upon their inner sense of integrity, rather than on outward pressure.
5. Build trust and integrity into all interactions between managerial and non-managerial personnel to develop a sense of the importance of individual contributions to the group effort.
6. Maintain few levels of authority in the organization and emphasize work groups to get jobs done because this maximizes an individual's sense of belonging to his or her group, and to the organization as a whole, and also increases individual and group accountability and performance.
7. Use informal rules and regulations, with formalized measures of performance to further encourage individual workers to internalize personal responsibility for achieving group and organizational objectives.

Theory Z takes the spotlight off the individual and puts each person in the context of the group, the organization, and the culture in which he or she is living. This gives the individual a sense of value and importance based upon the accomplishments of the overall organization, and takes some of the heavy pressure off each individual in each moment to perform all out. In Japan, this has created personal and corporate determination to succeed at functioning in groups to reach departmental, organizational, and even national cultural goals.

Critics of the Theory Z philosophy claim that it will not really work in North America because of cultural differences between here and Japan (Biggs, 1982).[4] However, some of the assumptions have seemingly been successful-

---

4   B. Biggs, "The Dangerous Folly Called Theory Z," *Fortune* (17 May, 1982): 48–53.

ly implemented, especially in some small family businesses, and in larger corporate structures like IBM, Hewlett-Packard, GM, and others (see Ouchi, 1981).

It is ironic to consider that North America, driven by predominantly Judeo-Christian historical and cultural roots, would find the values of cooperation, support, loyalty, family closeness, intimacy and caring so foreign to its way of leading businesses and organizations. Individual accomplishment, competition with others, confrontation between labor and management, and an emphasis on **self** in general, have come to the forefront of the value structure of so many people since the 1950s. One important reason for this could be that the reward system of the company is usually for individual performance and not connected to group achievement.

The Assumptions of Theory R: A Relational Approach

Alderson (1985)[5] has introduced a unique set of assumptions into the arena of leadership philosophies. These guiding assumptions have been given the name of Theory R. The assumptions underlying this philosophy are as follows:

1. That all people need love (*affirmation*), a sense of dignity (*appreciation*), and need to be treated with respect (*recognition* that they are of intrinsic value, and that their work is a valued contribution) in the workplace, not just at home, or in other environments.
2. That the building of a person's sense of self-esteem through meeting the above three key needs will have a positive impact on worker morale, quality of work, and productivity.
3. That reconciliation, not confrontation, in leader-follower relations will help to create the needed sense of mutual respect, dignity, and unconditional concern for one another as human beings.
4. That relationships between leaders and followers are the keys to productivity, morale, and quality concerns.
5. That people have the desire to work hard and take pride in what they accomplish.

---

5   W. Alderson, *Value of the Person: Theory R Concept* (Pittsburgh: Value of the Person, 1985).

6. That when people are placed in an environment that is sensitive to the "Value of the Person," they will be cooperative, creative, and productive.
7. That treating people "right" is the right thing to do, and that is reason enough to actively value people.

At first glance, these ideas seem too simplistic to have much credence in the "real," complex world. But, at least in the hands of Alderson, they worked stunningly well in a steel foundry in Pennsylvania called Pittron. Alderson found something that both labor and management could agree upon. Every man and woman in the entire operation had something in common: They all wanted to be valued.

Two years after the Value of the Person approach was implemented, the plant went from a 6 million dollar loss to a 6 million dollar profit, from 300 to 1,100 employees, from 600 grievances per year to 1 grievance per year, from 20% absenteeism to 1%, from poor quality production to high quality production, and productivity was up 64%! Such dramatic changes warrant our attention. Anyone wishing to read the published story, which outlines the whole case study of Pittron's turnaround, should see Sproul, 1980.[6]

Thus, we see a dramatic shift in the evolution of the guiding assumptions of leadership theories from the autocratic sweat shops of Theory X, to the humanistic Theory Y, to the group emphasis of Theory Z, to the value of people theory of Theory R. But there are more questions we must ask. In the next section we will compare these more traditional definitions of leadership with new insights into the nature of transformational leadership.

Comparing Traditional and Transformational Definitions of Leadership

Traditional Definitions

Leadership has been defined in many ways by people of varying perspectives over the years. Indeed, there are so many definitions that vagueness and confusion seem to prevail in the minds of many about the whole issue. It is not surprising then that many leaders question their roles, their effectiveness, even their importance, and are questioned by those around them.

---

6   R. Sproul, *Stronger Than Steel* (New York: Harper and Row, 1980).

Below you will see a brief summary of many definitions of leadership, most of which are traditional in nature, but some of which lead toward the more transformative (adapted from Stogdill, 1974)[7] and then give a specific definition of transforming leadership.

- Definitions and aspects of leadership: a potpourri
- Determining group structure, ideology, and activities
- Coupling leader behavior with the meeting of group needs
- Keeping one step ahead of the group
- Innovation in accomplishment of tasks
- Achieving the most with the least friction
- Inducing compliance, respect, and cooperation
- Goal directed communication which gets positive results
- Serving others and meeting their needs
- Persuading others to accept a particular view or strategy
- Exercising of positive power to get desired results
- Making the most of individual differences to reach goals
- Being perceived as legitimate, expert, trustworthy

As you can see by the range of definitions above, there are considerable differences among these various views of leadership. Few people search the literature to even come up with the above few. This lack of a *working definition of leadership* can be a problem for someone who wants to develop leadership potential and become more effective and successful in achieving goals.

In contrast, you will see below a focused definition of leadership which can assist you to develop a more integrated and applicable understanding of leadership and its more transformative nature.

Transforming Leadership: A Definition

Transforming Leadership is vision, planning, communication, and creative action which has a positive unifying effect on a group of people around a set of clear values and beliefs, to accomplish a clear set of measurable goals. This transforming approach simultaneously impacts the personal development and corporate productivity of all involved.

---

7   Ralph M. Stogdill, *Handbook of Leadership* (New York: The Free Press, 1974).

The **transforming leader** also transforms self and the nature of leadership itself in a continuing process of learning to better lead. Therefore, everything is affected by a transforming, developing leader who is by definition an *active agent of positive change*: The environment is affected, organizations are affected, groups are affected, interpersonal interchanges are affected, the nature of leadership is affected, others are developed, and the leader's understanding is developed in the process. The transforming leader is no "super person," but the subtle, ripple effect of positive leadership can affect all parts of an organization and all the people in it, and as a "spin-off," their families at home can be positively affected, and this can even impact the tone of the communities in which people live.

Transforming leaders could be people who are administrators, managers, supervisors, educators, health and medical professionals, counselors, clergy, criminal justice workers, parents, and others who might have the knowledge, skills, tools and abilities to impact and develop both an organization and the people in it at the same time. This is the case when a father or mother (the transforming leaders) in a family (the organization) facilitate themselves and their children to grow by combining structuring and nurturing behaviors. It is also the case when an executive structures an organization through long-range planning and policy development, and develops teams of people who grow toward increased morale and productivity. How many organizations do strategic planning to increase productivity? Quite a number. How many of those organizations *also* do strategic planning and budgeting to increase the quality of the work and interpersonal lives for the people who produce that hoped for productivity? Not nearly as many. Therefore, you can see the potential importance of defining leadership in terms of people who are the producers, rather than producers who also happen to be people instead of robots.

Traditional Theories of Leadership: An Overview

Now that we have reviewed some general definitions of leadership and compared them to the working definition of **transforming leadership,** it will be useful to review some general theories of leadership and compare them with **transforming leadership theory**. A theory is defined by Webster as: *A formulation of underlying principles of certain observed phenomena which have been verified to some degree*. Important aspects of leadership are contained in many of the traditional views of leadership, and some important lessons can be learned by identifying some of their limitations.

Biological — Personality Theories

The Great Man Theory: In 1960, Jennings[8] presented a comprehensive survey and analysis of the "great man" theory of leadership. In summary, this earlier theory advances the idea that certain people are born stronger, more intelligent, more able to lead. Heroes, royalty, and the more successful people in general were thought to have inborn talent and ability which enabled them to stand out from among the masses and achieve unusual successes. This idea that born leaders had certain characteristics gave rise to the related, trait theory of leadership, which was studied and popularized in the 1920s and 1930s by Bernard (1926),[9] Bingham (1927),[10] Tead (1929),[11] and Kilbourne (1935).[12]

Trait Theories: These theories were sometimes intermixed with racial, sexual, and class discrimination to promote supremacy of one race over another, one sex over another, or one social or economic class over another. A king would have his brother or son (or at least a daughter) succeed his throne because of the "good stock" inherent in the blood. Though it is possible that some strengths are hereditary (as revealed in medical research), it is clear that there are too many surprising exceptions to this theory for us to give it significant credence.

Environmental Theories

Leader-Behavior Theory: This position suggests that circumstances themselves cause a great leader to rise to the occasion. Under the "right" conditions, a leader will emerge as if by nature's necessity or invention. Bogardus (1918)[13] suggested that the type of leadership a group will develop or accept, will be determined by the nature of the group and the problems

---

8   E.E. Jennings, *An Anatomy of Leadership: Princes, Heroes, and Supermen* (New York: Harper, 1960).

9   L.L. Bernard, *An Introduction to Social Psychology* (New York: Holt, 1926).

10   W.V. Bingham, "Leadership," In H.C. Metcalf's *The Psychological Foundations of Management* (New York: Shaw, 1927).

11   O. Tead, "The Technique of Leadership," In *Human Nature and Management* (New York: McGraw-Hill, 1929).

12   C.E. Kilbourne, "The Elements of Leadership," *Journal of Applied Psychology*, 43, (1959): 209–211.

13   E.S. Bogardus, *Essentials of Social Psychology* (Los Angeles: University of Southern California Press, 1918).

it must solve. Victor Frankl, in his book, *Man's Search for Meaning*, cites examples of leadership emerging from the most frail of beings in the terrible conditions of a concentration camp. However, there have been many crises which have not produced a person equal to the occasion. Therefore, we cannot necessarily give great credence to this theory of leadership either.

Personal-Situational Theory: This theory is the first to propose a complex set of factors which are involved in the shaping and development of leadership, and is the first to be scrutinized by serious research efforts. Westburg (1931)[14] proposed that the critical factors involved in leadership were a combination of the "affective, intellectual, and action traits of the individual as well as the specific conditions under which the individual operates." The idea here is that success in leadership is dependent upon a leader's ability to understand the followers and the surrounding environment, and then react appropriately to those people and situations as they change.

Bennis (1961)[15] recommended that theory on leadership should consider the measurement of rationality, the impact of informal organization and interpersonal relations, the positive influence of a benevolent autocracy because it structures relationships between superiors and subordinates, job enlargement and employee-centered supervision that permits individual self-development; and participative management and joint consultation that allows the integration of individual and organizational goals. Bennis emphasized how important the interpersonal dimension was in determining the quality of the work life in an organization. He also emphasized the value of the person in relation to productivity.

Interaction-Expectation Theory: In this theoretical orientation, leadership is the act of initiating structure which is supported by group members because such structure solves mutual problems, conforms or positively trans- forms group norms, and causes members to expect that success will come from following a leader of such initiative. Leadership, according to this theory, involves both initiating and fulfilling the expectations of followers. Leader

---

14 E.M. Westburg, "A Point of View: Studies in Leadership." *J. Abnorm. Soc. Psychol.*, 25, (1931): 418–423.

15 W.G. Bennis, "Revisionist Theory of Leadership." *Harvard Bus. Rev.*, 39(1), (1961): 26–36, 146–150.

credibility is based upon the ability to fulfill expectations which were generated by the leader (Homans, 1950; Stogdill, 1959).[16],[17]

Humanistic Theories of Leadership

The theories of Argyris (1964),[18] Blake and Mouton (1964),[19] Likert (1967),[20] and McGregor (1960, 1966),[21],[22] are focused on the development of effective organizations through a "humanizing" process of structuring the work or living environment so that individuals can meet both personal needs and meet organizational objectives at the same time. This theory attempts to balance the needs of the individual with the goals of the organization, but has been accused at times of sacrificing organizational "bottom line" results for the sake of realizing human values such as employee morale, worth of the individual, quality of the work life, meaning and purpose in work, mutual trust, and productivity based upon the internal motivation of workers.

This approach can contribute much to our understanding of human needs in the workplace, and can cause us to be more cognizant of the "people" side of enterprise, the importance and dignity of human life, and the importance of personal meaning and purpose in work. It has also revolutionized thinking about productivity and performance as well; basically, it has clarified that people who like what they do, feel respected and valued, and are involved, will perform better.

Some major contributions from the these authors are:

Argyris: Pointed out the inevitable conflict between the individual and the organization. He claimed that organizations are most effective when leaders provide avenues for workers to make valuable contributions and be recognized for their efforts in reaching organizational objectives. He

---

16 G.C. Homans, *The Human Group* (New York: Harcourt, Brace, 1950).

17 R.M. Stogdill, *Individual Behavior and Group Achievement* (New York: Oxford University Press, 1959).

18 C. Argyris, *Integrating the Individual and the Organization* (New York: Wiley, 1964).

19 R.R. Blake and Jane S. Mouton, *The Managerial Grid* (Houston: Gulf, 1964).

20 Likert, R. *The Human Organization* (New York: McGraw-Hill, 1967).

21 D. McGregor, *The Human Side of Enterprise* (New York: McGraw-Hill, 1960).

22 D. McGregor, *Leadership and Motivation* (Cambridge, Mass.: MIT Press, 1966).

also explained how most organizations overplay the rational and under-emphasize the emotional—especially the negative emotions (1982).[23] In his opinion, the best organizations recognize and process negative emotions until resolution or at least compromise is achieved.

- **Blake and Mouton**: Presented a grid to illustrate the relationship between concern for people and concern for production. They created one of the first leadership style assessment instruments, and formulated a theory which suggested that a leader who scored high on both people and production concerns was most effective.
- **Likert**: Suggested that leaders need to seriously consider the values, expectations, and interpersonal skill competencies of those with whom they work. The positive leader, as defined by Likert, is one who appreciates an employee's efforts and builds self-esteem in others. Task and relationship factors are both important and inter-related.
- **McGregor**: I include McGregor in this section because some of his assumptions have been verified through observation and research over the years. He developed a theory of understanding leadership behavior along a continuum from "Theory X" to "Theory Y." The leader with a Theory X orientation is thought to be "old school," believing that followers are self-oriented and uncaring about the needs of the organization, and so attempts are made to directly influence and motivate them in the direction of accomplishing organizational goals, without much regard for their own feelings or motives. A leader with a Theory Y orientation is thought to be "new school," believing that people are self-motivated and self-actualizing by nature, and that what leaders should do is to arrange the organizational environment in such a manner as to capitalize on those internal motivations for employees to reach organizational goals.

All of the above humanistic theories suggest a single path for leader behavior, and are therefore now thought of as somewhat narrow. It has become increasingly clear that no one theory or approach really works best. Depending upon a whole host of variables, a wide range of interventions may work. This is not to say that there are not some key principles which can be applied throughout the leadership process, but for now we will examine the more situational approaches.

---

23 C. Argyris, *Reasoning, Learning and Action: Individual and Organizational* (San Francisco: Jossey-Bass, 1982).

Situational or "Contingency" Approaches to Leadership

These approaches reflect important advances over the more simplistic "one best way" methods to lead models. Contingency models suggest more complex diagnosis of the situation at hand, and more complex leadership interventions. Situational, or contingency approaches reflect the belief that there is a relationship between employees' satisfaction and performance, and their environments. The basic premise of these approaches is that if we understand the factors which have impact on employee morale and performance, and apply that understanding successfully, we can have more direct influence and control over morale, and (the belief of many is) productivity.

Fiedler (1967)[24] advanced a theory called *The Leadership Contingency Model* which serves at least three main purposes. First, it supports the idea that effective leadership is situational in nature, that a leader has to attend to a wide range of situational variables in order to make a wise choice of leader behavior. Secondly, Fiedler found that more directive leaders were effective in certain situations, and this finding was contrary to the philosophies of the 1950s and 1960s, which were dominated by human relations theories. Fiedler also opened up the issue of leader versatility, and the placement of a leader in a situation which he/she can build to fit her or his strengths—i.e., "engineer the environment to fit the manager."

A second theory which suggests that leader behaviors can influence worker performance and satisfaction is the *Path-Goal Model* formulated by House (1971).[25] This approach suggests that the leader's job is to increase the payoffs to workers for achieving work goals. The leader does this by clarifying the path to these goals, by reducing blockages that prevent workers from reaching the goals and by behaving in a way that will increase worker satisfaction while they are achieving those goals. However, if workers feel that they are capable of doing a good job without direction from the boss, directive leadership behavior will cause dissatisfaction or even resentment. House's model is important because it gives us insight into some things leaders can do to increase employee satisfaction.

---

24 F.E. Fiedler, *A Theory of Leadership Effectiveness* (New York: McGraw-Hill, 1967).

25 R. House, "A Path-Goal Model of Leader Effectiveness," *Administrative Science Quarterly* 16 (September, 1971): 312–338.

A third type of situational or contingency theory of leadership is contained in Vroom and Yetton's (1973) *Decision-Making Model.*[26] According to this theory, it is critical for the leader to decide on how much participation subordinates should have when making decisions. They provide guidelines for leaders to decide how much participation is appropriate in each situation. They stress the importance of decisions and information availability, and show that acceptance of decisions by subordinates is an important issue in regard to their productivity.

Finally, *Situational Leadership* was developed and popularized more recently by Blanchard and Hersey (1977, 1982).[27] Even though the roots of this approach go back to Westburg (in Stogdill, 1974),[28] it is fair to mention the impact and importance of this work as a major voice in communicating to many leaders (and trainers/educators of leaders) the value of carefully considering the developmental level of a follower or group of followers, and matching the leadership style to the ability of the follower to perform a particular task.

A concern for follower development is clearly voiced and this approach is continuing to be influential in shaping thinking and training in leadership flexibility for greater appropriateness and therefore greater effectiveness in face-to-face leadership situations.

Summary

As you can see, leadership theory has become more and more complex as time has moved on. The simple authority relationship of boss/employee has shifted greatly toward a realization of the importance of the *people* factors, factors in each *situation* which affect overall outcomes, and *people and situational factors which interact* to affect one another.

Only a few people in a situation rise to the top for a number of complex reasons, and succeed or fail for a number of complex reasons. Theories of leadership are each limited, none of them meta-theoretical (integrating and including many useful theories into one), and have been based upon inter-

---

26 V. Vroom and P. Yetton, *Leadership and Decision Making* (Pittsburg: University of Pittsburgh Press, 1973).

27 K. Blanchard and P. Hersey, *Management of Organizational Behavior: Utilizing Human Resources* (New Jersey: Prentice-Hall, 1982).

28 Ralph M. Stogdill, *Handbook of Leadership* (New York: The Free Press, 1974).

esting academic or valuable research trends, and upon the philosophical beliefs of a particular decade or era.

For a more complete account of the development of leadership theory see Stogdill (1974). It is useful to see the historical development of leadership in order to see the direction in which it has moved in past years, and thereby gain a sense of where it is likely to move in the next decade. Leadership, at all levels, from family to government, will have great impact on *how* we do move into the next century.

A Price to Pay for Complexity

Theories of leadership are moving from simple to the more complex as we move through time. However, there comes a time when the richness can become clutter, a time when the complexity goes beyond what is applicable by the average leader. This is the price we pay for more complex theories. They are more difficult to learn, more complicated in their applications, require more sophisticated training methods, and more intricate research methodologies are needed to study their effectiveness.

A Payoff for Integrating the Logically Useful Parts of Various Theories

As we develop more intricate but *integrated* models of leadership, there is a greater likelihood that these models will represent guidelines which can work in the real world. The challenge is to state them *clearly* enough so that they become *tools* which can be tested and used. Research on leadership effectiveness reveals that at this point we are still groping for the "magic formula," that there is some conflicting evidence about the effectiveness of leadership training (Fiedler, 1972),[29] and that each leader is still basically out there on her or his own to make a positive difference using the talents, knowledge and skills he or she has.

Hickman (1990)[30] does an excellent job of contrasting, comparing and integrating traditional and transformational definitions, roles and functions of management and leadership. In the preface of his new book, he states:

---

29 F. Fiedler, "How Do You Make Leaders More Effective: New Answers to an Old Puzzle," *Organizational Dynamics* (Autumn, 1972): 3–18.

30 Craig R. Hickman, *Mind of a Manager, Soul of a Leader* (New York: John Wiley and Sons, 1990).

In organizations this gravitation toward balance has encouraged business people to begin integrating incremental strategies with innovative breakthroughs, cultural values with corporate policies, stability and security with change and opportunity, flexible processes with structured systems, and short-term gains with long-term progress. The complex global business environment of the 1990s demands that we go much further in this direction. However, given the growing pressures, complexity, change, and competition facing business organizations today, most executives find themselves confronted with an escalating conflict and schism between the managerial and leaderhip requirements of organizations. An "either-or" mentality dominates at a time when organizations most desperately need the best of both.

Transforming Leadership is an emerging assessment and training model which has promise for providing a clearer vision of how powerful and enlivening leadership can be integrated with the wisdom of traditional management, and offers concrete ways we can grow into becoming better "leading managers" through expanding awareness and receiving training in deficit areas. Now we turn to developments in the late 1970s through the mid-1980s, and the emergence of this newer approach of *transformational leadership*.

Chapter 3

▼

FOUNDATIONS OF TRANSFORMING LEADERSHIP

...the basic philosophy, spirit and drive of an organization
have far more to do with its relative achievements
than do technological or economic resources,
organizational structures, innovation, and timing...

T. Watson of IBM

IN THIS CHAPTER we will look more deeply into the nature of transformative leadership by examining the following:

1. Examples of Transforming Leadership
2. The Emergence of Transformative Leadership
3. The Transforming Leadership Model
4. Principles of Transforming Leadership
5. Roles and Functions of Transforming Leadership
6. Attitudes and Characteristics of Transforming Leaders

Examples of Transforming Leadership

Some examples of leadership which have a transforming effect will help to clarify the important differences between traditional and transforming leadership.

1. **A father and mother** mutually decided to plan their lives more carefully, set goals and priorities, had family meetings which taught the children how to plan and structure life, and found that there was a payoff by the end of the first week. A psychologically closer family

---

ensued, the resolution of some unfinished conflict issues occurred, and two brothers planned to build a car together over the next few years. Traditionally, parents have tended to live more day by day, and deal with opportunities or problems as they arise rather than intentionally build a plan to enrich family life.

2. **A teacher** of an overcrowded 6th grade class decided to meet with interested parents to train them to work with "underachievers" and "gifted" children in the class. After just a few weeks of the new program, discipline problems diminished significantly, students performed better in class and at home on schoolwork, and at the end of the year the standardized test scores went up an unexpected 11% over the previous year for the underachieving students.

    The more traditional teachers have more often considered the parents "irresponsible" if they didn't help their kids at *home*, and tended to just accept the overcrowding as a "fact of life" they had to put up with, at least temporarily.

3. After consultation with her teachers and a local stress and health center director, **a principal of a junior high school** (where teachers had the highest absenteeism rate in the district) decided to offer health and wellness education programs to teachers, parents and students. These programs included deep relaxation training, computerized nutrition analysis and diet planning, weight reduction programs, quit-smoking programs, fitness training opportunities after school, and a team approach to scheduling on-duty time during recesses and lunch hours. She provided a quiet, smoke-free place to practice deep relaxation during the noon hour and held regular staff meetings to air concerns and solve problems. At the end of the second semester, there was a significant drop in absenteeism, a reported increase in morale, and significantly fewer stress symptoms reported among staff. Obviously, these results will not occur simply because programs are inserted into the environment—the people involved must accept and utilize such programs, and the programs have to be introduced in such a way as they are perceived as welcome additions.

4. **A top level government executive** realized that his management team lacked cohesion and harmony, that their meetings were fraught with tension and competition, and that some of the more important goals of the organization were not being reached because of poor relations among the management "team." He privately surveyed each of his managers, summarized their individual perceptions and concerns, and called them together to present his findings. The main troubles seemed to have stemmed from the fact that the team was thrown together in a hurry during a time of available funding, and no one spent much time discovering one another's strengths, clarifying roles, or agreeing upon goals in the organization. They called in a consultant to do a 3-day team development session, followed by a 3-day strategic planning session, and by the end of that year the group not only achieved its goals, but surpassed them. Tension levels dropped, job satisfaction increased, and cohesion and creativity developed within the group.

    Traditionally, there would have been no systematic intervention, with the resultant effects of either increased tension and backbiting with lowered performance, or increased turnover, or both.

5. **Lee Iacocca** had to change the feeling of Chrysler's employees from "losers" to that of "winners" at a time when Chrysler had a history of irregular performance, and at a time when they were suffering from the poor image of having to receive government money to stay afloat. Iacocca talked personally to the workers at Chrysler, hired back some sharp retirees to lend seasoning to the company, and even made personal appearances in Chrysler's advertising to help change the climate among employees and in the marketplace. Chrysler's increased quality, more effective marketing, increased sales, and government loan pay-back completion, was evidence that Iacocca transformed his intentions into reality with new vision, commitment, and follow through: The net result—a transformed Chrysler Corporation from top echelon executives to front line assembly workers. Iacocca transformed and magnified our vision of leadership.

    Traditionally, there had already been management and number crunching attempts to save the corporation from demise for over 5 years.

From these examples, you can get a better idea of what is the essence of transforming leadership in several different environments. Now, we will turn to gaining a better understanding of the theories which are foundational to transforming leadership.

Transformational Theories of Leadership

The Emergence of and Necessity for Transforming Leadership

Transformative leadership began to manifest itself as a distinct trend in the late 70s and early 80s and was made distinctive from the more usual type of "power" management which was more typical as we go back in history to the early 1900s. Both Bennis and Alderson (referred to in chapter one), and Hickman and Silva,[1] made similar distinctions between *managers* and *leaders.* A summary of some of the distinctions which have become increasingly clear during the past 20 years are outlined below:

A Traditional Manager

1. Tends to have a short-term profit mentality at the expense of longer term profits and relationships with employees and/or customers.
2. Often has an authoritarian, one-up approach to using power.
3. Is more satisfied with the status quo and reacts negatively to most changes.
4. Is often influenced by as little as 10% of the workers who apply pressure.
5. Tends to have an instinct for survival of the "fittest," and tends to be more self-oriented than "for others."
6. Stresses an efficiency philosophy of doing things "right."
7. Meets in a formal way with immediate subordinates.
8. Tends to be aloof, rational, critical and "cool" (people and new ideas get a reserved response).
9. Focuses on others' weaknesses.
10. Speaks about how well present goals are being reached.

---

1   C. Hickman and M. Silva, *Creating Excellence: Managing Corporate Culture, Strategy, and Change in the New Age* (New York: New American Library, 1984).

A Transforming Leader

1. Is more committed to long-term profits as a by-product of longer term service and/or relationships.
2. Uses personal *and* position power to make positive changes and influence others.
3. Initiates innovations, and encourages others to do the same.
4. Is more influenced by 90% of workers, not so much just the 10%.
5. Is more committed to positive relationships with others for the sake of their development, and the development of the organization as a whole.
6. Stresses the effectiveness philosophy of doing the right things for people *and* for the organization.
7. Articulates philosophy, beliefs and values.
8. Makes contact with employees at all levels.
9. Is receptive, expressive, supportive and warm (people and new ideas are of great interest).
10. Gives attention and recognition to others' strengths.
11. Speaks about a future vision, goals and plans.

The above views focus on the weaknesses of traditional management and the strengths of transforming leadership, and do not provide a balanced perspective on the relationship of good management to good leadership. In fact, Hickman (1990)[2] has written his most recent book in order to achieve this balanced perspective and approach, and heal the schism between leadership and management within and between individuals. From this excellent work, it is clear and keenly important that the tasks of leadership and the tasks of management are both attended to and performed successfully: but not necessarily by the same person. Let us now turn to an exploration of this concept of appropriate balance between good management and transforming leadership.

---

2 C. Hickman, *Mind of a Manager, Soul of a Leader* (New York: John Wiley and Sons, 1990).

Leadership and Management: Related but Different

There are clear differences between management and leadership orientations. However, as the chart below reveals, the integration of the two orientations presents a whole view of what is necessary for effective creation and transformation of an organization and the people in it. *Also, the re-cyclical nature of the transforming leadership approach illustrated in this chart gives you a sense of the fluidity of the process. Rather than a cycle, perhaps it could be better represented as a spiral moving through time.*

The Relationship Between Management and Leadership Functions

Management: Task/result Orientation

Evaluation, Research
Decision-making
Planning systems
Problem-solving
Data based decisions
Specifying procedures
Administering policy
Day-to-day operations
Present focus to ensure results

Leadership: People/process Orientation

Creatively applying research information
Motivating and rewarding others
Relationship and culture building
Team building and team development
Personnel selection, orientation, planning
Creative planning and shifting
Envisioning of end states process
It is also useful to think of management
Future focus for accomplishing a higher purpose

The Leading Manager: Integrating Diverse Orientations

As you look at the steps in the chart, you will see how important each of the tasks and functions are in management and leadership and how certain functions must be performed prior to others, in a step by step but flexible process. It is also useful to think of management and leadership as two separate but interrelated areas because there has been so much confusion about their separate identities and purposes. Without both working together in a balanced manner, each would suffer and be less effective. Without leadership as the foundation of management, management cannot function effectively because it is undermined by a lack of humanity, clarity, focus, adaptability and creativity. Without management, leadership might never follow through enough to get the results needed for long term success.

The Private Adoption Agency Case Study: A non-profit society had its origins in a group of peoples' concerns for unwed mothers who faced pregnancy, but for religious reasons did not want to abort the unborn. They formed a society by registering with the appropriate government office.

All the board members were dedicated professionals who were very sincere and very busy, without previous experience in the process of developing a new organization. There was a rough constitution written up but not agreed upon by all members, staff were hired, and the operation opened its doors. The staff agreed that the first priority was to conduct counseling sessions with the unwed mothers to assist them to make an independent but difficult decision as to whether to keep the child or adopt. Those who chose the adoption route had an opportunity to select the parents to whom their baby would go, and in nearly all cases it was with a couple who were unable to have their own children.

Things went well for a few months until conflicts began to emerge between staff members. Who should decide whom the baby goes to among the qualified applicants on file, the young woman who is the birth mother, or the director of the agency? Should prospective adoptive parents have to reveal whether or not they have ever induced an abortion in the past, used illegal drugs, had a criminal record, etc.? The staff members disagreed and could not resolve their disagreements on these issues.

The extent of authority of the director had not been spelled out to the other staff or even to the director by the board of directors. When the chairman of the board was informed of the conflicts, some arbitrary "management" decisions were passed "down," and the staff felt that their views were not being heard or respected, and that there wasn't really a team approach which had been so generously spoken of by all.

In the beginning, there was little transforming leadership to provide clarity of vision, purpose, philosophy, goals and policies about which people could agree. Therefore, it was very difficult for the board, director or staff to set forth procedures based on these vague organizational foundations. The moral of this story is: Where there is lack of clarity on issues which require leadership to facilitate a team or organizational consensus then various people withdraw their energies or try to over-manage so at least some decisions get made and action gets taken. Had there been clarity established from the beginning on the key organizational issues many of the problems of the new agency could have been averted.

The chairman of the board eventually exercised leadership and acquired the services of an external consultant who understood the social work oriented goals of the agency, and who was experienced in organization development and team development. He met with the board and the staff members in order to facilitate the specification of philosophy (beliefs, values and norms) based on policy statements to which the board and staff members could agree. This eliminated power struggles, bonded staff members together around a common purpose and values, and removed confusion and downtime due to disorganization or people working at cross-purposes. The consultative leadership intervention transformed the character and performance of the organization, and the people in it, for the sake of the parents and children being served. After this leadership intervention, the organization was ready to once again be managed.

Leading for a Change

The necessity of integrating management and leadership knowledge and skills within each key decision maker (or at least on each team) is becoming more critical as world history faces us with increasing complexity, spastic change and unpredictability. Each manager must lead and each leader must manage in a world where both leadership and management dimensions must be developed in order to respond to constant change and pressures, both internal to and external to an organization. Increasing pressures of a technical, interpersonal and organizational nature are on the horizon.

Change must be envisioned, anticipated, managed, and adapted to by numbers of key people in our world in order for us to globally cope with the acceleration and complexity which now is, and to cope with increasingly accelerated change which is likely to occur in the future. The best way to predict the future is to conceive of it, be aware of intervening forces, make adjustments along the way, and guide it into place as much as is realistically possible.

Transforming Managers Lead by Serving and Adapting to Change

Brown and Wiener (1984)[3] point out that Japanese managers have not been strategic planners who have operated by formula management, but have been sensitively accommodating to changes in the environment. They tend to distrust "master strategies" because they can limit a wider vision of changes occurring in clients, technologies, or with the competition.

Upper and middle management in Japan have tended to see their key task as responding to important input from "below" (front line staff and customers) rather than steering the organization from above along a predetermined course. This is closer to leadership than management. However, a Leading Manager effects a transforming impact by doing *both* the strategizing *and* the shifting or adapting simultaneously. Or, alternatively, agrees with another leader that one will play the leader and the other the manager for a purpose and for a period of time.

Naisbitt (1982)[4] outlines major changes in the chart on the next page that we can anticipate in the near future, some of which are occurring even now.

These changes are occurring to various extents in a wide range of environments, but it is clear that with the burgeoning of both technology and information that we are going to need adaptability, innovation, and creative leadership more than ever. An even more recent and revealing expose of the types of changes which will likely be advantageous in the future are outlined,

---

3   A. Brown and E. Wiener, *Supermanaging: How to Harness Change for Personal and Organizational Success* (New York: Mentor Books, 1985).

4   J. Naisbitt, *Megatrends* (New York: Warner, 1982).

NAISBITT'S TEN MEGATRENDS	
FROM	**TO**
Industrial Society	Information Society
Forced Technology	High-Tech/High Touch
National Economy	World Economy
Short Term	Long Term
Centralization	Decentralization
Institutional Help	Self-Help
Representative Democracy	Participatory Democracy
Hierarchies	Networking
North	South
Either/Or	Multiple Options

and to some extent forecasted, in Naisbitt and Aburdene's book (1986)[5]. This book paints a wave of new ideas regarding the transforming of jobs and companies for the new information society. Some of Naisbitt's forecasts include ten considerations for re-inventing an organization:

1. The best and brightest people will gravitate toward those corporations that foster personal growth.
2. The manager's new role is that of coach, teacher, and mentor.
3. The best people want ownership—psychic and literal—in a company. The best companies are providing it.
4. Companies will increasingly turn to third-party contractors, shifting from hired labor to contract labor.
5. Authoritarian management is yielding to a networking, people style of management.
6. Entrepreneurship within the corporations—intrapreneurship—is creating new products and new markets and vitalizing companies from the inside out.
7. Quality will be paramount.

---

5   J. Naisbitt and P. Aburdene, *Re-inventing the Corporation* (New York: Warner Books, 1986).

8. Intuition and creativity are challenging the "it's all in the numbers" business-school philosophy.

9. Large corporations are emulating the positive and productive qualities of small businesses.

10. The dawn of the information economy has fostered a massive shift from dependence upon natural resources, transportation and market proximity, to quality of life considerations (such as good climate, good schools, cultural opportunities, etc.).

These evidences of rapid and dramatic changes are important signals for us to heed when we prepare ourselves to meet the leadership challenges which lie ahead, or prepare others to better meet those challenges.

When so many changes are upon us, Naisbitt and Aburdene (1990)[6] outline another list of changes we can expect to see. They call these the "Millennial Megatrends—the gateways to the 21st century:"

1. The Booming Global Economy of the 1990s.
2. A Renaissance in the Arts
3. The Emergence of Free-Market Socialism
4. Global Lifestyles and Cultural Nationalism
5. The Privatization of the Welfare State
6. The Rise of the Pacific Rim
7. The Decade of Women in Leadership
8. The Age of Biology
9. The Religious Revival of the New Millennium
10. The Triumph of the Individual

These and other trends in our world will force upon us new demands and requirements that we become increasingly able to adapt to and become aware of our own potentials for growth and change, and lead the way with others who will need to undergo the same personal stretching process.

---

6 J. Naisbitt and P. Aburdene, *Megatrends 2000. Ten New Direction for the 1990's* (New York: William Morrow and Company, 1990), 13

A Time for Vision in an Era of Change

Such a complex and difficult time in human history our planet has likely never seen. For this reason, leaders need to understand the kind of leadership which stimulates positive transformation and breakdown prevention. Egan (1985)[7] most aptly states some basics of a theory of transformative leadership by describing clearly what a transformational leader *does*:

> *Transformational leaders are shapers of values, creators, interpreters of institutional purpose, exemplars, makers of meanings, pathfinders, and molders of organizational culture. They are persistent and consistent. Their vision is so compelling that they know what they want from every interaction. Their visions don't blind others, but empower them. Such leaders have a deep sense of the purpose for the system and a long-range strategic sense, and these provide a sense of overall direction. They also know what kind of culture, in terms of beliefs, values, and norms, the system must develop if it is to achieve that purpose. By stimulating, modeling, advocating, innovating, and motivating, they mold this culture, to the degree that this is possible, to meet both internal and environmental needs (p. 204).*

This clear vision of some ways a transformative leader can achieve positive results will assist you to further identify the somewhat elusive nature of transforming leadership. In addition to clarity of vision, the use of positive power is a necessary aspect of transforming leadership.

Power for Change

Bennis and Nanus (1985),[8] re-introduce the seemingly lost concept of *power* as a key to transformational leadership. They observe that many, if not most leaders, have visibly lacked wholehearted commitment to the challenge of leadership, have been overwhelmed by the rapid change and complexity of our era, and have lacked the necessary integrity and credibility to earn the trust and respect of followers. They claim that the kind of leadership which is needed is transformative leadership and that this leadership power is exemplified by what they call "the Iacocca phenomenon":

---

7   G. Egan, *Change Agent Skills* (Monterey, California: Brooks/Cole Publishing Co., 1985).

8   W. Bennis and B. Nanus, *Leaders: The Strategies for Taking Charge* (New York: Harper and Row, 1985), 66–67.

*Power is the basic energy needed to initiate and sustain action or, to put it another way, the capacity to translate intention into reality and sustain it. Leadership is the **wise use of this power** [emphasis added]: Transformative leadership. As we view it, effective leadership can move organizations from current to future states, create visions of potential opportunities for organizations, instill within employees commitment to change and instill new cultures and strategies in organizations that mobilize and focus energy and resources (p. 17).*

Leaders who are particularly successful in acquiring and sustaining power have a number of things in common. Kotter (1979)[9] observes in his studies on the use of leadership power that there are several keys to success for those who are effective in the use of power. They tend to be very sensitive to where power exists in their organizations. They use specific methods to develop power as long as the methods are ethical. They take calculated risks in which they "invest" some of their power in the hope of gaining it back with interest. They recognize that all of their actions can affect their power and they avoid actions that will accidentally decrease it. In their career development they try to move both up the hierarchy and toward positions where they can control some strategic contingency for their organization.

We can see that it is possible that one of the reasons some people are not very effective in developing leadership effectiveness is that they do not know how to establish their own "power" image in the minds of others. In order to do this, it is possible to assess the different kinds of power one could possibly have, and set about to develop these different types of power for positive purposes. Image management (managing our own self-images and self-presentations) can have a positive impact on the images others have of us in their minds. A comprehensive text on this subject of "impression management" was published in 1980 by Schlenker.[10] This is an excellent study of this issue of how self-presentation is linked to leadership effectiveness.

---

9   J. Kotter, *Power in Management* (New York: AMACOM, 1979).

10 B. Schlenker, *Impression Management* (Monterey, California: Brooks/Cole Publishing Company, 1980).

Kanter (1982)[11] found that formal authority was less important to managers attempting an innovation than power and influence which they exercised beyond the formal mandates of their organizational positions. Clearly, a greater understanding of power, how to develop it, how to keep it, and how to use it effectively, is important in transforming leadership.

The Subtle Nature and Potency of Transforming Leadership

Burns (1978)[12] further clarifies the character of transforming leadership when he expresses that it is more than mere power-holding, and is the *opposite* of brute power. He describes the relationship between most leaders and followers as *a transactional*, favor-for-favor type interchange. However, he points us to a view beyond the transactional tit-for-tat relationship of jobs for votes, subsidies for campaign contributions, or raises for more production:

> *Transforming leadership, while more complex, is more potent. The transforming leader recognizes and exploits the existing need or demand of a potential follower. But, beyond that, the transforming leader looks for potential motives in followers, seeks to satisfy higher needs, and engages the full person of the follower. The result of transforming leadership is a relationship of mutual stimulation and elevation that converts followers into leaders and may convert leaders into moral agents of change.*

> *...Moral leadership emerges from and always returns to, the fundamental wants and needs, aspirations, and values of the followers. I mean the kind of leadership that can produce social change that will satisfy followers' authentic needs.*

Greenleaf (1977)[13] had foresight in predicting the terrain of leadership theory today when he wrote:

> *A fresh look is being taken at the issues of power and authority, and people are beginning to learn, however haltingly, to relate to one another in less coercive and more creatively supporting ways. A new moral principle is*

---

11 R. Kanter, "Power and Entrepreneurship in Action: Corporate Middle Managers," *Varieties of Work* (Beverly Hills: Sage, 1982).

12 J. Burns, *Leadership* (New York: Harper and Row, 1978), 4.

13 R. Greenleaf, *Servant Leadership, A Journey in to the Nature of Legitimate Power and Greatness* (New York: Paulist Press, 1977).

emerging which holds that the only authority deserving one's allegiance is that which is freely and knowingly granted by the led to the leader in response to and in proportion to, the clearly evident servant stature of the leader. Those who choose to follow this principle will not casually accept the authority of existing institutions. Rather, they will freely respond only to individuals who are chosen as leaders because they are proven and trusted as servants. To the extent that this principle prevails in the future, the only truly viable institutions will be those that are predominantly servant-led (p. 9).

A more recent view on transforming leadership is presented by Kanter (1983).[14] She encourages a responsible, balanced leadership in serving the needs of the followers, *and* the needs of the organization simultaneously through participative leadership:

While encouraging participation, innovators still maintain leadership. "Leadership" consists in part of keeping everyone's mind on the shared vision, being explicit about "fixed" areas not up for discussion and the constraints on decisions, watching for uneven participation or group pressure, und keeping time bounded and managed. Then, as events move toward accomplishments, leaders can provide rewards and feedback, tangible signs that the participation mattered (pp. 275-277).

The Qualities Followers Want to See in Leaders

Kouzes and Posner (1987)[15] conducted a most interesting study of over 1,500 managers to discover what positive practices their leaders engaged in. They found four key qualities and 10 leadership practices which can be found in the behavior patterns of effective and admired leaders:

Most of us tend to admire leaders who have credibility, those who are:

1. Honest
2. Competent
3. Forward Looking
4. Inspiring

---

14 R.M. Kanter, *The Change Masters* (New York: Simon and Schuster, 1983).

15 J. Kouzes, and B. Posner, *The Leadership Challenge, How to Get Extraordinary Things Done in Organizations* (San Francisco: Jossey-Bass, 1987).

These credible leaders tend to be committed to consistently implementing 10 leadership practices:

1. Search out challenging opportunities to change, grow, innovate, and improve.
2. Experiment, take risks, and learn from the accompanying mistakes.
3. Envision an uplifting and ennobling future.
4. Enlist others in a common vision by appealing to their values, interests, hopes, and dreams.
5. Foster collaboration by promoting cooperative goals and building trust.
6. Strengthen people by sharing information and power and increasing their discretion and visibility.
7. Set the example for others by behaving in ways that are consistent with your stated values.
8. Plan small wins that promote consistent progress and build commitment.
9. Recognize individual contributions to the success of every project.
10. Celebrate team accomplishments regularly.

These ten practices represent central issues which are important to the understanding of transforming leadership. The *Leadership Challenge* book is recommended highly as one which has a very practical focus on understanding and integrating these 10 most effective leadership practices.

The Intertwining of Management, Leadership and Power

Kotter (1990),[16] in his most recent book, *A Force for Change: How Leadership Differs from Management,* outlines how subtly the various successful executives behaved as they artistically intertwined the various aspects of their approaches into a powerful force for positive change:

> *Specifically, the most effective executives created agendas for themselves, made up of loosely connected sets of short-term plans, medium-term*

---

16 J. Kotter, *A Force for Change: How Leadership Differs from Management* (New York: The Free Press, 1990), 103-104.

strategies, and long-term visions. They each built resource networks that could accomplish these agendas by staffing and structuring the jobs reporting to them, by communicating their plans and visions to people, and by establishing cooperative relationships with a broad range of individuals whose help they might need. They then actively sought to influence people in those networks when necessary to assure the achievement of their agendas, and did so in a wide variety of ways, sometimes trying to control people and activities, sometimes attempting to inspire others to new heights of performance. Overall, this behavior was extremely complex and, as has been reported in other in-depth studies of executives at work, did not look much like traditional management.

What these executives were doing, employing the language of this book, was a combination of management, leadership and still other things (chief among which was the development of sources of power that could help them manage, lead and get promoted). But all of these various aspects of behavior were highly intertwined. They did not manage for fifteen minutes and then lead for half-an-hour. Instead, in the course of single, five minute conversation, they might try to see if some activity was proceeding as planned (a control part of management), gather information that was relevant to their emerging vision (the direction setting part of leadership), promise to do someone a favor (an aspect of power development), and agree on a series of steps for accomplishing some objective (the planning part of management). As a result, to the observer, what they were doing did not look much like management or any other recognizable activity. The managers themselves even found their own behavior difficult to describe and explain.

With the kinds of complex demands placed upon those in positions of leadership, it is not surprising that a wide range of skills should be displayed in the behaviors of those who are most successful. A model which can capture the components of this complexity and render them transferable to others is needed. Such a model will provide guidance for self-assessment, planning for training, and for evaluating the effectiveness of your own or others' leadership behavior. *Transforming Leadership* provides a model which is an attempt at this integration of the various complex parts of the effective leadership behaviors exhibited by the executives Kotter studied, where their leadership helped turn around NCR, P&G, and Kodak; and stimulated business growth at American Express, PepsiCo, and ARCO.

The Transforming Leadership Model

In developing this model, an inter-disciplinary approach was taken in order to capture philosophy, theory, and scientific investigative results which have a range of practical applications. The following theory and practice bases should be recognized as being important in the formation of a more integrative and comprehensive model such as transforming leadership:

- Interpersonal Communication
- Counseling
- Human Development
- Human Resource Development
- Organization Development
- Transforming Leadership Theory and Principles
- Effective Personnel Practices

From the above bodies of research and theoretical formulations have emerged "chunks" of applicable knowledge or sets of learnable and teachable qualities and skills. As a result of learning these skills or developing such qualities it is easier to bring forward into reality not only competencies, but *some* sense of the "art" or charismatic (character) power involved in transforming leadership.

A model is an approximate map of what reality could look like, and it is clear enough to give us a reference point for evaluation of our own effectiveness when we try a particular leadership intervention. With this clarified reference point and increased evaluative ability, we are able to make the necessary shifts in order to fine-tune our responses to people and organizations so that we can have more positive and potent impacts.

Transforming Leadership: A Research and Philosophy Based Model

There are so many theories and philosophical assumptions about what one should do to become more effective that it is difficult to trust just anyone spouting off about another panacea, wonderful training or action-oriented program. The concepts in the model are based on validated theory in communication, counseling and consulting (OD and HRD). Philosophers and practitioners often attempt to simply convince others that their one school of thought is the correct one. A visual overview of the Transforming Leadership Model is presented on the following page.

Knowledge and Skills which Develop and Transform People and Organizations

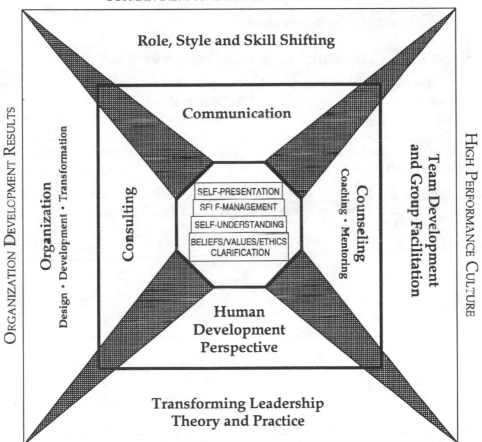

HUMAN RESOURCE DEVELOPMENT RESULTS

ORGANIZATION DEVELOPMENT RESULTS

HIGH PERFORMANCE CULTURE

Role, Style and Skill Shifting

Communication

Organization
Design • Development • Transformation

Consulting

SELF-PRESENTATION
SELF-MANAGEMENT
SELF-UNDERSTANDING
BELIEFS/VALUES/ETHICS
CLARIFICATION

Counseling
Coaching • Mentoring

Team Development and Group Facilitation

Human Development Perspective

Transforming Leadership Theory and Practice

EFFECTIVE PERSONNEL PRACTICES

Leaders who utilize the skills "chunks" and knowledge areas in the model have greater potential to shape organizational climate and the interpersonal environment in order to achieve the desired results. Except for the management functions, these skills and knowledge areas will be discussed in greater detail in chapters four through eight. This book does not have as its purpose to introduce the reader to the knowledge and skills of effective management because there are a wealth of good books which accomplish this goal more than adequately. But first it is important to understand that in reality transforming leadership is not a rigid, linear, step-by-step process, even though there are a series of steps which can be outlined to assist in understanding how the process can work.

Steps in the Transformative Leadership Process

We can see leadership as a complex *process* involving a fluid series of steps (which may overlap or reverse into one another, depending upon the circumstances). When this process is understood, it can assist leaders to develop people and to bring a vision of human and organizational transformation into reality. Without a compelling and clearly communicated vision, the status quo often remains, and innovation and development are arrested.

Learning to use the steps in the transforming leadership process model can increase your leadership behavior appropriateness "score."

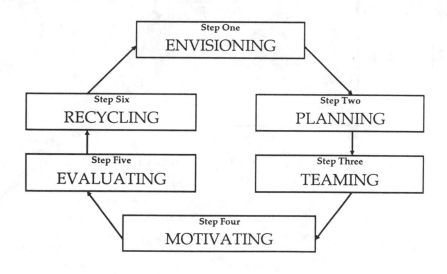

A further delineation of what is entailed in each of these steps is presented below:

1. **Envisioning**: This first step requires imagination, creativity, and an understanding of the history of a group or organization so that what is possible in the future can be more accurately and realistically specified and articulated. For most people, this is the most difficult of all of the steps because it requires originality, stepping out of the ordinary ways of thinking and doing things and, since habits are strong and new ideas are accepted slowly, there is more risk involved than many people are willing to take. It is the critical step, however, because innovation and improvements usually happen because some person conceived of a better way to work or a better way to live. Envisioning *must* also be *based* upon the specifying and meeting of some kind of human need, or there will be no market for the new service or product being offered by a person or an organization.

2. **Planning**: Once a vision is captured (with or without dialogue with others), it can be built upon through carefully specifying just how, where, and when a thing can best be done, and by whom it might best be done. This may involve family or committee meetings, brainstorming sessions, team development sessions, conflict resolutions, and negotiations. As the plan develops, if it is to succeed there must be enough acceptance of the plan, and enough enthusiasm about the plan *and* the vision for it to be truly shared by all involved. Otherwise, the likelihood of it succeeding can be seriously diminished. When the followers involved have an opportunity for involvement which challenges them personally, they are more likely to invest themselves at a deeper level in making it work. Finally, this planning process must include highly specific and concrete goals, objectives and programs for the timely accomplishment of worthy and realistic aims.

3. **Teaming**: Selectively giving responsibility to others involves building harmonious and productive teams by placing people in appropriate groupings they see as desirable (whenever possible), giving them tasks appropriate to their strengths and interests, and supporting them emotionally and physically in the process of their taking on responsibility. This ensures that they will more likely meet the challenges they hopefully chose to meet. Matching the *nature* of a person with the *nature* of the job, and matching people with people is an effective way of exercising leadership discernment.

4. **Motivating** *to Action*: Once there is some acceptance established, motivation must develop inside of people (for internal or external reasons) *on a continuing basis*, or the plan will not be realized to the level of quality originally envisioned, or within the time allotted. A system of rewards must be established *and valued* for motivation to be kept at a challenging and yet comfortable peak. People won't work hard when they feel what they give is a great deal more than what they get—they find it demoralizing. Many things act as rewards, and identifying people's "hot" buttons, a whole range of them, and giving them reasonable rewards and opportunities which encourage them to stay motivated are key factors in transforming people and organizations. Motivation leads to the most important aspect of organizational life: action. Higher levels of motivation and achievement can be accomplished by meeting the deeper needs of people: needs of recognition, accomplishment, challenge, belonging, meaning and purpose. To do this is not manipulation, but respect for people to have a sense of need for both internal and external rewards in return for the sweat of their lives.

5. **Evaluating**: Evaluation of the results of a change effort is tricky but necessary business. It is important both in terms of making improvements on the plan but important also in being able to jointly celebrate a specific level of success. The more carefully specified the plan is in terms of identified accomplishments to be reached for, the easier is the evaluation of the results. In designing the plan, evaluation criteria should be made a part of the plan. They should be realistic, desirable, concretely defined in terms of accomplishments, and measurable.

6. **Recycling the Process Through Evaluation**: Periodically, after a time of evaluation, all the steps in this process need to be repeated so that false assumptions are not made about how events are going, or how they should best go. Re-thinking the vision, reformulating and re-negotiating the plans, finding new motivators, re-grouping for greater harmony and productivity, and re-evaluation all keep people and organizations alive to what is real, and to what has positive change potential.

Using the Transforming Leadership Model and process steps as a backdrop, we can now examine the twelve principles which lie at the heart of *Transforming Leadership*.

Principles of Transforming Leadership

As a summary of *Transforming Leadership,* an outline of principles involved in the model are important. Principles of Transforming Leadership are general operating guidelines which can be applied in a wide variety of situations. These principles are listed below:

1. **Every person in every situation is having an impact,** for better or worse, on the people and the situations which are present.

2. **Learning to observe this impact alerts us to the reality of positive or negative leadership opportunities** and events. Increasing our level of awareness of people and events can be fruitful for everyone.

3. **Every person can choose to try and make a positive difference in each moment** with each other person, and at least within that immediate sphere of influence can likely exert some positive, and therefore transforming leadership.

4. **The use of positive and respectful power and influence is necessary** for leadership to have enough impact to be effective. Knowing one's own strengths, gaining strategic position power, developing a power network of like-minded people, and communicating your personal and position power in a positive way to others will assist you to reach higher goals.

5. **Everything begins with the initiative of each individual.** Privately, inwardly, individuals determine in their own selves what to do, how to act, and how to treat people. If we are each clear within about our own beliefs, purpose, goals, and objectives, we will much more likely achieve them from this solid and well defined center within ourselves.

6. Leadership, in it's deepest sense is the **understanding and meeting of the deeper needs of the people** being led/served. Even when achieving goals of increased innovation or productivity, our meeting of the deeper human needs of worth, recognition, reward, accomplishment, and personal development of others are cornerstones of motivation and satisfaction.

7. **Transforming leadership has a moral component** which is centrally important to all other aspects of leadership, because few people will trust a leader who has lied, one who has embezzled, one who hurts others.

8.   **Transforming leadership understands and involves others,** so that they can gain a critical sense of belonging, and experience the mutual sense of respect and trust which follow. Personal ownership in any venture can potentially increase motivation, morale, creativity, energy and productivity.

9.   **There is opportunity for leadership in every environment, in every interaction, in every situation, in every moment.** Leadership is intentionally making a positive difference in the development of organizations and individuals for a specific purpose. Being awake to these opportunities and seizing them increases our personal meaning and impact in life and work.

10. **Transforming leadership looks for *long-term* impact and long-term development,** rather than just immediate results. Satisfaction increases when we can see a continuing positive development over longer periods of time, rather than just short-term successes.

11. **Transforming leadership begins deep within a person's belief and value structures,** and a solid sense of purpose or mission in life is necessary for leadership effectiveness to be sustained. Have a well defined, achievable sense of purpose which "sets you on fire" distinguishes you from the herd of people who follow along with a more vague purpose of some relatively unknown leader-heroes (such as political, sports, scientific heroes, etc.).

12. **Transforming leadership** is open to the potential that there could always be another, higher or deeper understanding of reality beyond that which is presently comprehended. An attitude of humility which is not "puffed up with pride" characterizes a transforming leader.

I believe that these principles, when internalized and implemented in a leader's life, will result in greater leadership impact in the wide range of roles which leaders must play. These roles will be examined further in the next section of this chapter.

Comparing Traditional and Transformational Roles and Functions of Leadership

Classical theories as outlined by Stogdill (1974) in his monumental review of leadership theory and research suggest that the primary functions of a leader are planning, organizing, and controlling. Various theorists have added coordinating, supervising, motivating, and others to the list. Functions which have been identified by behavioral theorists and researchers include:

- Defining objectives and maintaining goal direction
- Facilitating group task performance
- Facilitating group action and interaction
- Maintaining group cohesiveness and member satisfaction
- Providing and maintaining group structure
- Providing means for goal attainment

Functions of transforming leadership are in addition to the above and are necessary for greater impact to be made on the development of individuals and the organizations in which they live and work. These are:

- Creating and communicating vision and purpose
- Doing strategic, versatile thinking and planning
- Facilitating peer, subordinate, and team development
- Facilitating the development of the organization
- Protecting individuals from destructive forces
- Protecting the organization from destructive forces
- Seeking and communicating consensus between groups
- Specifying philosophy, values and creating culture
- Creative insight

Traditionally, the roles of leadership have been divided into three main categories (Mintzberg, 1973).[17] These are interpersonal, informational, and decisional roles. Transforming Leadership Theory asserts that the informational and decisional roles are primarily management functions, even though they can be handled creatively from a leadership as well as from a "hard line" management perspective. Therefore, these three traditional roles exclude some important dimensions which can make a critical difference to leadership effectiveness and potency. These important roles which encompass some of the traditional roles and introduce some new ones form the structures and avenues for the effective execution of transforming leadership. These roles are graphically introduced and expanded upon in the graphic illustration on the next page.

---

17 H. Mintzberg, *The Nature of Managerial Work* (New York: Harper and Row, 1973).

Although these roles and functions are not exhaustive, they capture some of the essence of what is believed to produce a transforming effect on individuals, groups and organizations. It should be remembered also that effective management practices form the solid platform from which these additional functions can be carried forward.

Now that we have reviewed these roles and functions which are central to transforming leadership, we can examine the critical attitudes and characteristics of transforming leaders.

Attitudes and Characteristics of Transforming Leaders

This part of the chapter can be used as a way for you to look at yourself in relation to what has been discovered to be effective attitudes and characteristics of transforming leaders. In doing this self-examination, you can discover areas which are in need of development, and can devise a short term and long term plan for your development as a leader. Highlight or underline parts of the following which you think will help you to formulate such a plan.

A Portrait of the Transforming Leader

General Characteristics

The transforming leader is critically involved in envisioning, communicating and creating an *improved future* for self, any other person, group or organization. The transforming leader has clear personal beliefs: without clarity about one's own life stance on life's major questions, an individual can be easily swayed by situations (which are becoming increasingly complex, unstable and unpredictable).

The transforming leader also has a well-defined sense of mission, purpose, values, goals, and strategies which are based upon a deep understanding of the people and aims which are being served, and a clear understanding of the cultural, political and economic environment surrounding the change endeavor being attempted. The transforming leader is able to *arouse a sense of excitement* about the significance of the organization's contribution to society, or the group's contribution to the organization. The transforming leader has working knowledge and skills in the areas of human develop-

Roles and Functions of Transforming Leadership

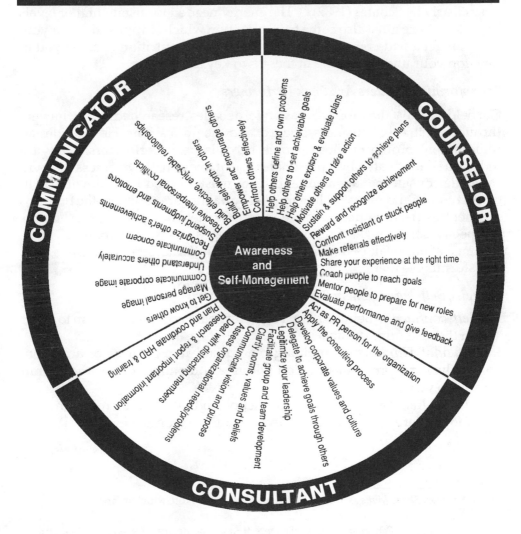

COMMUNICATOR

COUNSELOR

CONSULTANT

Awareness and Self-Management

Empower and encourage others
Confront others effectively
Build self-worth in others
Build effective, enjoyable relationships
Resolve interpersonal conflicts
Suspend judgments and emotions
Recognize other's achievements
Communicate concern
Understand others accurately
Communicate corporate image
Manage personal image
Get to know others
Plan and coordinate HRD & training
Research & report important information
Deal with distracting members
Assess organizational needs/problems
Communicate vision and purpose
Clarify norms, values and beliefs
Legitimize your leadership
Facilitate group and team development
Delegate to achieve goals through others
Apply the consulting process
Develop corporate values and culture
Act as PR person for the organization
Evaluate performance and give feedback
Mentor people to prepare for new roles
Coach people to reach goals
Share your experience at the right time
Make referrals effectively
Confront resistant or stuck people
Reward and recognize achievement
Sustain & support others to achieve plans
Motivate others to take action
Help others explore & evaluate plans
Help others to set achievable goals
Help others define and own problems

ment, organization development, interpersonal communication, counseling, consulting and problem management/solving.

Transforming Leaders Need Exceptional Physical Health

To be in leadership positions often requires an ability to deal with stress and
difficult situations with some degree of resilience. The fitness required to
sustain higher levels of energy and performance is described and prescribed
very clearly by Schafer (1987).[18] The energy needed to sustain higher levels
of performance must also come from nutrition which is appropriate for you.
You can get a wide range of books on fitness and nutrition to assist you to
develop your understanding in these two key areas.

Transforming Leaders Are Peak Performers

Garfield (1986)[19] has for the past two decades researched top achievers
through all strata of business, science, and the professions. He provides an
illuminating profile of those people he calls peak performers: They are
individuals motivated by a personal sense of mission, they possess the twin
capacities of self-management and team mastery, and have the ability to
correct course and manage change. These qualities are similar to the findings
of other theorists mentioned above, except Garfield has gone to great lengths
to specify some of his findings. Summarized below are some of these
findings about peak performers which are similar to others' findings, that
transforming leaders:

Exercise Self-management Through Self-mastery

- *Self-confidence*: Being willing to go out, hear "no," and move on to focus
  on the next opportunity.
- *Bimodal Thinking*: Combining macro and micro forms of attention.
  Analyzing a problem situation within a company requires the overall
  macro view.
- *Mental Rehearsal*: Preparing for action so that both the mind and the
  emotions are conditioned positively for the upcoming events.

---

18 W. Schafer, *Stress Management for Wellness* (New York: Holt, Rinehart and Winston,
    1987).

19 C. Garfield, *Peak Performers: The New Heroes of American Business* (New York: William
    Morrow and Company, 1986).

Use Course Correction

- *Mental Agility*: The flexibility to change perspective and do the creative thinking necessary to deal with challenges.
- *Concentration*: Consisting of: the stamina to work long, adaptability to change, and the hardiness that could also be called resilience under stress.
- *Learning From Mistakes*: Taking appropriate actions based upon updated information.

Have a Results Orientation

- *As Individuals*: Envisioning and communicating a clear mission, following up with a plan of action that includes specific goals, complete with benchmarks necessary for assessing timing, quality, and quantity of results.
- *As Collaborators*: Using a "magnet mentality" to draw in what they need from other people.
- *As Innovators*: Understanding that there is no guaranteed path from A to Z, and being prepared to make new paths in the service of results.

Cultivate Necessary Skills

- *Develop New Skills*: Assessing what new skills are needed and then developing those skills though readings, courses, workshops, and tapes. Then asking for and getting feedback.
- *Use Leverage*: Maximizing opportunities to use the skills they already have so they stay in their "peak performance" zone.

Develop Teams to Accomplish Results

- *Delegate to Empower Others:* Empowering (releasing power in and from) others by giving them tasks and assignments they do best, and never doing what others can do better.
- *Stretch the Abilities of Others:* Challenging others to develop to their potentials and offering opportunities and projects for them to do so (with the necessary support to succeed).
- *Encourage Educated Risk-taking:* Encouraging others to take higher-payoff risks if there is reasonable chance for success.

Manage Change for Future Success

- *Are Students Forever:* Seeking lifelong learning opportunities which means that there is a willingness to admit sequential ignorance, that a degree is not the end of the game.
- *Expect to Succeed*: Having confidence and the ability to visualize at least one way in each moment that things can work.
- *Map Alternative Futures*: Having alternate game-plans to shift into if the present one(s) does not materialize as expected.
- *Update the Mission*: Having an open mind to restating the mission, or critical paths to it, can be a necessary ability in times of spastic change.

Refined Self-awareness and a Broad Base of Self-development

The transforming leader has a refined self-awareness, is able to acknowledge and compensate for limitations, has ability to use self as an instrument for change, has developed good interpersonal communication skills, counseling skills, problem solving and problem management skills and has an optimistic attitude in general.

The transforming leader takes initiative in transforming all parts of an organization *where there is opportunity for positive change.* Ideally, the person(s) who has been placed "in charge" of any family, group, department, or organization would facilitate development at the *personal, interpersonal, and organizational* levels. All too often, traditional leaders attempt only one level of impact, or at best two, and fail to comprehend the breadth of influence they *could* have (Egan, 1985).[20]

Consciousness: An Openness to New Perspectives

The transforming leader values increasing consciousness of self and others without overloading awareness with clutter and detail. An ability to see patterns in the past and project them into the future to sense new directions is important. The transforming leader understands that a personal commitment to become a more conscious, clear minded and intentional person results in important personal growth which attracts others and wins their

---

20 G. Egan, *Change Agent Skills* (Monterey, California: Brooks/Cole Publishing Co., 1985), 204.

trust. Some call this personal "presence," presence of mind, alertness, or expanded awareness (beyond the average).

Caring: The Critical Factor

Most of all, the transforming leader *cares* deeply about self and others, is committed to the higher goals of developing both the inner lives and worth of individuals, and is committed to developing positive organizational climates and productivity. The transforming leader knows that increased morale in general means increased productivity, and, to (only) a certain extent, increasing productivity and quality of products or services can boost morale. Facilitating the personal development of people as individuals adds depth and character to an organization over the long term, and workers are more likely to have a positive self-image, which often results in improved performance in producing quality goods or delivering quality services.

Bennis (1985)[21] quotes Irwin Federman, president and CEO of Monolithic Memories, one of the most successful of the high-tech companies in Silicon Valley:

> *If you think about it, people love others not for who they are, but for how they make others feel. We willingly follow others for much the same reason. It makes us feel good to do so. Now, we also follow platoon sergeants, self centered geniuses, demanding spouses, bosses of various persuasions and others, for a variety of reasons as well. But none of those reasons involves that person's leadership qualities. In order to willingly accept the direction of another individual, it must feel good to do so. This business of making another person feel good in the unspectacular course of his daily comings and goings is, in my view, the very essence of leadership.*

Caring about the well-being and development of others is a quality which is not only necessary, but when absent from an otherwise good leader, most of us feel a sense of having being deceived, or at least having been let down, or sadly disappointed, as is exemplified in the extreme by such leaders as Napoleon, Hitler, and Nixon. It would seem that the tragic flaws of *deceptiveness*, *lovelessness*, and the insane tragedy of *destructiveness* are, to most of

---

21 W. Bennis, and B. Nanus, *Leaders: The Strategies for Taking Charge* (New York: Harper and Row, 1985), 17, 66–67.

us, unacceptable, no matter what the promises or other accomplishments of a leader are.

The Secret of Leadership Success

Posner and Kouzes (1987)[22] claim that love is the secret of leadership success. They define love as encouragement, loyalty, teamwork, commitment, respect of others' dignity and worth, and claim it is an affair of the heart and not of the head. If any one thing will cause people to be distrustful of a leader, it is when they sense that the leader does not care. In contrast, Kouzes and Posner write, "When we encourage others, we give them heart. And when we give heart to others, we give love."

Assessment: Identifying Your Own Position in Relation to Transforming Leadership Principles

Rate the extent of your agreement with the 12 Principles of Transforming Leadership. This will give you an opportunity to discover the extent to which you "buy into" these basic "beliefs" of transforming leadership. Doing this assessment will assist you to identify how much you are committed to the idea of seeing yourself more and more as an agent of positive change. You can rate each of the 12 principles from 1–5 to indicate your acceptance of these principles into your value structure:

> 1 = rejection
> 2 = avoidance
> 3 = neutrality
> 4 = general acceptance
> 5 = complete acceptance and agreement

---

22 Kouzes and Posner, *The Leadership Challenge, How to Get Extraordinary Things Done in Organizations.*

Are You in Agreement with Transforming Leadership Principles?

Circle the number which indicates your acceptance level:

1.	Every person in every situation is having impact	1	2	3	4	5
2.	Observing this impact helps leaders to lead	1	2	3	4	5
3.	Anyone can choose to make a positive difference	1	2	3	4	5
4.	Using positive power and influence is necessary	1	2	3	4	5
5.	Responsibility for success lies inside each person	1	2	3	4	5
6.	Meeting human needs facilitates bottom line results	1	2	3	4	5
7.	Leadership has a moral component	1	2	3	4	5
8.	Leadership involves and empowers others	1	2	3	4	5
9.	There is leadership opportunity in each moment	1	2	3	4	5
10.	Long-term development is better than short-term gain	1	2	3	4	5
11.	Effective leadership begins deep within the values and beliefs of people	1	2	3	4	5
12.	There is always a reality beyond that which we presently understand	1	2	3	4	5

Total the twelve scores above   Total = _____

Rejection	Avoidance	Neutrality	Acceptance	Agreement
0–12	13–24	25–36	37–48	49–60

Knowledge and Skills which Develop and Transform People and Organizations

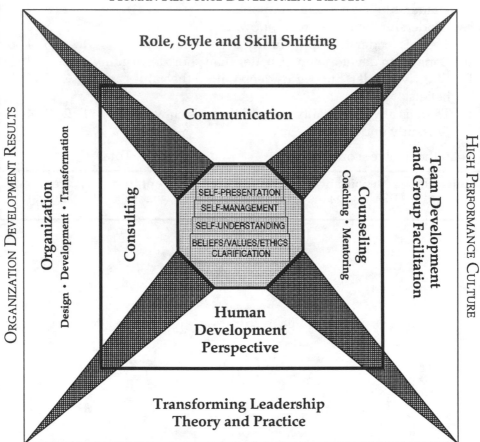

HUMAN RESOURCE DEVELOPMENT RESULTS

Role, Style and Skill Shifting

Communication

ORGANIZATION DEVELOPMENT RESULTS

HIGH PERFORMANCE CULTURE

Organization
Design • Development • Transformation

Consulting

SELF-PRESENTATION
SELF-MANAGEMENT
SELF-UNDERSTANDING
BELIEFS/VALUES/ETHICS
CLARIFICATION

Counseling
Coaching • Mentoring

Team Development
and Group Facilitation

Human
Development
Perspective

Transforming Leadership
Theory and Practice

EFFECTIVE PERSONNEL PRACTICES

Chapter 4

▼

AWARENESS AND
SELF-MANAGEMENT SKILLS

I knew who I was this morning,
but I think I must have been changed
several times since then.
Alice, in *Through the Looking Glass*

THIS CHAPTER WILL ASSIST YOU to gain a more in-depth understanding of the skills you will need in order to have greater positive impact in the process of developing yourself and others. When you complete the reading of this chapter you will have surveyed the terrain of what key self-management and interpersonal communication skills you now have, identified which ones you may need or want to add to your repertoire, and devised a tentative plan to develop your weaker skill areas. In the future, when you see a workshop or course outline which you think may be relevant for your development, you will be able to evaluate immediately whether or not that particular professional development opportunity fits your individual learning needs in this foundational area of personal and professional development.

Of all the areas of awareness and skill in focus for this chapter, the most difficult are those of beliefs and values. Most of the people I have had in university and college classes have given up to some degree on the hope of inner clarity and resolution regarding personal beliefs or life stance. They have become somewhat numbed to the challenge of tackling life's most difficult of questions. Many have even consciously resorted to a kind of waning scientific materialism which they also describe as lacking in vitality and inspiration. Srivastva and Cooperider (1990)[1] have so aptly described the precipice near which so many stand:

While the voices sometimes clash and the arguments reel in complexity, there is one powerful consensus that reverberates throughout: The scientific materialism that so confidently dominated the postindustrial era and so thoroughly insinuated itself into virtually every aspect of institutional life is now a dying orthodoxy. While there is little agreement as to exactly what we are moving toward, there is no question that the shift now taking place in society's dominant metaphysic—Who are we? What kind of universe are we in? What is ultimately important?—will have a transforming effect on all our institutions.

With this ominous prospect of huge paradigm shifts in the minds and belief positions of large numbers of people we turn to the process of self-assessment which will trigger a beginning of a new and conscious clarification within.

The need to take up the challenge of gaining clarity is emphasized by Vaill (1990)[2] in his chapter titled, *Executive Development as Spiritual Development.*

The primary emphasis among contemporary writers seems to be the exhortation of executives about the sense of mission, the new vision, vitality, and spirit they are supposed to impart to their organizations. I see very little attention being given to the question of where this vision, vitality, and spirit are going to come from in the leader who is imparting them.

I think it is a scandal that there should be so little discussion of them in the mainstream of management education and development. At best, we tend to treat the subject as primarily a matter of ethics. The practice of any system of ethics, though, makes all kinds of assumptions about the spiritual condition of those who are going to do the practicing. I am genuinely embarrassed for myself and my colleagues that we should, by and large, be leaving these deep questions of executive character unaddressed, all the while calling for a new vision, vitality, and spirit in Western organizations.

---

1   Srivastva and Cooperrider, *Appreciative Management and Leadership*, 5.

2   P. Vaill, in Srivastva, Cooperrider, and Associates, *Appreciative Management and Leadership*, 323-324.

In this book, an opportunity to begin your search for clarity and resolution is provided. If you have not consciously begun your search, you can do so with the assistance of some structure and process provided in the pages to follow. If you have already intentionally begun your search process, you can more easily monitor your clarity and progress.

Values are perhaps the next most perplexing area of life to clarify and resolve so that a sense of inner peace and integrity is in place within each person. Since there are so many criteria for judging which values are more correct or appropriate, which criteria shall we trust? Our inner sense of what should be our priorities? Evidence from history regarding the consequences of certain values being implemented? Are there any absolute values? Or should we adjust our values to the situation? Or, are some values situational in nature and others absolute? These questions, and others, are very difficult for most people to answer to their own satisfaction. Even so, the need for clarification and regeneration of values is nevertheless greatly needed. As pointed out by Gardner (1990)[3]

> The truth is that disintegration of the value framework is always going on—but so are regenerative processes. Some people see little hope that such processes can be effective, believing that we have lost the capacity to generate a new vision. A still gloomier view is that we may have lost the capacity to tolerate a new vision. The debunking reflex is powerful today. We are sick of past hypocrisies. We have seen the fine words of morality used as a screen for greed, for bigotry, for power seeking. Granted. But to let that estrange us from all attempts to regenerate the moral framework would be petulant and self-defeating.
>
> Creating value systems is something that the human species does. "It's our thing" as the recently popular saying goes, and without that irrepressible impulse civilization would not have survived. Destroy every vestige of law and morality, demolish every community, level the temples of justice, erase even the memory of custom, and one would see—in the midst of chaos, savagery and pillage—an awesome sight: the sight of men and women, bereft of all guiding memory, beginning to forge anew the rudiments of order and justice and law, acting out of the mysterious community-building impulse of the species.

---

3   J. Gardner, *On Leadership* (New York: The Free Press, 1990).

If it is true, and I agree with John Gardner that it is, that we by instinct seek order, peace and benevolent control, then let's get on with the task of clarification and teach others to do the same.

The first step toward clarification is an initial self-assessment. It is with this foundational concern regarding the need for clarity of beliefs and values within and between individuals that we begin the process of self examination and skills assessment in this chapter.

Inner Skills of the Transforming Leader: A Self-assessment

Below, you will be doing a self-assessment of the extent to which you believe you have the various skills. Each skill will be explained and you will then rate your own competency level in each area after you read about it. The skills will be explained below in the order in which they are developed, from the more simple to the more complex.

Instructions for Self-ratings:

In the box below and to the right of each skill description write in a number (from 1–5) which represents your evaluation of your present level of ability in performing each skill:

1 = Skill is new to me, cannot do it
2 = Understand it but cannot perform it
3 = Can begin to do it, but not naturally
4 = Can do it naturally in many situations
5 = Can do it well and teach others if I want

Self-management Skills for Transforming Leaders

Grounding: Focusing Awareness in the Present

This awareness skill of *grounding* involves your taking responsibility for placing your attention in each present moment, and not in memory about past events or in fantasy about future events. When you focus your attention in the "here and now" you are grounded in the present, fully available for interaction with self, the environment and people in each passing moment. People who are grounded have more personal presence, and people who are in fantasy or memory seem to be "spaced out," somewhere else, or in some ways "out of it." You can probably think of a person whom you know who is very "spaced out" most of the time, and another person whom you know who is very grounded most of the time.

This skill is the foundation of all other skills, for if we are psychologically unavailable to present events, our interactions with others will be interrupted or blocked. Take a moment to notice the extent to which you are steadily focused in the present, and rate yourself on how you generally function by writing in the appropriate number in the box to the right below:

Grounding
1 = Skill is new to me, cannot do it 2 = Understand it but cannot perform it 3 = Can begin to do it, but not naturally 4 = Can do it naturally in many situations 5 = Can do it well and teach others if I want

Centering: Including Self in the Context of Events

Centering is an important pre-requisite for being a conscious, alert, and *intentional* person, especially when exercising leadership. It is an awareness skill which enables you to intentionally be conscious of your own presence as a person with specific beliefs, biases, creative ideas, intuitions, revelations, emotions, physical experiences, and judgments in each moment. This awareness level is distinct from your awareness of external events. This deeper self-awareness can develop more quickly through self-conscious effort, and through the practice of being very still (deep relaxation, meditation, or prayer states). Centering is the opposite of selfishness because this part of yourself which can be more aware of *you*, is the same part of yourself which can be more receptive and sensitive to others. Take a moment now to check yourself and see how aware of your own feelings, thoughts, beliefs, physical sensations, and intuitions you are. Rate yourself on how you generally function by writing in the appropriate number in the box to the right on the next page:

Centering
1 = Skill is new to me, cannot do it 2 = Understand it but cannot perform it 3 = Can begin to do it, but not naturally 4 = Can do it naturally in many situations 5 = Can do it well and teach others if I want

Beliefs Clarification and Resolution: Taking a Stance on Life's Basic Issues

This awareness skill area will be the longest section in this chapter to explain because of its importance and complexity. This area of skill, or "wisdom" in discerning the nature of things, is the primary cornerstone for the development of the other skills to come. If when a person looks inside there is fog or "mush," that is too vague or soft a foundation to build on. We all could benefit from further clarification or a deepening of understanding of our operating assumptions about life.

Science defines and explains the "what and how" of observable life, and in the last 100 years has delved more into the powers of the previously unseen forces (radio, electronic and atomic). Beliefs (philosophy and religion) deal with the questions of "who and why?" These questions are much more difficult to answer but are at the same time more essential to our integrity because the answers we give to key questions determine our whole approach to our lives, to others, and to life itself.

This awareness "skill" is developed by examining carefully the main questions of existence, and (over time) searching and discovering workable answers to them. However, if we are to have any confidence in our answers they must have their validation in at least some of the ways of knowing (epistimology): through empirical investigation (science), historical evidence, personal experience (phenomenology), archeology, intuition (psychological), revelation (spiritual), etc. Otherwise we have little confidence that our assumptions about the nature of life are grounded in any kind of reality that is substantial and therefore believable. That our positions should be validatable at all of the levels listed above may also be of critical importance because if there is historical evidence to support the validity of our belief position but there is no other evidence (or conflicting evidence) we should be suspect! Perhaps our beliefs should be true at every level or they are only partly true?

For example, most people in the free world believe absolutely in the sanctity of life, that murder is wrong, and that the only justification for the use of force is to stop unjust, immoral or illegal killing (but only with the appropriate and necessary amount of police or military use of force). Evidence that murder for self-gain has negative consequences can be supported by historical documentation, empirical investigation, archeological findings, intuition, and possibly revelation (depending upon the belief system of the investigator). Therefore, I assert for the sake of discussion that murder is truly and absolutely wrong because under no circumstances does it have validatable positive consequences on the long term.

However, some people maintain that addressing the most difficult of life's "belief" questions is irrelevant to a meaningful existence in the here and now, and that mere values and goals are adequate for living (Ellis, 1976).[4] Values and goals are very important but the presumption that it is irrational for us to expect to clarify metaphysical issues and arrive at resolute beliefs does nothing for those of us who want to grasp some further essence of life, to go beyond what is visible, to comprehend life in new and deeper ways.

Beliefs are by their nature intensely personal. They are our *operating assumptions* about life, love, safety, happiness, leadership, management, etc. If we want to know a person intimately, we might first ask what he or she believes to be most real, true, good, unreal, false, bad. Then we will begin to get a picture of their position on some of the basic issues of life, which are really the *big questions* in life. In an annual survey (over 4 years) of my college and university students I have delineated 20 of what they think are "life's most unanswered problem questions" in their order of estimated difficulty to answer:

1. What is really happening here on this planet? What is the purpose of matter and existence, if any?
2. Is it possible to know at all, or should I just skip it as an issue I can't resolve?
3. What criteria do I use to discern what is true from what is not true, good from bad, real from unreal?

---

4   A. Ellis, *A New Guide to Rational Living* (Hollywood: Wilshire Book Company, 1976).

4. How can I know whether these criteria are reliable and true, and what are the sources of these criteria?

5. Who am I: In relation to others, the world, the universe, God, etc.?

6. What should I do with my life: A purpose for living, goals to accomplish, a career or "life calling" (vocation)?

7. What is truth? What is my definition of truth, where did I get it, and how do I know it is true?

8. What is the nature of human beings? Good? Evil? Neutral? Where did I get my belief? How did this human nature I believe in get to be the way it is: Creation, the environment, the "fall into original sin," conditioning, parents, etc.?

9. Is there a supreme being or ultimate cause, or did everything just evolve from nothing, and how do I know?

10. Where did matter come from? Creation by some conscious designer, or statistical happenstance, evolution?

11. Is everything absurd, or is there underlying and inherent purpose in life and in the universe?

12. Are there any absolutes (truths that are immovable) or is "reality" relative to each person's perspective?

13. What is the source(s) or cause(s) of negativity ("evil") and positivity ("good") in life? Are there many sources, one, none?

14. Is there life after death? If so, what kind, where, and with whom? If not, what happens, and how do I know this?

15. Is it possible to communicate with a higher being(s)? If so, how? If not, what difference does that make in my life?

16. What should I value? What is most important in life and what are my priorities?

17. Whom should I join up with in life: To marry, live with, work with, etc.? What criteria should I use to choose these people with whom I ally myself?

18. Where (geographically) on this planet do I want to live and why?

19. How do I prepare myself to fulfill my purpose and goals?

20. How do I know if I am doing OK in life?

These questions are among many critical questions which people ask, attempt to answer, or attempt to avoid answering. The fact that different people come up with clashing answers to these questions accounts for much of the discord, misunderstanding, and conflict in relationships, in organizations, and even between nations.

For most people, getting to the bottom of the above kinds of questions is a meaningful task (or quest, depending upon their view of the issue). However, when I asked over 300 students during the past 4 years how many of them had generally either given up on answering these kinds of questions or found them to be irrelevant, approximately 32% of them said "yes." The reasons they gave for giving up trying to answer the difficult questions of life were:

1. Confusion, or a feeling of being overwhelmed by the complexity of both the questions and the diversity of answers.
2. Lack of satisfying criteria for validating what is true or good.
3. Lack of interest in the issue of clarification.
4. Lack of understanding of the benefits of being more clear.
5. Lack of information and knowledge about alternatives.
6. Laziness, or fear.

About 28% of these 300 students reported that they were determined to "crack the code" to some kind of "higher reality." They said that they had already had some experiences which had led them to believe that there was a discernable reality beyond that which they could see with the eye.

Another 35% of the 300 claimed to have satisfying answers to these and other more difficult-to-answer questions. They seemed to have some kind of clear frame of reference, stance, faith, or belief about the questions of death, a supreme being, the nature of humans, why we are here, who we are, and where we are going. Approximately 5% decided not to respond to the questions put to them.

It would seem in one way that those people in the 35% group have an advantage over those who haven't, or somehow can't deal with these questions. In this state of conscious awareness, they act on specific assumptions and are more likely aware of the consequences of taking action based on each specific belief position. This enables them to gain feedback from their environments about the validity and workability of their assumptions. Contrast this clarity of mind with the person who is unsure and unresolved, or who wavers from situation to situation and gets mixed feedback.

Some of those who claim to know specific answers were criticized by others for not having ever really searched and opened their minds in the first place, because they may have simply "swallowed" what was "fed" to them.

It would appear from this informal study that the issue of beliefs is a highly charged and intensely personal one to most people. When challenged to rate the importance of this issue of beliefs clarity on a scale from 1–10 the average person gave the issue an 8.6 out of 10 (with a range of 4–10).

It is for this reason that I have developed a self-guided process of clarification of beliefs. The process is clearly a developmental one and usually there is not a sudden flash of blinding light on the road to Damascus as St. Paul is reported to have had, although slightly over one third of those who claimed to have achieved some clarity of beliefs said that there was a definite time that an internal "light went on."

Before outlining what I call steps in the search process we will examine my summaries of the developmental stages delineated by Fowler (1981).[5]

Clarification: A Developmental Process

Fowler describes the clarification and development of clear beliefs from a developmental perspective, by outlining what he calls "stages of faith:"

Stage 0: This is a pre-stage called *UNDIFFERENTIATED* faith. The seeds of trust, courage, hope and love are sown here during infancy and correspond somewhat to Erikson's psychosocial stage of Trust vs. Mistrust. When thought and language begin to converge, then the child moves through the transition to Stage 1.

Stage 1: This first stage is called the *INTUITIVE-PROJECTIVE* faith stage. Between ages 3–7, fantasy and *imitation* form powerfully and possibly permanently some basics of a belief system. Fluid thinking, the beginnings of self-awareness, and the verbalization of learned doctrines and concepts (mixed with imagination) are expressed, and the child begins to become more concrete in thought, separating fantasy from "doctrine," and getting ready to move into Stage 2.

---

5   J. Fowler, *Stages of Faith: Psychology of Human Development and the Quest for Meaning* (New York: Harper and Row, 1981).

Stage 2: *MYTHICAL-LITERAL* faith is characterized by the emergence of concrete, causal thinking, which is able to separate fantasy from the stories, doctrines, beliefs and observances that have been taught in order to *belong* to the family or surrounding community. Symbols are taken literally, as are moral rules and attitudes. This is the faith stage of the school child (ages 7–12), though this stage is found in many adolescents and adults.

People at this stage are able to be deeply affected by stories and dramatic presentations (highly vulnerable to influence, therefore) but are *not able yet to consciously reflect on the meaning or possible errancy of such presentations* (T.V. included). Because of a lack of reflective or relative-thinking capacity they may seem to be "legalistic," black-and-white thinkers.

The transition to Stage 3 is marked with a breakdown of literalism; and contradictions in stories or reflective logic can cause disillusionment with previous teachers or teachings (including parental influences and early religious training). Formal operational thought makes such reflection possible and necessary.

Stage 3: This stage is called *SYNTHETIC-CONVENTIONAL* faith. It emerges most often in adolescence, but for many adults, becomes a place of non-responsible comfort, fun, or avoidance of further development. This is a "conformist" stage because one's security and identity are defined and dependent upon others. It *does not have enough inner—and autonomous—judgment or solid faith to build and maintain an inner resolution about beliefs.* The Stage 3 person believes, but often not in a wholehearted, well-examined manner, and constantly scans the environment (especially the social environment) to see if what is believed is popular, accepted.

The adolescent is using the beliefs and assumptions which were acquired in childhood in a sense to "get by" during the turbulent and insecure teenage years, until full formal operational thinking capacity develops; then, a full and thorough examination regarding the source, validity, and utility of a belief system (and therefore an inner identity) can be independently begun. Quite often crises occur (such as the failure of a love relationship, the parents' marriage, or leaving home), which precipitate the breakdown of stage 3 and the need to move into the "crisis of the deeper life" which can prove to be the most critical, but also most rewarding, transition.

Stage 4: Stage 4 is called *INDIVIDUATIVE-REFLECTIVE* faith. At this time a person realizes how alone he or she really is in deciding everything, even if there has been relegation of that responsibility to others, one's self-awareness causes a painful realization that "my decisions are in my own hands." Many adults do not reach this stage, perhaps because they are for a number of reasons unable, or if they do, they turn away from the burden of responsibility for their own consciously chosen life, and turn to the age old philosophy of *Numbism,* supported in full force by the increasingly available forms of "soma" (alcohol, drugs, eating, T.V. and other "give up" paraphernalia described by Glasser, 1984).[6]

This level is extremely difficult to face, and especially difficult to face alone. There are fewer and fewer people who are more developed than you are to give you help as you move up the stages of development! If the call to higher belief definition is heeded, *the reward is a sense of one's own being beyond the definitions others give us, and beyond the roles one happens to be in at the time.* For many people in this stage, a certain sense of the *reality* of a *"higher being"* has been reported to be especially strong and clear in a personal way.

At this level, the ability to critically reflect on one's own self identity and upon various outlooks or ideologies is greatly enhanced. The ability to be increasingly objective is a *danger* however, in that there can come a kind of *cognitive self-assurance* which closes off a continuing deeper search, and trades it in for "settling for security." However, for many people there creeps in a certain restlessness, a sense of flatness, or sterility to life that prompts or even urges a higher search for greater meaning and intimacy with what ultimately is to be discovered: This stage has been called by many the "mid-life crisis," and seems to often occur for many people in their early to mid-forties.

Stage 5: Stage 5 is called *CONJUNCTIVE* faith. Often the potential power in symbolic meanings comes alive for people in this stage. Ricoeur calls it a "second naivete" where the emotional and/or spiritual impact of one's beliefs becomes quickened, or alive in each moment ("becoming as a little child," if you will). A reworking of the fabric of one's past into the garment of the future must be attended to. In mid-life, when this stage usually occurs, *there is a seriousness which emerges* and it knows the realities of defeat, the irrevocability of certain commitments and acts, and is in full appreciation that life is more than half over (at best).

---

6   W. Glasser, *Taking Effective Control of Your Life* (New York: Harper and Row, 1984).

This is the sobering, deepening time when the search for inner resolve and resolution is contrasted with a curious openness to new depths of spirituality and the possibility of personal revelations. A sense of the ironic, the paradoxes of life, the unsolvable mysteries, makes life both more magical and the individual more able to be in a state of wonder and awe. On the other hand, some people become bitter or get into a state of complacency or cynical withdrawal if the power of faith is not sufficient to withstand a more full awareness of the inescapable presence of death and the unknown.

While many people in this stage report deep peace, inner resolution and interrelatedness to their supreme being and loved ones, others report a sense of hopelessness and futility and excruciating hollowness when they arrive near the top of this developmental climb. In only a few cases, people who arrive at this stage are moved or committed to move on to the stage of radical actualization called *Universalizing Faith* (Stage 6).

Stage 6: *UNIVERSALIZING FAITH* is characterized by the person's radical commitment to the sanctity of all being, all life, justice, love, and of selfless passion for a transformed world. They aren't pushing what they personally wish to see happen (as Hitler or the Reverend Jim Jones), but are committed to a transcendent vision as was Gandhi and Martin Luther King, Jr., and as is Mother Theresa; and many others who had "no greater love than this, than to lay down their lives for their friends" (Jesus, approx. 33 AD). They seem to have a "subversive" character which challenges the status quo, governments, and/or individuals to reach past their own usual patterns of self-orientation to the higher path of love for others. Fowler states of these Stage 6 people:

> *It is my conviction that persons who come to embody Universalizing faith are drawn into those patterns of commitment and leadership by the providence of God and the exigencies of history, heated in the fires of turmoil and trouble and then hammered into usable shape on the hard anvil of conflict and struggle (p. 202).*

These people in stage 6 have a clear vision of what life is "meant to be," are able to feel the injustice and suffering imposed on others, are nearly always heralded for their uncommon courage and faith, and are willing to die for the cause of justice and the liberation of any and all people. Not many of us are able or perhaps willing to take the full leap into Universalizing faith.

Admittedly, the six steps outlined above are "western" in their orientation, much as are the developmental stages of Piaget. These stage specific theories do not seem true to some people in other cultures. However, Fowler has at least given us a starting place in understanding the development of what many people would call the spiritual part of people.

Steps in the Process of Clarification of Your Belief Stance

The process of clarifying your beliefs involves several steps. By following these steps, your own belief stance will become more clear as time passes. The steps for clarifying beliefs can be done with your own self, or you can help an individual or group of people to gain resolution by coaching them through the following steps.

1. As best you can, specify in writing your present answers to life's major questions which were outlined above (or attempt to answer your own problem questions);
2. Search out their sources, where you got your beliefs, and write down these sources for later comparison;
3. Examine your criteria for accepting these beliefs as true, and write down the various validations for your beliefs which you accept;
4. Write a clear and concise position paper about your stance on life's major questions and issues;
5. Read this paper over once a week while you consistently attempt to take on this position in a real way, living it out on a daily basis as congruently as you are able;
6. Review your position statements every 3–6 months, and examine how your position helps you to deal with problems or better appreciate the joys of life;
7. Note any "holes" or inconsistencies in your belief positions which you think may be invalid, incomplete, or problematic;
8. Examine other differing belief positions (ones you think are incomplete, or false, if any) which validate for you how true your position is; or, note how there are parts of other positions which seem to have truth in them on the premise that "truth is truth wherever it is found." To assist you to get started with this step, I would suggest that you consider reading Chapter 9 in Naisbitt and Aburdene's book,

Megatrends 2000.[7] This book will give you a factual overview of what is occurring in the world of beliefs. Using this chapter as an introduction, you could move ahead with a more thorough study of each of the various philosophical or religious belief positions.

Students who have generally followed this series of steps in my courses on self-awareness and interpersonal communication have reported in the course evaluations at the end of the terms that this exercise was the most challenging and meaningful of their semester, and some of them even reported that it was the most important step in their whole lives.

The Downside of Failing to Clarify a Lifestance

People who avoid this whole issue of belief clarification, or give up on its resolution, perhaps are less deeply "rooted" in a life position, are more easily influenced to move in a number of directions depending upon which way a personal, social, political or economic "wind" is blowing at the time, and they often claim that "flexible" tendency to be a strength, that they are "open minded," willing to "change with the times." However, they also often say that they have little inner peace, that decision making is difficult without a clear reference point, and that their relationships suffer because they often clash with people who have clear beliefs.

I believe that those who have a metaphysical understanding of and orientation to life (answers to the "why" questions) have a distinct advantage, even if their orientation may ultimately be incorrect in the end. I believe they are more solid, act more consistently, can get feedback from the environment as to the validity and workability of their actions (because they *have* a position as a reference point) and many times are better able to understand others' positions, a "tolerance" skill which is important when leading people.

Beliefs form the solid foundation of a clear purpose in life, and a clear set of values are structures upon which to build goals, strategies, and actions. With only values to live by, the "why" of life is not addressed, explored, or resolved in the least. Beliefs address the "why" and "what" questions of life directly. The hierarchical relationship between beliefs, purpose, values, goals, strategies and actions is illustrated as follows:

---

7   J. Naisbitt and P. Aburdene, *Megatrends 2000: Ten New Directions for the 1990's* (New York: William Morrow and Company, 1990).

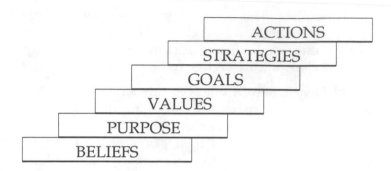

When people can share some basic beliefs they are more likely to join together to create something productive. This is true for marriage partners, or any other type of endeavor in business, health, education, community development, or human services, where team effort is required.

Furthermore, if you understand others' beliefs, you are more likely to comprehend why they have given their "hearts" to them, why they feel they need them, why they need to keep their own beliefs, and even be more tolerant.

Rate how much you have developed this awareness skill, and how much you have gained a clear and resolved sense of your beliefs in relation to the 20 (or other) questions outlined earlier in the chapter.

Beliefs Clarification and Resolution

1 = Skill is new to me, cannot do it
2 = Understand it but cannot perform it
3 = Can begin to do it, but not naturally
4 = Can do it naturally in many situations
5 = Can do it well and teach others if I want

Specifying Your Personal Purpose: A Critical Life Skill

As you gain a greater sense of clarity about what you believe or assume to be real and true it is easier to move ahead to specify a keener sense of purpose in your life which is in harmony with your beliefs. If your beliefs are fuzzy or unresolved you will have more difficulty in specifying a definite purpose.

A desire for clarification, and a belief that it is possible are good requisites for making progress in this area.

Finding or developing a clear sense of personal purpose is not an easy task. I personally tried for a number of years to state my purpose for living on paper without having a sense that I had actually captured the essence of it. My life was less focused and organized because of this. I found myself saying "yes" to things which others wanted me to do, or to things which I couldn't see a good reason to say "no" to, and as a result my life became filled with tasks, goals, and even obligations which didn't "click way down deep." I would get up in the morning and say to myself, "What am I *really* up to today, anyway?"

In the French language, the phrase which roughly translates as "purpose" is *raison d'etre*: Specifically, it translates as *reason for BEING*. Why should you even *BE*? If we can answer that question so that we have a burning sense of mission, purpose or desire, then we will be internally motivated, we will be able to better clarify and set priorities, and better able to specify high-drive goals which match our strengths and abilities. My own personal purpose statement reads as follows:

> *"My purpose in life is to increasingly become a transformative leader, facilitating the spiritual, mental, emotional, physical, and interpersonal development of others who can become transformative leaders in the lives of others, and in organizations or groups, for the same purpose."*

So, I am an author, encourager, facilitator, helper, knowledge resource, consultant, and supporter of other leaders (or leaders-to-be) who have as their purpose to impact human and organization development for positive ends. I include my family in this purpose; my wife and two boys are leaders and becoming better at it. My identity is steeped in this purpose. I plan my days around this purpose, set my priorities and goals around this purpose, and encourage and assist willing others to do the same. I have also learned to have fun in the midst of all of this endeavoring, something which many people forget when they get too goal-oriented. However, I admit that I fall short in certain areas, lose balance at times and neglect one or more parts of my life—sometimes it is my fitness schedule, sometimes my wife, my sons, or even God whom I claim to an extent to know and love. I want to make sure that I don't give the impression that I "have it all together" when I don't.

I consider my two sons as transforming leaders in their schools and on their sports fields. I encourage and support my wife to grow because I care for her and because of the positive impact she has on my children, on me, and on others. I consider my college and university students as transforming leaders, many of whom are developing abilities to develop others. I consider managers and executives with whom I do consulting to be potentially more transformative as leaders. I treasure each person, and each one of us has a great potential to make positive impact, however seemingly small at the moment. I have at times been shocked years later to find that even a "low-achiever" who was in one of my college classes has made a signficant impact on people and the organizations they live and work in. I was shocked at how I had obviously prejudged these people!

I feel fulfilled with this purpose, and get a charge of excitement when I see it realized. It is highly motivating to me. You may want to try writing your own purpose statement in the space provided below:

My Personal Purpose Statement:

If you are having difficulty in specifying your sense of purpose, a course in career and life planning or personal life planning counseling can be a very worthwhile investment. Readings in this area could also be useful.

Rate below your ability to specify a clear, satisfying, motivating purpose for your own life.

Specification of Personal Purpose

1 = Skill is new to me, cannot do it
2 = Understand it but cannot perform it
3 = Can begin to do it, but not naturally
4 = Can do it naturally in many situations
5 = Can do it well and teach others if I want

Values Identification Skills: Setting Priorities

The more clear your purpose is, the greater ease you will have in identifying what is important to you. Confusion rules when our sense of purpose is vague. Clarifying and identifying values (importances) is a somewhat difficult matter of prioritizing various things in our lives, such as spirituality, family, career, education, money, geographic location, etc. When we know what we find to be most important, more valuable in relation to other values, it becomes easier to set goals.

My highest value is human life and human development. I value the quality of the inner life of myself and other individuals more highly than anything else. Developing quality inner life, and learning to express high quality to others through caring and the use of knowledge and skills is very important to me. I value high impact activities where the payoff is primarily human development. It is because of these values that I set the goal of writing this book.

Another way to get at our values, especially in relation to work, is to assess our patterns of interest in relation to others. Testing in this area with interest inventories is available in most counseling centers at colleges and universities for free.

If you wanted to go through a more complete values preference prioritization exercise you could obtain a copy of Robinson's (1990)[8] *Values Preference Inventory.*

If you have difficulty with this area you could take a values clarification or identification course or workshop, do readings in this area, or seek professional consultative advice or counseling from a career or personal counselor.

Rate your ability to identify and prioritize your values in order of importance as a preparation for setting clear and motivating goals:

Values Identification Skills

1 = Skill is new to me, cannot do it
2 = Understand it but cannot perform it
3 = Can begin to do it, but not naturally
4 = Can do it naturally in many situations
5 = Can do it well and teach others if I want

Education, Career and Life Planning Skills: Setting Motivating Goals

As you gain clarity of purpose and identify your values in order of priority, you will be able to more easily and clearly set motivating goals. Effective goals are based upon clear beliefs and assumptions, a deep sense of purpose, and clear values; and must be desirable, concretely defined, realistically achievable within the time you have available, measurable so that you know when you have reached them, owned or chosen by yourself instead of imposed on you by others and celebrated when achieved.

One of my goals is to complete and publish this book by next July, so I can prepare to use it in a leadership course I teach to 3rd and 4th year university students who are entering the fields of business, human services, or education. This goal fits my beliefs, fulfills my purpose, is guided and shaped by my values, and is achievable within a realistic time frame for balance in life (if I stick to my work schedule I have created for a balance in my life between leisure/family, work, and education).

---

8   E. Robinson, *The Values Preference Inventory* (Abbotsford, B.C. Canada: Consulting Resource Group International, Inc., 1990).

Rate your own ability to set clear goals and achieve them within the time frame you allow:

Education, Career and Life Planning Skills	
1 = Skill is new to me, cannot do it 2 = Understand it but cannot perform it 3 = Can begin to do it, but not naturally 4 = Can do it naturally in many situations 5 = Can do it well and teach others if I want	

Time Management Skills

After teaching this skill for years, I estimate that few people actually want to practice time management skills to increase their own productivity and balance in life. Most of us tend to just live from day to day, get done what we can, and avoid what we can avoid in terms of stress. Many people get discouraged when they first try to plan their personal and work lives because at first they aren't very realistic, their plans don't work out as expected, they often try to do too much in too short a time, experience some "burnout," and give up on any kind of systematic approach to planning and living. This is unfortunate because it is possible to find a comfortable and productive way of becoming more effective in the use of time. I have discovered very practical approach to dealing with the complexities we face in our work and personal lives by using three "bins" into which each task gets placed:

Priority 1: Must be dealt with today;
Priority 2: Would like to do today if there is time for it;
Priority 3: Will get to it if I can, someday.

As time goes by, various tasks can be moved up into a higher priority "bin." If everything just keeps piling up, then of course we have to ask ourselves if we really want to live or work in that way!

Another important way to manage time is to "chunk" out time blocks by the type of task: All phone calls returned between 9 am and 10 am, all letters written between 10am and 11am, etc. For some people, this approach is very effective and eliminates distraction and complexity which can interfere with effective performance.

When your beliefs, purpose, values, and goals are clear it is much easier to decide in which of the three piles things belong. My experience is that I become better at managing time as I do it over and over. It is an art as well as a logical planning activity. Sometimes I structure in time that is not structured or goal-oriented, except that my goal during that "loose" time is to get loose from any regimen.

Rate your ability to plan your activities and manage your time:

Time Management Skills	
1 = Skill is new to me, cannot do it 2 = Understand it but cannot perform it 3 = Can begin to do it, but not naturally 4 = Can do it naturally in many situations 5 = Can do it well and teach others if I want	

Personal Energy and Stress Management for Improved Health and Performance

Energy management is the focus here because it is a preventive approach to stress management. If you can get the "jump" on stress accumulation in your mind and body by nourishing, strengthening, and resting yourself physically, then you will have a much greater reserve of energy with which to cope resourcefully with more difficult or demanding situations. In addition to avoiding harmful substances such as tobacco, alcohol in moderate to large quantities, and various medical and non-medical drugs there are four areas where increased knowledge and development can result in a greater resilience and hardiness.

The Four Lifestyle Management Keys to Increased Energy and Performance: Optimum Nutrition, Exercise, Deep Relaxation, and Restful Sleep

The wide range of opinions about what makes up the optimum amounts and best types of nutrition, exercise, deep relaxation, and sleep is overwhelming and confusing for most people. Just what sources or experts should one rely on when attempting to establish an appropriate balance in these four energy resource foundations? After reviewing the literature in the four resource areas that has been published in the last 20 years, the following basic learnings and guidelines become evident:

1. There is little disagreement among various experts in the fields about things one might best do in general to increase baseline energy and performance levels;

2. Individual differences between people are significant enough that any one prescription for anyone could be arbitrarily effective or ineffective;

3. Assessments of a particular individual's unique physiology, needs, and style are prerequisites to any appropriate health and fitness program design that could be made for that person;

4. A monitoring of progress on any program is necessary if one is to know if in fact changes made in diet, exercise, relaxation practices, or sleep patterns make any worthwhile difference;

5. Life style changes (clarity of purpose, values, goals, plans, and activities) often accompany increased control and balance of energy resources which result in higher performance and vitality, and these lifestyle changes need to be protected and supported if the programs are to promote sustained higher energy and performance;

6. Once new and more effective habit patterns have been well established which are more preferable to the old patterns, there are side benefits of increased self-awareness, self-esteem and therefore self-confidence;

7. A combination of professional medical advice and personal experimentation with various programs yields the results of improved health, wellness, increased performance and well-being.

It is not the purpose of this book to look in depth at this area, but to introduce you to the importance of learning to manage this part of life well. The benefits of healthful practices are obvious, and the limitations which can occur when we allow stress to overtake us are also obvious.

Two books which could be beneficial reading in this area are by Schafer (1987)[9] and Roglieri (1980).[10]

---

9   W. Schafer, *Stress Management for Wellness* (New York: Holt, Rinehart and Winston, 19).

10 J.L. Roglieri, *Odds on Your Life* (New York: Seaview, 1980).

Rate yourself overall, in your ability to manage and practice the four skill areas of nutrition, exercise, deep relaxation, and effective sleep.

Lifestyle Management Skills	
1 = Skill is new to me, cannot do it 2 = Understand it but cannot perform it 3 = Can begin to do it, but not naturally 4 = Can do it naturally in many situations 5 = Can do it well and teach others if I want	

Positive Mental Attitude: The Inner Skill of the Winner

In his studies of professional athletes, Waitley (1979)[11] found that there were specifically identifiable patterns of thought and action which distinguished winners from losers. The major differences were found in mental attitude, and other less significant differences were found in physical ability. He studied winners from many fields and found similar success patterns.

The ability to face an apparent problem and see it as a positive challenge is one internal ability winners have. They inwardly control their reactions to an event and assign it the weight of importance which is appropriate to the situation, rather than assess the situation by the intensity or depth of their emotions at the moment.

Winners take failure and use it to improve their next performance—their rationale is, "The more times I fail, the more practice I get, the better I get." Because they practice more often without presuming that they cannot achieve a particular goal, they succeed more often.

Rate your ability (on the following page) to stay focused with a winning attitude:

---

11 D. Waitley, *The Psychology of Winning* (New York: The Berkeley Publishing Company, 1979).

Positive Mental Attitude

1 = Skill is new to me, cannot do it
2 = Understand it but cannot perform it
3 = Can begin to do it, but not naturally
4 = Can do it naturally in many situations
5 = Can do it well and teach others if I want

Total of Awareness and Self-management Section

Total of the awareness and self-management section
(Add all numbers in the boxes above and place the total here)

Conclusion

The results you will see on the self-assessment graph (on the following page) will help you to plan your future professional development activities, or identify specific training needs if you decide to engage in the Leading Manager Program. The skills which are rated "3" or below are ones which you assess as needing definite development.

Graphing Your Self-assessment Scores

Now that you have completed this section of the comprehensive self-assessment, graph in all of your individual scores so that you can get a visual summary of what skills you see are stronger and weaker. Graph in your self-rating scores on each skill using the "bar graph" method of drawing lines from left to right on each scale.

1 = Skill is new to me, cannot do it
2 = Understand it but cannot perform it
3 = Can begin to do it, but not naturally
4 = Can do it naturally in many situations
5 = Can do it well and teach others if I want

	1	2	3	4	5
Grounding: Focusing Awareness in the Present					
Centering: Including Self in the Context of Events					
Beliefs Clarification and Resolution					
Specifying Your Personal Purpose					
Values Identification Skills: Setting Priorities					
Education, Career and Life Planning Skills: Setting Motivating Goals					
Time Management Skills					
Personal Energy and Stress Management for Improved Health and Performance					
The Four Lifestyle Management Keys to Increased Energy and Performance: Optimum Nutrition, Exercise, Deep Relaxation, and Restful Sleep					
Positive Mental Attitude: The Inner Skill of the Winner					

Knowledge and Skills which Develop and Transform People and Organizations

HUMAN RESOURCE DEVELOPMENT RESULTS

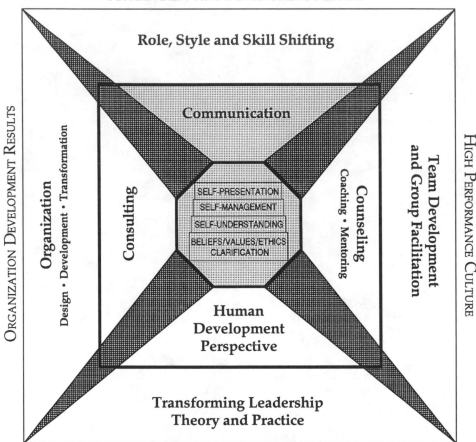

ORGANIZATION DEVELOPMENT RESULTS

Role, Style and Skill Shifting

Communication

Organization
Design • Development • Transformation

Consulting

SELF-PRESENTATION
SELF-MANAGEMENT
SELF-UNDERSTANDING
BELIEFS/VALUES/ETHICS
CLARIFICATION

Counseling
Coaching • Mentoring

**Team Development
and Group Facilitation**

HIGH PERFORMANCE CULTURE

Human
Development
Perspective

Transforming Leadership
Theory and Practice

EFFECTIVE PERSONNEL PRACTICES

Chapter 5

▼

THE SKILLS OF INTERPERSONAL COMMUNICATION

To care for another person,
I must be able to understand him and his world
as if I were inside it. I must be able to see
as it were what his world is like to him and how he sees himself.

M. Mayeroff

Instead of merely looking at him in a detached way from outside, as if he were a specimen, I must be able to be with him in his world, "going" into his world in order to sense from the "inside" what life is like for him, what he is striving to be and what he requires to grow (Mayeroff, 1971).[1]

THIS SELF-ASSESSMENT SECTION will introduce you to the interpersonal skills necessary to facilitate effective communication between self and others at home, at work or at play.

---

1   M. Mayeroff, *On Caring* (New York: Perennial Library, Harper and Row, 1971) 41–42.

Introduction

What Are Communication Skills?

Interpersonal communication skills are the vehicles by which all interactions between you and other people are made clear. Much of the communication which occurs between people is one-way, without either party truly hearing the other and accurately understanding the feelings, thoughts, or reasons for these feelings or thoughts. In fact, if you think about it, our modern culture, especially in cities, teaches many people not to have two-way communication because it is too personal and imposing.

Have you ever had a course where you were *trained* in interpersonal communication skills so that it was confirmed that you had competencies, not just knowledge? Where do people go to get such training? There aren't very many places to go: Not at most schools, not in most families, not at most churches, not even in most business schools, medical schools, or law schools.

Self-assessment in Communication Skills

The practice of good communication skills results in two-way communication which builds intimate relationships or solves practical problems, whichever is the intent. This chapter will assist you to review and self-assess the extent to which you have the skills which have been researched as critical to the development of effective interpersonal communication in any setting (Carkhuff, 1971);[2] and Ivey (1983).[3]

Self-disclosure: Appropriately Sharing Yourself With Others

Self-disclosure refers to the ability to appropriately reveal deeper and deeper levels of self to others, as the other person in the relationship earns trust which warrants such deeper and more genuine disclosure. This skill is one which is critical in the development of both your self-concept and your relationships with others.

---

2   R. Carkhuff, *The Development of Human Resources* (New York: Holt, Rinehart and Winston, 1971).

3   A. Ivey, *Intentional Interviewing and Counseling* (Pacific Grove, CA.: Brooks/Cole, 1983).

It seems that we earn trust and intimacy as a trade-off for depth of self-disclosure. Being visible, but not unwisely risking too much information too soon, promotes this type of trust, and can even promote intimacy. If no one knows you very well, you will likely not feel much of a "connection" to others. Perhaps a sense of "belonging" with others is one deep need we all have, and if that need is frustrated, some people experience emotional difficulties. If you are shy, fearful that others will "use" any knowledge they have about you against you, then you will likely have difficulty with this skill of appropriately sharing yourself with others.

Self-disclosure, in order to be most effective must be well timed, not too deep or too shallow, for the purpose of improving the relationship and be shared in confidence and trust.

Rate your ability to share yourself at the appropriate depth in a wide range of social and business situations, and eventually deeply become psychologically intimate with some special others; or to distance yourself appropriately where intimacy is not called for.

Self-disclosure	
1 = Skill is new to me, cannot do it 2 = Understand it but cannot perform it 3 = Can begin to do it, but not naturally 4 = Can do it naturally in many situations 5 = Can do it well and teach others if I want	

Image and Impression Management Skills: Taking Responsibility for How You See Yourself and for How Others See You

Image Management: This skill refers to your ability to be conscious of how you are seeing your own self, monitoring the development of any negative images which would undermine your effectiveness as a person or leader, and managing them in a number of ways to ensure that they remain positive no matter what external circumstances occur. This is a very critical skill area often neglected by many people. It is mainly a skill which is activated by awareness and by carefully choosing and affirming a positive self-image. Also, it is important to live congruently (with integrity) to that image so that it can develop as a part of the very fabric of your being. Studies on successful people reveal that this inner capacity and strength of managing self-image is an important contributor to success in career and life (Glasser, 1984, and Waitley, 1983).[4],[5]

Rate your ability to apply this skill in your own life.

Image Management
1 = Skill is new to me, cannot do it 2 = Understand it but cannot perform it 3 = Can begin to do it, but not naturally 4 = Can do it naturally in many situations 5 = Can do it well and teach others if I want

Impression Management: This skill involves awareness of the impact of your behavior on other people, and control of your behavior in order to alter this impact in a desired manner. It is related to the above skill in that it involves the bringing forward of the positive images of self which have been created or discovered. The skill includes the following: Learning to dress appropriately for various social situations, learning to speak effectively and articulately, expressing strong, effective and pleasant non-verbal messages to others, creating the image in others minds which you desire them to have of you, and avoiding being "pigeonholed" by others' limited perceptions of you. The research and practical applications of this skill area are extensive and can be reviewed (Schlenker, 1982).[6]

Rate your ability (on the following page) to apply this skill in your own life.

---

4   W. Glasser, *Take Effective Control of Your Life,* (New York: Harper and Row, 1984).

5   D. Waitley, *Seeds of Greatness* (Old Tappan, New Jersey: Fleming H. Revell Company, 1983).

6   B. Schlenker, *Impression Management* (Monterey, California: Brooks/Cole Publishing Company, 1982).

Impression Management
1 = Skill is new to me, cannot do it
2 = Understand it but cannot perform it
3 = Can begin to do it, but not naturally
4 = Can do it naturally in many situations
5 = Can do it well and teach others if I want

Attending: Giving Undivided Attention to Others

Attending involves both your appearing to be attentive to others and your actually (inwardly) giving your undivided attention. Attending behaviors which give you the *appearance of being interested* in others are: Facing the other person, squaring your shoulders, appropriate eye contact, open and relaxed posture, leaning into the relationship (instead of leaning back) and appropriate distancing (usually 3–6 feet in North American culture, further away in Asian cultures, and often closer in Mediterranean, some European, and South American cultures). Genuinely giving attention to others is something which others can sense as well as observe. *Focused attention* from the "heart" is what most people want and expect from one another, but receive all too seldom. Attending forms the basis for observing another person accurately, and is a pre-requisite skill for observing without distorting your perceptions. Make a review of your attending behaviors and your ability to inwardly direct your attention where you want it to go on a continuous basis.

Rate your ability to apply this skill in your own life.

Attending
1 = Skill is new to me, cannot do it
2 = Understand it but cannot perform it
3 = Can begin to do it, but not naturally
4 = Can do it naturally in many situations
5 = Can do it well and teach others if I want

Observing: Seeing Another Person Without Distorting

Observing skills involve your *conscious* receiving of information about another person from all visible sources: A person's physical tension and energy levels, facial expressions, skin flushes, body posture, manner of dress, expressive mannerisms, hand movements, gestures, and the sum total of all other "body language." When you can just simply *see* what another person *is* doing, and keep those observations separate from any judgments you might be having, then you are being more objective in your understanding of others. Observing skills prevent the development of assumptions and alert us to judgmental tendencies we all seem to have at times. Observing is the pre-requisite skill for effectively and temporarily suspending your own frame of reference (judgment or value system). Evaluate your ability to observe accurately and keep your personal reactions separate from what you see.

Rate your ability to apply this skill in your own life.

Observing
1 = Skill is new to me, cannot do it 2 = Understand it but cannot perform it 3 = Can begin to do it, but not naturally 4 = Can do it naturally in many situations 5 = Can do it well and teach others if I want

Suspending Frame of Reference: The Key to the Golden Rule

The skill of temporarily suspending frame of reference is perhaps the most critical and important of all other skills in that our credibility and effectiveness can rest *solely* on our performance of this skill. Your frame of reference is made up of your beliefs, assumptions, values, feelings, judgments, emotions, advice, moods, thoughts, and stress levels at any given moment. Because our *frame of reference* is so personal and deeply imbedded in each of us, it is very difficult to practice suspending it on a regular basis. Most interpersonal, counseling and leadership problems stem from this difficulty we all seem to have of needing to interpret reality from our own vantage point, and reacting in a self-oriented manner. It is very important that we learn to react in such a way that we take into consideration others' points of view and feelings, as well as our own.

This skill, simply put, is inner strength for self-control of emotions, judgments, and premature advice. Practicing this *suspending* skill involves putting others first before self, checking things out before jumping to conclusions or reacting emotionally, and giving others the benefit of any doubts which we might have about them. Making snap judgments, reacting emotionally to a situation before we really understand it, "writing a person off" before we give him or her a fair chance, or assuming that something is true before we check it out, are all signs of *not* suspending. Suspending is appropriate especially when others need to be understood in order for their tension or stress to be defused. In this way we can help them to become ready to hear our own thoughts, feelings or points of view. Suspending is the foundation of patience, gentleness, kindness, respect and effectiveness in all leadership, counseling and communication situations.

Rate how well you see yourself performing this skill in your interactions with others.

Suspending Frame of Reference	
1 = Skill is new to me, cannot do it 2 = Understand it but cannot perform it 3 = Can begin to do it, but not naturally 4 = Can do it naturally in many situations 5 = Can do it well and teach others if I want	

Questioning: Appropriate Gathering of Information

Questioning is a much overused skill which often puts others on the defensive. It is appropriate to use *open* questions (such as, "What do you think about that?") when we want a person to expand on a particular topic without influencing the direction of their talk. However, as we will see, active listening and checking for what people intend to convey to us is often more effective than questioning. Questioning makes us seem that we are the ones who are controlling the situation, much like interrogations during a police interview. *Closed* questions, such as "How many times did you beat your wife?," leave little room for discussion and force a person into the answer we hope to hear from them.

Effective questioning is used when we need to gather information about a person's address, what he or she thinks about a specific issue, or when we want directions to get to a particular place. In general, questions are less personal than active listening, and should be reserved for less personal interchanges when correctness or completeness of information is the main focus. Questions are risky to use on a habitual basis because when we question others, we are often taking the ball from them and leading the direction of the conversation, usually unconsciously, in the direction we think it should go (and thereby we fail to suspend frame of reference). Though it is possible to be effective and appropriate in the use of questions, more often than not, questions can interfere with good communication because they can be misused, and overused so easily.

Rate yourself below in how effectively and appropriately you use questioning skills.

Questioning
1 = Skill is new to me, cannot do it
2 = Understand it but cannot perform it
3 = Can begin to do it, but not naturally
4 = Can do it naturally in many situations
5 = Can do it well and teach others if I want

Listening: Checking for What Others Intend to Mean

A person who listens well *actively checks* for the intended meaning from the sender's point of view. A good listener is grounded, centered, gives undivided attention, temporarily suspends emotions, advice, and judgments, uses questions in a limited and appropriate manner, and checks with the sender to see if there is mutually understood meaning.

The skill of active listening also involves *letting others finish* even when you *feel* like "butting in" to make a point. Helping others to feel heard and get finished with what they are saying only increases the chances that their "door" will be open when we do send a message to them from our own frame of reference.

To some people, letting others finish and feel understood seems to be a "phony" way to interact (because they are holding themselves back), and they are uncomfortable with it as a skill. Perhaps it can be seen that way, but nevertheless *careful listening works to clarify confusing* messages and defuse tensions which are often at the root of conflicts or misunderstandings in all kinds of relationships. One language format which can be used for active listening is:

"You mean_____?"

Check yourself now to see how well you practice this skill in your interchanges with others, and rate yourself below.

Listening
1 = Skill is new to me, cannot do it
2 = Understand it but cannot perform it
3 = Can begin to do it, but not naturally
4 = Can do it naturally in many situations
5 = Can do it well and teach others if I want

Responding With Understanding: Getting on the Inside

The skill of responding with understanding is a more powerful, personal and intimate skill which can require the other person's permission for use. Many people will resist or even resent your responding to their feelings directly. Many others will experience relief or satisfaction when you understand their feelings in a specific way. Yet, one of the most frequent complaints we hear from employees, spouses, children, and relatives is "he/she doesn't even understand how I *feel*." In order to carefully understand what someone is feeling, all of the above skills must be applied first. What is important here is that this particular skill is best used *when others want* us to use it with them. Otherwise we might be accused of being like "phony bleeding heart social workers."

To use this skill requires more expertise and sensitivity than any of the other skills reviewed to this point because careful observation of non-verbal cues is required, and this is how responding gets you inside of another person's emotional world. Responding with accurate understanding also enables you to see and feel things from others' points of view.

That is why this skill is the foundation of the quality called "empathy." Empathy is defined as *communicated understanding*, so that you can prove to other people that you understand what they feel and think and why they feel and think the way they do. One language format which can be used for conveying empathy is:

"You seem to feel ___*(feeling word)*___ because ___*(reason)*___."

Formats are just general guidelines, and may be changed to fit the situation or person, but must contain a direct and accurate response to a person's feeling state and the appropriate reason why he or she feels a particular emotion. Empathy training is available as a part of most communication skills training courses or workshops.

Rate yourself below in your ability to use this skill.

Responding With Understanding
1 = Skill is new to me, cannot do it 2 = Understand it but cannot perform it 3 = Can begin to do it, but not naturally 4 = Can do it naturally in many situations 5 = Can do it well and teach others if I want

Assertiveness: Speaking Honestly and Kindly, Simultaneously

The skill of being assertive means that you send a part of your frame of reference to others in a respectful manner, letting them know your feelings, ideas, opinions, reactions, beliefs, judgments, or points of view. It is important for you to be "up front" (without being overly pushy) to avoid getting walked on by others' behaviors, false expectations and assumptions about you. Assertiveness involves speaking the "truth" about yourself to others in a patient, kind, and understanding manner, giving others the opportunity and the right to do the same thing. It involves not getting your frame of reference "hooked" and then over-reacting emotionally in anger (which can add fuel to an already blazing fire).

Combining assertiveness (genuineness) with responding skills (empathy) prevents your communications with others from seeming aggressive, or passive, and promotes *two-way completed communication which can result in problems getting solved.* Therefore, if you are angry with someone because of her or his behavior, you might use a format like:

"When you *(describe behavior)* I end up feeling *(one word)* , and then *(describe what else tangibly happens to you)* ."

If the other person is having difficulty receiving your message, you could respond empathically, "You seem upset when I tell you how I feel;" and help the other person to process your message. Combining the skills of assertiveness and responding enables you to *manage your half* of the communication and gives every opportunity for two way communication to take place. Your taking this responsibility can more often than not result in problems getting solved and relationships getting developed. However, some people may choose not to enter into two-way communication for a number of reasons, but at least you will have done your part well.

Self-control: A Worthwhile Responsibility

A major goal of personal development and the key to effective assertiveness is self-control. It only makes sense that the more self-control people have the better they will be able to use what abilities and skills are at their disposal. Control is achieved through knowledge and practice. For an individual to develop tennis skills he/she needs to exercise control over her/his body on the tennis court. The same is true for personal relationships in that those individuals who have solid relationships usually also have self-control and interpersonal skills.

A very important part of controlling self is self-discipline. Egan (1977) states, "Discipline means, at least in part, self-control. A person is disciplined if he or she makes whatever sacrifice is necessary in order to achieve a goal. Thus, discipline often involves some kind of hardship—doing things that aren't pleasant and giving up things that are."[7] This kind of self-control and self-sacrifice is an essential ingredient for personal satisfaction and successful relationships. Individuals who lack control over their frames of reference become more self-centered and tend to have shallow relationships with others.

---

7   G. Egan, *The Skilled Helper* (Monterey, CA: Brooks/Cole, 1977), 23.

People who behave assertively, rather than aggressively or passively, tend to be more in control of self. This occurs because these individuals accept both their rights and responsibilities. They do not aggressively take what belongs to others or passively let others blame them for what is not their responsibility. Assertive individuals think of others as equals and attempt to treat them as they would like to be treated.

On the other hand, people who are aggressive are usually not in control of their thoughts, feelings, and behaviors. They either cannot or will not take charge of their frames of references, and therefore have trouble controlling their actions, and others suffer as a result. These types of individuals are labelled "aggressive" or "hot heads" because they often take others' rights away from them so that they can have more control. They also attempt to make others assume their responsibilities so that they will not have to do so. These individuals often put themselves before and above others.

People who are passive tend to go to the other extreme in that they often over-control their "frames" to the point of self-suppression. They place others before themselves even if they (or others) have to suffer for doing so. While this sounds noble often it is for selfish reasons. Passive individuals, like those who are aggressive, are most worried about their needs first, and others second. Notice in the chart on the following page of interpersonal characteristics some of the qualities, behaviors and skills of the three style characteristics.

Interpersonal Style Characteristics

	AGGRESSIVE	ASSERTIVE	PASSIVE
Qualities	Insecure	Secure	Insecure
	Insensitive	Sensitive	Oversensitive
	Domineering	Respectful	Submissive
	Impatient	Patient	Patient
	Self-Oriented	People-Oriented	Other-Oriented
	Win-Lose Attitude	Negotiable Attitude	No-Win Attitude
	Dishonest	Honest	Dishonest
	Decision maker	Decision maker	Indecisive
	Unreliable	Reliable	Reliable
Behaviors	Verbal/Physical Abuse	Respectful Communication	Manipulative Negative Messages
	Lies	Truthful	Lies
	Power-oriented	Respect-oriented	Escape-oriented
Skills	Physical	Centered	Attends
	Verbal	Attends	Observes
		Observes	Giving
		Listens	Listens
		Understands	
		Communicates	
		Challenges	
		Solves Problems	

Rate your ability to be assertive and respectful at the same time.

Assertiveness

1 = Skill is new to me, cannot do it
2 = Understand it but cannot perform it
3 = Can begin to do it, but not naturally
4 = Can do it naturally in many situations
5 = Can do it well and teach others if I want

Confrontive Communication: Giving Constructive Feedback and Challenging Others

Assertiveness is mainly concerned with your presenting yourself honestly and realistically in "tight" social situations. Confrontive communication on the other hand is more focused on *other* peoples' problem behaviors or attitudes, and your need for them to change in order for them to be more effective with you, in their own lives, or with others.

Sometimes it is important or even necessary to give critical feedback to others about how their behavior is ineffective, stressful, or inappropriate. This is a difficult skill to perform effectively because it is required that a certain level of trust is developed in the relationship before others will receive your feedback in a positive manner. In a sense, you have to earn the right to confront by proving ahead of time to others that you care about their development as persons, that you are seeking to develop a relationship with them, that you are attempting to build rather than tear down, and that you are willing to accept confrontive feedback as well as dish it out.

It is possible to get agreements in advance with others that your relationship with them will be characterized by genuineness and honesty for the purpose of mutual personal development, and for the purpose of your developing your work or personal relationship with them. With this advance permission, giving difficult and challenging feedback can be much easier and more effective. Also, using responding skills to assist others to process your confrontive feedback to them can be helpful to defuse the stress and tension often involved in giving and receiving feedback.

Rate your ability to be respectfully critical when confronting others about their attitudes or behaviors.

Confrontive Communication
1 = Skill is new to me, cannot do it
2 = Understand it but cannot perform it
3 = Can begin to do it, but not naturally
4 = Can do it naturally in many situations
5 = Can do it well and teach others if I want

Conflict Management: Putting All the Skills Together

When managing an interpersonal conflict, all the skills we have examined above must be utilized to the fullest in order to have as positive an impact as possible. Conflict management involves managing your own frame of reference, your feelings, words, wants and needs, and assisting the other person to feel respected and yet understand your position at the same time. This is why this skill is the most difficult of all the interpersonal skills: Often you have to manage your half and the other person's half at the same time. This is the case because most people do not have well developed interpersonal skills.

Research on conflict management (Burke, 1977)[8] has produced a general list used in managing conflict. These methods, which form parts of the conflict management skill, are outlined as follows:

1. Forcing: using power to cause the other person to accept a position; each party tries to figure out how to get the upper hand and cause the other person to lose;
2. Withdrawal: retreating from the argument;
3. Smoothing: playing down the conflict (differences) and emphasizing the positive (common interests), or avoiding issues that might cause hard feelings;
4. Compromise: looking for a position in which each gives and gets a little, splitting the difference if possible; no winners and no losers;
5. Confrontation and/or problem solving: directing energies toward defeating the problem and not the other person; encouraging the open exchange of information; best solution for all: the situation is defined, the parties try to reach a mutually beneficial solution, and the situation is defined as "win-win."

A problem-solving approach to conflict management is an ideal one to implement when attempting to resolve a conflict. It should be your first choice. Then, if it doesn't work, back off to method number four, compromise, and so on.

---

8 R. Burke, "Methods of Resolving Superior-Subordinate Conflict: The Constructive Use of Subordinate Differences and Disagreements," In *Readings in Interpersonal and Organizational Communication*, eds. R.C. Huseman, C.M. Logue, and D.L. Freshley, 3rd ed. (Boston: Holbrook Press, 1977), 234–255.

In the problem-solving approach you begin your communication by *making a date to communicate* with the person you are having a conflict with at a mutually convenient time instead of "dumping" your tension and demanding that the problem be solved "now."

Then, whenever possible, you *take into consideration your personal style and the other person's style*, and get ready to shift styles if necessary to encourage the other person to engage in two-way communication and problem solving with you.

Agree together on a clear definition of the problem by redefining it several times from one another's points of view, using listening and understanding skills. Express your own points of view when the other person is able and willing to listen or the session will turn into a power struggle (a lose-lose position).

Then *agree on mutually satisfactory goals* for your session. State and come to consensus about what you hope to achieve at the onset of your session so that there are no expectation gaps which lead to disillusionments and even bitterness.

Take turns sharing honestly, but not in a blaming tone, each person's views, needs, wants, etc.

Explore alternative solutions to the problem which could potentially be satisfactory to both parties. Consider the consequences of each alternative both short and long term.

Implement the agreed upon solution(s) by agreeing on who will do what, when, where, etc. *Set a date to review* how things have gone and see if there need to be adjustments made in order for the plan to work better in the future.

When you cannot agree or come to a plan which is satisfying to both parties, it is acceptable to negotiate time for re-evaluation and then plan another meeting. If, after a time of further exploration, this is not possible then withdrawal from the situation, putting the conflict into others' hands for management, or proceeding in your own direction may be the only alternatives possible. There are always consequences to pay when you decide to walk away, get help from a person in a position of authority, or just take your own course of action without compromise. Weigh the consequences carefully before acting. You want to be as constructive as possible without giving up your own sense of integrity.

Conflict Management

1 = Skill is new to me, cannot do it
2 = Understand it but cannot perform it
3 = Can begin to do it, but not naturally
4 = Can do it naturally in many situations
5 = Can do it well and teach others if I want

Total of the Communication Section

Add all numbers in the boxes above.

Conclusion

In this chapter, we have examined interpersonal skills particularly from the point of view of establishing a base of mutuality, respect and openness in personal and work relationships. Those leaders who are most respected are those who are honest without putting others down, willing to solve a problem so that as many people are respected as possible and show caring about other people without getting manipulated (the "bleeding heart" syndrome).

In the next chapter, we will examine the skills of counseling and problem management. These skills are different in character in that quite often it is difficult to maintain the predominant mutual quality in the relationship. In counseling and problem management, the transforming leader is exercising a more dominant influence and accepting more of the responsibility for directing the relationship.

The results you will see on the self-assessment graph below will help you to plan your own future professional development activities, or delineate a specific training needs analysis if you decide to engage in the Leading Manager Program. The skills which are rated "3" or below are ones which you assess as needing development.

Graphing Your Self-assessment Scores

Now that you have completed this section of the comprehensive self-assessment, graph in all of your individual scores so that you can get a visual summary of what skills you see are stronger and weaker. Graph in your self-rating scores on each skill using the "bar graph" method of drawing lines from left to right on each scale.

1 = Skill is new to me, cannot do it
2 = Understand it but cannot perform it
3 = Can begin to do it, but not naturally
4 = Can do it naturally in many situations
5 = Can do it well and teach others if I want

	1	2	3	4	5
Self-disclosure: Appropriately Sharing Yourself With Others					
Image Management Skills					
Impression Management Skills					
Attending: Giving Undivided Attention to Others					
Observing: Seeing Another Person Without Distorting					
Suspending Frame of Reference: The Key to the Golden Rule					
Questioning: Appropriate Gathering of Information					
Listening: Checking for What Others Intend to Mean					
Responding With Understanding: Getting on the Inside					
Assertiveness: Speaking Honestly and Kindly, Simultaneously					
Confrontive Communication: Giving Constructive Feedback and Challenging Others					
Conflict Management: Putting All the Skills Together					

Knowledge and Skills which Develop and Transform People and Organizations

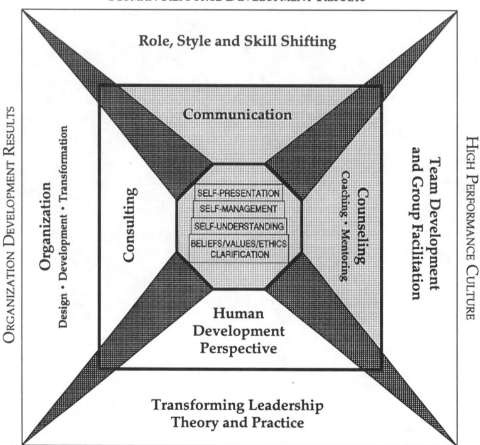

Chapter 6

▼

COUNSELING AND PROBLEM MANAGEMENT SKILLS

*Helpers are effective
to the degree that their clients,
as a result of client-helper interactions,
are in a better position to manage
their problem situations.*

Gerard Egan

Introduction

Counseling and problem management are process skills which go together to form a battery of potent elements for positive change. They are important aspects of the practice of transforming leadership because these skills can move people ahead toward greater self-understanding, self-responsibility and performance. Each leader needs to develop these skills for personal use and to encourage others to develop and perform at their full potential.

Personal applications include self-examination and problem solving (counseling one's self), and assisting family members to gain self-understanding and to solve problems they may encounter in everyday life. These skills can also be used with others in service organizations so that people in these settings may become more effective and enjoy a greater sense of well being. Corporate applications may include counseling, coaching and mentoring others who may need assistance in overcoming blocks to performance, help in dealing with personal or work-related crises, or guidance in career planning. Counseling and problem management skills are necessary prerequisites to effectively coaching others' performances and mentoring to facilitate their development.

What Are Counseling Skills?

Counseling skills are specific, observable and helpful leader behaviors which can be explained, modeled, practiced, learned and integrated into everyday life and work situations. The practice of counseling skills in a wide range of settings is meaningful because it emphasizes the importance of human development and change in our "mega-trend" world which requires increasing adaptability each year.

What Is the Problem Management Process?

The problem management process is a step by step manner of approaching and solving all kinds of problems. It emerged from theory, research and models of problem solving and decision making. This process is becoming more popularly integrated into counseling, leaderhip *and* managment practice because of its logical and systematic approach to defining problems, setting goals, exploring and implementing action alternatives, and evaluating the results.

Effective counseling or helper training programs have effectively used a problem management approach (Egan, 1990).[1] In his book, Egan offers a theoretical backdrop for the model he has developed. He reviews and integrates applied behavioral psychology, applied cognitive psychology, applied personality theory, social influence and decision making approaches and weaves them into a comprehensive counseling model. This model has a three stage process which assists practitioners in assessing what they are doing and what they need to do next in the problem management process.

Expertise in the use of a step-by-step process model such as this is developed as you apply it to real problems. The problem management process gives structure to the application of appropriate skills at various stages. We will examine the stages, steps and skills in this process later in this chapter and

---

1   G. Egan, *The Skilled Helper*, 4th ed. (Monterey, California: Brooks/Cole Publishing Company, 1990).

you will do a self-assessment of the extent to which you see yourself as having developed counseling and problem management skills.

Who Needs You To Be a Skilled People Problem Manager, Anyway?

Nearly anyone may need you to assist them in some way. The knowledge and techniques for facilitating problem-solving within and between individuals is perhaps more subtle and advanced than any other problem solving body of knowledge. It can be applied to personal and interpersonal matters which affect overall human performance and morale in families and in work settings. If there is truth in the above statement, then everyone we contact (including ourselves) could potentially benefit from others who possessed these skills.

During a consulting contract where my job was to assist 28 managers to better understand and deal with high stress levels on the job, I heard one manager say:

> *Managers don't have time to deal with "whiners" or people with problems. We are too busy dealing with more important issues and decisions and shouldn't be slowed down by ineffective people. If people can't hack it, get rid of them and get people in there who can do the job.*

This general attitude of impatience, seeming unkindness and intolerance is a signal that this person lacked what the research of Kouzes and Posner (1988) report that employees like very much in their leaders: A *heart* for people.[2] The insensitive "bottom line" response to people with "problems" is what I call the "transistor approach" to management: "if it is defective, just unplug it and push in another one that works." Sometimes, because of collective agreements or labor legislation, managers are forced to make the best of employees with problems. Parents are leaders who definitely are "stuck" with their children who seem to nearly always have some kinds of problems prior to leaving home.

---

2   Kouzes and J. Posner, *The Leadership Challenge* (San Francisco: Jossey-Bass Publishing Company, 1988).

Someone Close May Need Your Help: It May Be You

It is realistic to say that some of the personal relationships managers or leaders have may *require* a deeper level of helpful understanding and skills. Certainly for one's self, family and friends they are enviable skills to possess. Problems don't really happen between people in relationships, they happen inside of each person who is interacting within the context of a relationship, and that is where they have to be solved—on the inside. This is the great contribution counseling skills can make toward strengthening our personal and even our business relationships. Another encouraging point is *that you can learn the skills of solving (and helping others to solve) internal personal problems* which interfere with personal relationships and work performance.

Often, it is someone in our immediate family or the person working beside us who is going through a separation which could end in divorce, a battle with alcoholism, drug abuse, grief, depression or "mid-life crisis." Leaders are in strategic positions to support, problem-solve and intervene in the lives of many people. The results of counseling others can be increased morale, increased productivity and a more positive organizational culture. Sometimes each of us is in an advantageous position of having established trust with someone which can enable us to assist in more powerful and deeper ways than anyone else could.

One of the most impressive studies I have seen on the efficacy of good communication, problem management and effective culture-building (these three areas build upon one another) to produce bottom line results and positive worker morale are those done by Kravetz (1988).[3] A total of 150 well established companies were evaluated as to their human resource effectiveness practices and attitudes, and the ones which came out on top were also the ones assessed as having the highest morale and greatest revenues (compared to the other companies surveyed).

There is also some evidence that the best counseling that is given occurs right in a person's own environment; and that most people who are facing a per-

---

3   D. Kravetz, *The Human Resources Revolution* (San Francisco: Jossey-Bass Publishing Company, 1988).

sonal problem will not or do not seek the help of a professional (Carkhuff, 1971).[4]

Furthermore, it is also true that even if everyone who needed help were to go to a professional helper (and no one else) to gain assistance in solving problems that there would likely be more than 200 people crowded into each psychologist's waiting room at any given time. This is yet another reason why it would appear that perhaps it could ideally be everyone's responsibility to learn to help everyone else for everyone's benefit.

Lastly, you may need to help yourself solve a problem. Perhaps there are some problems too personal to share with some people. Watson and Tharpe (1981) have devoted a whole book to self-management and problem solving, which outlines how to apply the problem management process to one's self.[5]

Leading Managers Do Not Have Time?

Because managers often do not have time to become involved in longer term or in-depth counseling relationships it is important that they continually seek a balance between task and relationship factors in the environment. If supportive and helpful relationship factors are neglected for too long a time this can affect performance. If the task aspects of the environment are not attended to properly then they simply won't get done as well. This type of balance is much like surfing: If you step too far ahead in trying to catch the wave it will come crashing down on you; and if you step back too far you miss the wave entirely.

It is true that leaders cannot deal with **all** people who have personal problems just because they happen to cross their paths, but it is very desirable and advantageous for good leaders to selectively understand and be able to show genuine and skilled caring for some of the people who get the work done. This can increase trust, commitment, morale and productivity.

It is also a fact that people who are ordinarily effective go through periods of time when they face developmental crises, times of grief when perfor-

---

4   R.R. Carkhuff, *The Development of Human Resources* (New York: Holt, Rinehart & Winston, 1971), 167–168.

5   D. Watson, and R. Tharpe, *Self-directed Behavior*, 3rd. ed. (Monterey, California: Brooks/Cole, 1981).

mance is lower, times of personal, family or marital stress when concentration is distracted or times of physical health difficulties when performance is temporarily on the decline. An attitude of support, encouragement, tolerance and compassion is what most of us would deeply appreciate from others around us, and perhaps especially need from those "above" us who are in leadership positions.

When time or pressure does not allow a leader to take on counseling responsibilities, then a transforming leader will develop other helpers within the organization or effectively refer the burdened person to a professional helper.

Does Counseling Really Help?

A review of research literature on counseling outcomes reveals basic themes which might be best summarized by saying that *some approaches do help some people, with some problems, in some situations, some of the time.* We are not able to say with confidence that all helpers are helpful, but can say with some confidence that some helpers have been and can be destructive!

Following is a summary of three statements from the literature on counseling effectiveness which were reviewed to provide you with a clearer picture of some relevant findings that have been established through research:

1. *Counseling can be effective and can encourage personal development and can also enhance job performance* (Bergin, 1971[6]; Emrick, 1975[7]; Landman and Dawes, 1982[8]; Smith and Glass, 1977[9]; Smith, Glass, and Miller 1980[10]).

    In view of the evidence in the studies referenced above, that counseling can be *valid* and helpful is not really in question. However, in view of

---

6   A.E. Bergin, "The Evaluating of Therapeutic Outcomes." In A. E. Bergin and S. L. Garfield (eds.), *Handbook of Psychotherapy and Behavior Change* (New York: Wiley, 1971).

7   C.D. Emrick, "A Review of Psychologically Oriented Treatment in Alcoholism," *Journal of Studies of Alcohol*, 1975, 36, 88–108.

8   J.T. Landman and R.M. Dawes, "Psychotherapy Outcome: Smith and Glass' Conclusions Stand Up Under Scrutiny," *American Psychologist*, 1982, 37, 504–516.

9   M.C. Smith and G.V. Glass, "Meta-analysis of Psychotherapy Outcome Studies," *American Psychologist*, 1977, 32, 752–761.

10 M.C. Smith, G.V. Glass, and T.J. Miller, *The Benefits of Psychotherapy* (Baltimore: Johns Hopkins University Press, 1980).

the evidence in the studies referenced below it would appear that the *reliability* of counseling is in question.

2. *Counseling can also be questionable because there is some evidence that it can be ineffective and/or destructive* (Levitt, 1963[11]; Bergin, 1980[12]; Mays and Franks, 1980[13]; Orwin and Cordray, 1984[14]).

This statement may summarize why so many managers, leaders and others are fearful of trying to help people solve problems which interfere with morale or performance at home or on the job. It is clear that if you don't know what you are doing when you enter others' personal worlds you might inadvertently damage self-worth, morale and performance; and perhaps even increase turnover and absenteeism at the same time. Therefore, it is important to be able to recognize the major mistakes of counseling, and develop the key skills to be a facilitative helper.

Three Major Mistakes Untrained Leaders Make

In video taping sessions I have conducted of untrained (in counseling skills) leaders and managers at the beginning of a counseling skills training session there are several frequently made mistakes.

Mistake #1: The first one was simply that most leaders were so task-focused that they *failed to actually hear* the content and check for the intended meaning of the messages which were being sent to them.

Mistake #2: The next most frequently made mistake is that they *presumed that they accurately understood*, without checking with the other person.

Mistake #3: The next mistake made in sequence was that they *gave premature advice* without jointly arriving at a specific definition of the problem. This advice was usually not followed by the other person because the solution offered did not fit the real nature of the problem.

---

11 E.E. Levitt, "Psychotherapy With Children: A Further Evaluation," *Behavior Research and Therapy*, 1963, 1, 45–51.

12 A.E. Bergin, "Negative Effects Revisited: A Reply," *Professional Psychology*, 1980, 11, 93–100.

13 D.T. Mays and C.M. Franks, "Getting Worse: Psychotherapy or No Treatment—The Jury Should Still Be Out," *Professional Psychology*,1980, 11,78–92.

14 R.G. Orwin and D.S. Cordray, "Smith and Glass's Psychotherapy Conclusions Need Further Probing: On Landman and Dawes' Re-analysis," *American Psychologist*, 1984, 39, 71–72.

There were other problems which showed up less frequently, such as failing to temporarily suspend personal judgmental reactions, emotions, and the giving of inappropriate or even destructive advice.

The Good News About Transferable Skills Training

However, we know from many other studies on the efficacy of training people in interpersonal and counseling skills that it is possible to train them in a relatively short period of time to be effective in counseling others to solve problems which are not long term and pervasive in nature. We know that it is possible to help most trainees to quite rapidly give up ineffective patterns.

1.   *Helper Training Programs which bring forward core facilitative conditions through systematic skills training have been demonstrated to be most effective*

(Carkhuff (1971)[15]; Carkhuff and Berenson (1967)[16]; Ivey and Authier (1978)[17]; Larson (1984)[18]).

Based on the positive statement of skills training outcomes like the ones above, counseling skills have powerful potential to assist transforming leaders to produce positive changes in self, in others and therefore in organizations.

Gain Self-confidence and Self-esteem

After managers developed a minimum level of competency in counseling skills in my college and university courses, they reported on the evaluations at the end that they felt a greater sense of calm, confidence and self-esteem because they knew they could now really be of help to others in need without feeling like they were "fumbling around in an area I don't know anything about." They also reported being glad to learn how to make effective

---

15 R.R. Carkhuff, *The Development of Human Resources* (New York: Holt, Rinehart & Winston, 1971).

16 R. Carkhuff and B. Berenson,. *Beyond Counseling and Therapy* (New York: Holt, Rinehart & Winston, 1967).

17 A. Ivey and J. Authier, *Microcounseling: Innovations in Interviewing, Counseling, Psychotherapy, and Psychoeducation.* (2nd. ed.) (Springfield, Ill., Charles C. Thomas, 1978).

18 D. Larson, *Teaching Psychological Skills: Models for Giving Psychology Away* (Monterey, California: Brooks/Cole, 1984).

referrals to professional helpers when it is appropriate to do so, a skill which we will review and you will assess your knowledge of at the end of this chapter.

Dispel Fears of Judgment and Earn Trust

By developing a culture in your group, organization (or family) where people agree in advance to face problems openly, and people see one another as resources rather than judges, there can be a resultant increase in morale and performance. You can observe decreases in productivity, and increases in absenteeism, turnover and stress-related illnesses where people are supervised in negative-culture environments by managers who are overly task-oriented and miss out on the people side of enterprise. When they fail to attend to the relationship dimensions of supervision or management, they contribute to a higher level of corporate stress. The same is true when children are put down and undervalued: They often rebel or even run away from home.

Problem Solving Not People Blaming

Many, if not most, problems are a result of a person's not having a more effective response to a given situation. In most cases people can learn new ways of perceiving, thinking and acting which will enable them to solve problems. This approach of defining the situation as a problem to be better faced through learning and development avoids having people feel like they are losers, "basket cases" or "unpromotables."

When Is Counseling Appropriate?

It is inappropriate to counsel people when there has not been any trust established, when there is no cause to counsel and when there is no permission to counsel. Peters (1985)[19] suggests that counseling is most needed when an individual follower:

1. Has a solid track record but isn't performing.
2. Has been educated and coached but without results.
3. Asks for help in solving a personal problem.

---

19 T. Peters, *A Passion for Excellence: The Leadership Difference* (New York: Random House, 1985), 367–368.

---

4.   Is "stuck," unsure about how to proceed.
5.   Is having difficulty coping with organizational change.
6.   Cannot bounce back after a failure or loss experience.

More specifically, there are several ways that counseling can be used constructively:

For Improving Performance: It is appropriately used for leadership impact when co-workers, colleagues, subordinates or learners are having personal difficulties which are interfering with their performance on a task or in relationships with others. Assisting them to specify and take *ownership* for their own problems in relation to a problem situation is germane. Supporting or guiding them to set realistic goals and take effective action can also be a great help in keeping people, groups, and organizations "unblocked."

For Supporting Others: The problem management process and counseling skills are also appropriately used with those who are seeking or needing brief personal assistance in your own family, with friends, or in work situations. These skills do not replace professional counseling or long term psychotherapy when it is needed. By understanding and practicing the skills of counseling, you can better specify, manage, and solve problems yourself.

When You Get Permission to Counsel: Most people have to be willing to enter into a *helpful type of communication* with you and often will do so only because they trust you. They will more likely trust you if you have integrity, are genuine, respectful, empathic, and are skilled. You must have their permission to enter into a deeper level of communication with them which can involve your seeing their personal difficulties which are interfering with their relationships at home or performance at work.

Getting and Giving Mutual Commitment Through Formalized Mentoring Relationships

As reported by Gray (1987)[20] it was clear that a key set of skills that have been identified as effective in the process of formalized mentoring are the skills of supporting and helping protégés through the stages of the problem management process. The mentor/protégé relationship is a further development and extension of the leader-helping-follower relationship in

---

20 W. Gray, *International Journal of Mentoring* (Vancouver, B.C.), vol 1, no. 1, 1987.

that there is an *agreement in advance* to engage in problem management, personal growth and professional development. This agreement avoids the often uncomfortable crossing of the "line" into what is traditionally considered to be the personal territory of the follower. The importance and impact of developing a mentoring or consultative type relationship with subordinates will be discussed more fully in chapter seven.

Example of a Major Problem and an Appropriate Counseling Intervention

The Assessment

A Senior Executive Officer in a large government department became aware of a serious stress problem among most of the managers in his region. They were ill more often than usual, and did not deal well with problems he thought should have been dealt with swiftly and effectively; he was suspicious that there was a "hidden" problem.

The Senior Executive talked with some of the managers in an attempt to identify the causes of the problem, but not one of the managers wanted to come right out and say what the real problem was. The Senior Executive sought assistance from a consultant who interviewed him and the five top managers in the Region. Aside from the fact that there was a "trimming" of management positions due to budget cuts, it became clear from the interviews that all five managers felt scared that their job security was threatened. This was because they had received virtually no feedback from the Senior Executive in over a year, had observed him firing two other managers for "confidential" reasons, and experienced his leadership style as being very authoritarian (he did a great deal of *telling*), was distant (he had only one weekly meeting with them where he informed them of new developments and changes), and threatening (he yelled frequently and listened very little).

The Intervention

The consultant confidentially presented his findings in summary written form to the Senior Executive, and asked him for his assessment of the validity of the findings. Surprisingly, he responded very openly, and said that he had been very domineering all of his life, had felt close to hardly anyone, had alienated his wife and three children with his intimidating stance to the point of her threatening to leave him, and asked for direct counseling assistance in overcoming this problem.

Then, with the CEO's permission, the consultant shifted into a supportive counseling mode (because he had the skills and ability to do so), and had several productive two-hour sessions with him. After these sessions, the consultant shifted back into the consultant "mode" so he and the CEO could plan and arrange a team development session where he and all twelve managers clarified the purpose and concrete goals of the team for the first time, assisted them to clarify each of their roles and the goals they were attempting to reach, and negotiated an appropriate and agreeable leadership style for the Senior Executive to use with this group of managers.

Transforming leaders can be "outside consultants," as in this case, or can act as this type of flexible counselor-consultant within their own organizations if they have the knowledge and skills to do so. Most preferably, the CEO himself would have had the personal and interpersonal development and counseling skills to deal with these problems himself.

The Results

The absenteeism levels dropped, two-way communication was established among nearly all members, problems were managed more effectively, goals were reached more swiftly, and the CEO sought continuing marriage and family counseling outside of the work setting. This is an unusually ideal series of events where most everything worked out well, but without the transforming leadership intervention, the outcome could otherwise have been far worse.

The main point in the above example is that the consultant was able to shift into a helpful, supportive, developmental mode to assist the Senior Executive to develop in a problem area which was causing distress among twelve managers (and their employees, and their families, etc.). If the Senior Executive would have had these skills from the beginning, the stress and morale problems would likely not have developed to nearly the degree they had. The advantage is clear when communication and counseling skills are present within individual leaders, regardless of their role.

Counseling Skills Training Is Becoming More Recognized

On the basis of extensive research on the impact of counseling in various environments Carkhuff (1969)[21] has stated two propositions which suggest that counseling can be a potent tool for leaders. The first one states, "all interpersonal processes may have constructive or deteriorative consequences." This implies that management, leadership, psychotherapy, counseling, parenting, teaching, training, and all other significant relationships are not neutral, and may effect people (and performance) for "better or for worse."

The second proposition is, "all effective interpersonal processes share a common core of conditions conducive to facilitative human experiences." Those leaders, managers, counselors, psychotherapists, teachers, parents, trainers, and significant others who demonstrate adequate levels of conditions which are supportive, facilitative, and action-motivating will be more effective than those leaders/helpers who do not.

These propositions, and the research on which they were based, roughly cut the edge of a new movement within counseling, one *towards the education and training of a wide range of people* in the skills only counselors and therapists had previously learned. The new focus on skills training for members external to the "expert" psychologist community marked the beginning of a new awareness of the need for facilitative interpersonal and counseling skills in many fields.

It used to be that managers appreciated the value of communication skills, and "communication" was the training buzzword for management training, and often still is. Now many managers want further training in how to deal with followers' deeper issues and problems in their own personal and professional lives. When there is a rich body of transferable knowledge and skills available to managers to help them develop personal effectiveness and leadership potency, then why not avail ourselves of it?

Since the late 1960s, this movement has taken these face-to-face human resource development skills into a wide range of environments from elementary school classrooms to corporate boardrooms. Most colleges and universities now offer competency-based courses in interpersonal and problem management skills. But these skills-oriented courses are often limited

---

21 R. Carkhuff, *Helping and Human Relations*, vols. I and II, (New York: Holt, Rinehart, & Winston, 1969).

to social work, counseling, corrections, and education departments. In more progressive business, law and medical schools systematic competency-based courses have begun to appear during the past 10 to 15 years.

In response to demands from the professional community, Ivey (1987)[22] has developed a well-researched and effective helper training program which has been taken by a wide range of people from executives, managers, doctors, social workers, nurses, social services workers, correctional workers, to parents and volunteers in community service agencies.

The need for all people to become good people problem managers is on the increase as problems in our world increase in intensity and frequency. Transformative leaders can pass on some of these important skills to others whom they help and lead as we move into the 1990s, perhaps the decade of most rapid change when problem management will likely be most needed.

The Conditions Which Facilitate Effective Problem Management

The "core conditions" which have been found to be effective when present in the behaviors of leaders who are helpful are:

Genuineness: The willingness and ability to be role-free, honest in a kind way, and open about one's self to others makes them freer to open up and explore themselves without fear of judgment.

Empathy: The willingness and ability to perceive others' world views, to see through their eyes, and to communicate back to them accurate understanding of their feelings and ideas encourages them to trust you and to explore problems more deeply and specifically.

Respect: The willingness and ability to actively show that you highly value the people you work with (regardless of their present performance) is an important quality to communicate to others when you need their respect and participation toward reaching goals.

Specificity: The willingness and ability to be highly specific when using language to describe others' views and experiences can help them to increase the clarity of their understanding and solve problems more effectively.

---

22 A. Ivey, *Intentional Interviewing and Counseling*, 2nd ed.. (Monterey, California: Brooks/Cole, 1987).

Transforming Leadership and Counseling Are Integrally Linked

When leaders learn to apply counseling skills and the problem management process to themselves and in their work with others, they internalize a powerful set of knowledge and skills at a deep and personal level.

Good leaders understand the problem management processes both cognitively when analyzing an organizational problem and affectively when understanding the inner workings of self or another person. They understand the stages and steps in the process, and are able to deal with their own personal and interpersonal problems. It is important that a leader's personal life be in good shape so that he or she is not distracted by internal unresolved emotional or interpersonal problems at home or at work. Good leaders are personal, interpersonal and organizational problem solvers and managers, directly in their own lives.

Transforming leaders also help other people solve problems. If an employee is facing a personal problem but not seeking outside help for it (which often is the case) a transforming leader is able to respond with genuine caring and effective counseling skills. This leader may be a principal of a school counseling a student, a teacher or counselor on staff, or a parent. The leader may also be an executive who intimately and quietly assists an executive team mate who is having marriage, family, drug, alcohol or stress problems (problems typical to some executives).

Counseling skills are an integral part of a Leading Manager's problem management skill repertoire because some problems are simply *inside of individuals*. Whether a leader is managing a problem within self or others, or between self and others; mediating a conflict between others; doing a performance appraisal counseling interview, a career planning interview or assisting a person or employee to overcome a personal difficulty, basic counseling/problem management skills are invaluable.

Style-Shift Counseling: A Developmental Approach

Anderson (1987)[23] has developed a theoretically integrated and developmentally based helper style assessment and training instrument and leader's manual. While Style-Shift Counseling integrates familiar concepts from a number of theoretical approaches, it is novel in its usage of them because assessment and intervention are presented from a developmental perspective. In this chapter we will briefly discuss the Developmental Level Assessment Grid, which integrates developmental theories into a counseling tool for assessment, intervention planning, and tracking progress.

Style-Shift Counseling is a systematic counseling plan that organizes psycho-therapeutic methods into a working model which provides guidelines for the appropriate use of helping and developmental approaches and interventions. For the purposes of this book, a review of the the basic assumptions of the approach are summarized below.

1. No one approach works with all people.
2. No one approach always works with the same person.
3. It can be difficult to decide which approach will work best.
4. It is difficult for most helpers to use more than one approach at one time, or shift from one approach to another.
5. It can be easy to get discouraged and give up when working with failure-oriented or undeveloped people.
6. A more practical and flexible approach to counseling that would allow for client individuality and facilitate development and performance was needed.
7. A method for assessing a person's developmental readiness to receive help is needed which would also allow for helper flexibility in shifting to fit people's helping style preferences and ability levels.
8. Helper training often acquaints students with a wide range of counseling theories, but seldom gives them a framework for the appropriate application of those theories and methods in a systematic and integrative manner.

---

23 T. Anderson, *The Therapeutic Style Indicator* (Amherst, Mass.: Microtraining Associates, 1987).

Style-Shift Counseling offers such a framework for the effective application of theory. The developmental theories and counseling approaches which form the basis of Style-Shift Counseling can be examined in Anderson's *Leader's Manual* (1987) which is referenced below.

Understanding Developmental Levels for Situational Effectiveness

The following developmental levels are presented for you to gain additional understanding that there exist different levels of functioning due to varying levels of development. This is a very important reality to observe in people because it will help us to learn to adapt our methods and approach to the level of the person we are dealing with.

Level One — Resistant or Undeveloped Individuals: People who function at level one are distinguished by low levels of individual readiness and willingness which often result in their becoming detractors in the helping and problem-solving process. They are predominantly preoccupied with self, underdeveloped, reactionary, unaware of problems and/or deny ownership of and responsibility for personal problems. People who function at this level sometimes attempt to escape reality by trying to live in fantasy.

Some examples of level one client populations might include: pre-school children, drug addicts, alcoholics, severely mentally retarded or mentally ill people, autistic children, "hard-core" juvenile delinquents who are highly resistant, and potentially violent prisoners.

Level Two — Rational Individuals: People who are functioning at level two demonstrate some readiness and willingness to be helped but usually at a cognitive level only. They are *willing to think and talk about behavior change* but need help defining problems in concrete terms, and often need follow-up support and reinforcement programs. Often these people can be good observers who notice many things but seldom take corrective action without support and follow-up from others.

Some examples of level two client populations might include: under-developed teenagers, "soft-core" juvenile delinquents, immature high school, college and university students, underdeveloped adults in general, mildly mentally retarded or mentally ill people.

Level Three — Reflective Individuals: People who function at this level tend to seek self-understanding, are willing and able to explore internal personal problems that may interfere with performance, are often more willing to take ownership for personal problems and behaviors, have the ability to learn independently with occasional support, are often concerned about interpersonal development and problem-solving, care about others as well as self, and are more able to make lasting commitments to change.

Some examples of level three clients might include: mature teenagers, responsible adults, some college and university students, and personal development seekers in general. These are the employees who make ideal employees and followers because they are ready and willing to learn, and take responsibility for their own performance.

Level Four — Resourceful Individuals: People functioning at this level tend to be independent learners, good decision-makers and creative problem solvers. They are often able to teach others, have developed a self-responsible lifestyle, and often are only in need of additional information, resources or additional perspectives. They seek and use expert consultative advice.

Some examples of level four clients might include: successful professionals, creative homemakers, educators, plumbers, electricians, managers, artists, etc.

The Style-Shift Counseling model provides a clear way to assess levels of development and functioning. Each level has corresponding helping styles, behaviors, and interventions which best match levels of readiness, ability, willingness, and preference. A foundational concept of the model is that it is the helper's responsibility to shift counseling style to fit the client's willingness and ability to receive that approach. For a review of the literature which forms the base for this approach see the *Leader's Manual for the Therapeutic Style Indicator.*

The Developmental Level Assessment Grid

The Assessment Grid presented below can be a useful tool to do a quick assessment of a person's general level of functioning in relation to a specific task which they are attempting to do or which you may be asking them to complete. The developmental level of a person is task-specific. It includes the following dimensions: general functioning level, cognitive, affective, interpersonal, ego development and needs hierarchy level. An example of a person who has different levels of functioning in two areas of life is a prisoner I know of, who is doing a life sentence for molesting and murdering children and is also an accomplished concert pianist. At controlling his abnormal sexual impulses, he is functioning at level one, but functions at level four on the piano.

As you can see from the grid, it is possible to estimate what levels of functioning or development a person moves in and out of depending on the situational context. Assessing a person's functioning level will assist you to plan which approach you should generally take with them in relation to a specific problem which they are facing.

Four Intervention Styles

There are four styles of intervention which correspond to the four functioning levels. What we do to help people move ahead in their development must be more appropriate to their readiness and ability levels in order for our interventions to be more catalytic to their development. In *Helping Tasks Appropriate to the Four Development Levels*, below, you will see four levels with appropriate strategies of intervention.

These guidelines are meant to be a useful beginning—a starting place for you to learn to use developmental considerations when approaching people who are facing problems. If you wish further study in this area of using developmental considerations to plan your interventions you could take courses in developmental psychology or counseling theory and practice, or read Ivey's recent book (1986).[24]

Facilitative Leaders Are Not Psychotherapists

The field of psychotherapy (not counseling or helping as the terms are used in this chapter) includes those therapists who use predominantly one or two orientations of therapy and generally work with emotionally disturbed or mentally ill people over longer periods of time (months or years). Psychotherapists, at least in the beginning, tended to work with institutionalized patients including both inpatients and outpatients. Helpers are people who have developed counseling skills and work with members of the general public concerning issues of social adjustment and/or minor emotional and

---

24 A. Ivey, *Developmental Therapy* (San Francisco: Jossey-Bass, 1986).

The Developmental Level Assessment Grid

D-Levels	D-LEVEL 1	D-LEVEL 2	D-LEVEL 3	D-LEVEL 4
Assessment Dimensions	*Resistant/ Undeveloped*	*Reasonable*	*Reflective*	*Resourceful*
GENERAL CAPABILITY	Unable, unwilling, and/or insecure	Unable as yet, but willing	Able, but somewhat insecure	A degree of competence with creativity
COGNITIVE FUNCTIONING (Neo-Piagetian)	'Magical,' unrealistic, or illogical thinking	Concrete, rational thinking— linear, simpler	Formal operational, self-reflective thinking— more complex	Dialectic, abstract, creative thinking
EGO/ AFFECTIVE FUNCTIONING	Lacks inner controls or denies emotions— lacks self-worth and self-confidence	Begins responsible integration and controlled expression of emotion	Integrates own emotion with appropriate control and responds to others' emotions	Has integrated emotion and can understand and care for others' feelings
INTER-PERSONAL FUNCTIONING	Self-oriented detractor	Self-oriented observer, interacts for self-interest	Minimally capable of intimacy and two-way communication	Seeks to develop relationships and to develop others
CONSCIOUS-NESS LEVEL	Blind belief or imagining	Unvalidated rigid belief based on understanding of a system of belief	Validated belief based on examination of alternatives	Direct sense of 'knowing' self and 'life'

Helping Tasks Appropriate to the Four Developmental Levels			
STRUCTURE WITH RESISTANT PEOPLE	COACH WITH RATIONAL PEOPLE	COUNSEL WITH REFLECTIVE PEOPLE	CONSULT WITH RESOURCEFUL PEOPLE
Design safe environments	Gain credibility	Establish rapport in relationship	Do problem management
Structure therapeutic environments	Clarify problem behavior	Explore problem situation with the person	Consult and give expert info
Control violent people with restraints	Coach problem thinking	Assist person to own personal responsibility	Provide life planning consultation
Provide constructive releases	Plan for improved behavior	Specify internal problems of person	Personal development (advanced)
Provide positive reinforcement	Plan for improved thinking	Focus on problem which has good potential	Focus on new perspectives
Administer humane discipline	Confront irrational assumptions	Confront person's internal discrepancies	Challenge in a mutual way
Temporary isolation programs	Set action goals and programs	Mutually set action goals and programs	Explore goal options
Evaluate and communicate progress	Mutually evaluate progress	Mutually evaluate progress	Explore possible scenarios

behavioral problem solving. It is usually short-term in comparison to psychotherapy and often is educationally related. Leaders can have a transforming impact without pretending to be psychotherapists.

The differences between counseling and psychotherapy can be summarized in the following statement by Pietrofesa, Hoffman and Splete (1984)[25]. Counseling focuses more on developmental-educational-preventative concerns, whereas psychotherapy focuses more on remediative-adjustive-therapeutic concerns. *Transforming Leadership* focuses mainly on the developmental, educational and preventive concerns.

Performance Appraisal and Discipline Interviews Require Facilitative Counseling Skills

The one situation where you do not need "permission" to shift into a counseling mode is when you are doing performance appraisal or reprimand interviews. Then, it is your role and job to assist employees to specify problems which block performance and even job security. Your position gives you the right to specify problems, goals, and action plans with employees. Under these more difficult circumstances, it is even more important that you be positive, skilled and wise in your approach.

Understanding the Problem Management Process

It is a logical inference that people who are more effective are less encumbered with unsolved personal or family problems, and that these same people will therefore be more effective and productive on the job. The process outlined below can be used with self or others. The problem management process has been outlined clearly by Egan (1990)[26] but will not be specified in great detail in the self-assessment below because it would require too much space to do this effectively. However, it is interesting to see the three stages of the process as Egan breaks them down into substeps.

---

25 J.J. Pietrofesa, A. Hoffman and H.H. Splete, *Counseling, an Introduction*, 2nd ed. (Boston: Houghton Mifflin Company, 1984).

26 G. Egan, *The Skilled Helper*, 4th ed. (Monterey, California: Brooks/Cole Publishing Company: 1990).

1. **Identifying and clarifying** problem situations and unused opportunities.

   a) Helping people tell their stories

   b) Identifying and challenging blind spots

   c) Focusing: Helping people to identify and work on problems which will make a difference

2. **Goal setting**: Developing and choosing preferred scenarios

   a) Exploring preferred scenario possibilities

   b) Creating viable agendas

   c) Eliciting choice and commitment

3. **Formulating Strategies and Plans**

   a) Brainstorming strategies for action

   b) Choosing the best strategies

   c) Turning strategies into a plan

Egan suggests that "the stages and steps of the helping process are, at best, triggers and channels for client action." He emphasizes the importance of *action* in all three of the stages of the problem management process. In stage one, helper-leaders facilitate followers to take an active role within the counseling or coaching sessions. In stage two, action can be taken as well, as people explore outside the counseling sessions various possibilities which could lead to problem resolution or management. Stage three, of course, has as its main purpose the propelling of the client into more effective action with clarity of vision, enhanced motivation and encouragement.

The three stage process for managing problems was introduced earlier by Carkhuff (1969)[27] and has been developed, streamlined and refined by many others since then. Egan has developed a refined training technology

---

27 R. Carkhuff, *Helping and Human Relations*, vols. I and II (New York: Holt, Rinehart, & Winston, 1969).

which provides the structure of a workable model, but the versatility needed to adapt to real demands of live counseling sessions.

Assessing Your Skills for Helping Others

The counseling skills below are presented in the order required for successful progression through the steps of the problem management process. However, as indicated above, the process does not usually progress in a neat, step-by-step fashion. Counseling is unpredictable, sometimes very difficult, often rewarding and requires a great deal of assertiveness, skill, sensitivity, creativity and openness to the unexpected. First, we will examine the skill of specifying problems.

Problem Exploration and Specification

Exploring External and Internal Problems

This skill requires that you follow other people through their *own* understandings of their problem situations first, and, if they are ready or developed enough, assist them to see the personal internal problems they are having with those external problems—prior to setting goals, exploring alternative courses of action, and before you give advice. The facilitative process of helping others see and take ownership of problems is much like the quarterback leading the runner by throwing a football—if the ball is thrown too far ahead the runner will miss it; and if the ball is thrown too far behind no yardage is made. You may have to lead a bit but only in the direction that the other person is already going. Difficult confrontations, of course, are exceptions to this general guideline of "following" clients.

You can offer your own hunches about what you think is the "real" problem and see if the other person can use your view of it, but only if you are not so busy doing this that you interrupt the other person's self-examination process with your "wise" ideas. People receiving help, especially premature advice (before the problem is specified and owned) often find it more difficult to use others' ideas when they are busy seeking to define and understand their own thoughts and feelings.

Perhaps the ideal time to share your ideas with others is when they are stuck, or when you want to add some alternative ways for them to consider a problem or a solution to the ideas which are presently available to them. Do this tentatively and watch, in order to *check* with the other person for the usefulness of your ideas or responses.

The more thoroughly a problem is explored and the more specifically it is defined, the greater probability there is for a high impact solution to be reached. The exploration of an internal or external problem with another person (or with self) begins by using all of the skills outlined above in the section on communication. As you understand meanings, feelings, and define the situation which has occurred, you will begin to get a sense of a pattern emerging. As you lay a base of understanding using the communication skills, especially the skills of listening and responding, you are in a better position to formulate a specific problem statement using a format such as:

Now you realize that you can't/haven't *(specify what person cannot or has not done)* because *(specify reason)* , and that makes you feel *(specify predominant feeling, using one word)*.

Or, you may choose to use a somewhat different format which gets at the same issue:

You seem *(identify main feeling)* because you can't *(specify what cannot be performed)* due to *(identify internal lacks or causes of problem which could be overcome if identified)*.

Example of a Problem Specification Dialog

Presented below is an example of a problem specification dialog a leader (Helen) was engaged in with a manager (Merle) who was having a difficult time sticking to time lines. He has turned in most things two weeks late. Merle was a highly functioning employee in his previous job where he moved around and talked to people. Now he is in a job role where much of what he does is an audit function at his desk. He has more critical managerial responsibility in his new role but less opportunity for innovation and human contact. He is also having medical problems in his family, his parents are aging rapidly 1,500 miles away, and he doesn't really like the stress of living in a big city where there is a lot of traffic and smog.

Helen:
Merle, I've noticed that you have been turning in several projects late during the past few weeks. Could we talk about this now, or do you want to set up a time to meet tomorrow sometime?

Merle:
Yes, we can talk now. I know I have been late on three important projects, but I'm in a slump and can't seem to keep myself on track. I don't really know what is wrong.

Helen:
I noticed you looking down a bit just now, Merle *(a response to immediate, observable feeling to facilitate a supportive climate of emotional intimacy)*. I'm not trying to make you feel guilty, but I'd really like to work through this with you if I can be of any help: your previous contributions have been on time and high quality and I want to do what I can to support you to continue the super job you normally do *(recognizing previous strengths and achievements in the context of confronting weakness is a respectful and supportive leader behavior)*.

Merle:
I've even been avoiding trying to face why I am repeatedly late with the projects. It's been bothering me a lot since the first one was late 2 weeks ago. I just feel depressed and I don't know why.

Helen:
Yes, when I have glanced at you during the past few weeks I have noticed that your energy level is down and you seem to be in a slump, even sometimes your posture is actually slumping over, and it is even now. You seem to be sort of in pain, somehow. Does that fit for you? *(A response to the predominant feeling that is non-verbally exhibited is often facilitative of deeper self-disclosure.)*

Merle:
Yes! I feel pain in my neck and back when I sit down to do these projects. I thought I would be motivated in this new area, but now that I am into it, I don't find it challenging; it's too repetitive, and I don't see any promotions sideways or up for quite sometime. I feel trapped, like I'm just doing time here all day long, not using my talents like I was in my other role.

(At this point, Helen could have become "hooked" and said, "...but I thought you wanted this job, you dork...," but she suspended her frame of reference.)

Helen:
Ok, Merle, I think I am getting a clearer picture. Right now you seem down on yourself because you haven't taken responsibility for processing this "off

key" feeling for over two weeks and you have allowed your performance to drop because you can't see any way out of your dilemma.

Merle:
Yeah. I know I'm stuck because I said I would take on this job for 2 years. And I can't go back on my word.

Helen:
So you feel trapped because you believe you can't have integrity if you change your mind, due to your high standards about giving your word?

Merle:
Yes. If I say I'm going to do something, I do it. No whining.

Helen:
So it's like you're sapped of enthusiasm because you can't see another way to maintain your integrity other than making yourself march through this job for a few years even though you now realize it doesn't fit your goals and talents?

Merle:
Is *that* what I'm doing?! I'm not that rigid, am I? I guess I am. I think I want to do something about that! I don't think I will be doing myself or the company the best I can by being so rigid. What other options do I have?

Helen:
I'm not sure because I haven't thought about it. Maybe we could both jot down some ideas between now and Monday and see what we come up with. Can we meet at 10 in the morning?

Merle:
Yes. Definitely. Thanks for supporting me on this one, Helen. It's not everyone who is willing to look at more than one way things can work out for the better.

Helen:
I need to be in the right spot too if I am going to use my talents and enthusiasm to produce good results. I'm thinking about making a move in about a year too. I'll be ready for a change by then. Thanks for your trust in going through this personal area with me. Do you think you can get the report in on time tomorrow afternoon now that we have a better idea of what is happening?

Merle:
Count on it.

Helen:
Thanks.

It Doesn't Have to Take a Long Time

This sequence of problem identification responses gives you a clear idea of some interventions which could be appropriate in a 3 to 5 minute conversation. It doesn't have to take a long time to facilitate a person through the process. In the long run, it will save many lost person-hours if Merle's performance goes up, or if he gets into a more fitting job role, or even if you help him find another company so you can replace him with a person who has a nature that fits the nature of the job.

Problem Specification: The Most Complex Skill

This specification skill is the main skill which nearly everyone who attempts to develop counseling skills has difficulty implementing effectively. This is the case because problem exploration requires a complex set of qualities and abilities: patience, temporarily suspending (personal "hunches," judgments, emotions, and premature advice), careful empathic listening, a creative mind, a perceptual receptivity to the other person's non-verbal cues, ability to craft language which defines the problem clearly , and a preference that "root" causes of a problem should eventually be explored when the person being helped can handle more depth. Although difficult to master, the skill of problem specification is very powerful in assisting others to move ahead in their understanding of their problems and solve them, which can improve their morale and their work performance.

Example Problem Statement — An example of language which could be appropriate for a problem statement which a leading manager might make to a co-worker in trouble is: "You seem to be saying that you're depressed because you realize that you can't stop drinking too much, because it's so difficult right now for you to face the reality of your wife's cancer." As you can see, this is a complex sentence, capturing the problem behavior, the difficult inner self-control problem, and the harsh external reality. The statement also contains no words which could be accusatory—just the facts as presented, for the most part. You can see why these statements are so difficult to formulate, and therefore why many people tend to over-simplify problems and give trite advice which they honestly hope will be helpful.

The More Solvable Problems Are Best Addressed First

It is also important that problems which have a high probability of being solved or managed effectively be focused on first so that motivation will be higher to take action. Searching for supports in the environment, strengths within the person, and problem solving potentials inherent within the problem itself are important. Success will then more likely be the result.

Rate your ability to help yourself or others to explore and define a specific internal and/or external problem.

Problem Specification	
1 = Skill is new to me, cannot do it 2 = Understand it but cannot perform it 3 = Can begin to do it, but not naturally 4 = Can do it naturally in many situations 5 = Can do it well and teach others if I want	

Goal Setting: Identifying Realistic and Motivating Targets

Goal setting is the "what to do" part of the problem management process. Action planning, which is the skill we will examine after goal setting, is the "how to get there" part of the process. For now, let's turn to your self assessment of your goal setting skills.

Attacking *high yield problems*, where there is opportunity for *both* personal development and improvement in external circumstances is preferable to setting goals which will alleviate only a personal problem *or* improve external circumstances. This is the case because often personal difficulties cause problem situations, and problem situations can in turn cause additional personal difficulties. The skill of goal setting is important because it provides a focus for defining future accomplishments which, when reached, can ideally alleviate the problem inside a person and improve the external problem situation at the same time. Goal setting is a practical and powerful skill for becoming a more intentional and successful person yourself, and in your leadership interventions with others to assist them to do the same.

Goals should be set which are specific enough to solve a defined problem and give direction to action. They should be:

1. measurable and verifiable;
2. realistic and achievable within a reasonable time;
3. genuinely owned by the person with the problem;
4. in accord with the values and beliefs of the person;
5. clearly envisioned and attractive enough to be motivating;
6. desirable enough to give rise to genuine commitment;
7. evaluated on an ongoing basis to check for realism.

Thus, specific and careful goal setting which challenges our own or others' unused potentials are often not easy to specify. Often people offer one another premature advice or "pat answers." Goal setting however, requires time and careful consideration for effective formulation. By providing yourself and others with a clear sense of direction for managing problems, stress can be alleviated, and constructive action, increased energy and improved performance can result.

An example of a clear goal statement might be the one that Merle made to Helen during their next meeting when he realized that for a number of reasons he had to change jobs and geographic locations. After Helen and Merle met the next Monday morning, Merle realized that he was not only disillusioned with his new job role, but was facing the fact that he did not want to live in the city where he now lived, wanted to move closer to his aging parents, and live in a city where pollution would not be such a problem. His problem was related to a complex set of factors which were pushing him away from not only the job he was in, but away from the company he was working with as well. After Helen helped him to sort through a more clear understanding of these factors, she helped him re-specify his problem as a career and life planning problem—then Merle formulated his own goal statement based on the increased clarity he found in his dialog with Helen:

> *I want to take the initiative to explore other career options and other cities, so I can relocate to start a new life by next summer where there are ample career opportunities, good family emphasis, clean air, and affordable housing.*

Note how clearly the goal is defined here, with a time line and Merle's values considered in the statement. Helen did a good job of helping Merle to be quite specific and concrete in his goal setting.

Helen began searching for another employee who could better fill Merle's position instead of keeping him in the same job or switching him to another job in the same company in the city where he did not want to live. Helen is likely to see an overall increase in corporate performance if she does more careful staff selection for that same position and other positions next time she has the opportunity.

Rate your ability to be specific and careful in the goal setting process as outlined above:

Goal Setting
1 = Skill is new to me, cannot do it 2 = Understand it but cannot perform it 3 = Can begin to do it, but not naturally 4 = Can do it naturally in many situations 5 = Can do it well and teach others if I want

Action Planning: Exploring and Evaluating Specific Pathways for Achievement

Exploring Alternative Strategies to Reach the Goal

Once the goal has been defined, it is time to examine alternative pathways to reach it; then it is time to develop a realistic plan to implement that goal in a step by step fashion.

Quite often, people fail to achieve goals because of a number of reasons. Some of the main reasons are that their strategies are not clear, the steps involved are too large for the time-line which has been set, or because of lack of either material or emotional supports. It is important therefore to ensure that all possible alternative strategies be explored and evaluated before one is decided upon prematurely. Often, there is a better way to "get there," but people tend to do what is familiar and not explore other options thoroughly enough to evaluate better action alternatives. Being exhaustive in searching out alternative courses of action nearly always reveals attractive, motivating, and encouraging steps to take which previously were not clear.

Evaluating and Selecting Alternative Strategies to Reach the Goal

Once alternative strategies have been explored, it is important to evaluate which ones best fit your own or others' values and motivational structures. The action plan simply has to "turn us on" for some reason or we do not want to "go for it." Therefore, in order to evaluate the potential of an alternative action plan, we need to specify what is important to the person with the problem, and assess how much each alternative course of action fits what is felt to be important.

For example, Merle wanted to choose a new location to live, and after exploring what was important to him, his family, and others in his social setting, he made the following type of comparison chart and rated each city on a scale of 1–5 in terms of how much it might fulfill the values he deemed as important:

| | **Alternatives** | | |
Importances	Chicago	Denver	Dallas
Clear Air	2	5	3
Family City	2	4	3
Good Economy	3	4	4
Affordable Housing	2	4	2
Proximity to Aging Parents	2	5	3
TOTALS	**11**	**22**	**15**

It may be entirely unnecessary to actually make a chart on paper unless the problem is quite complex, but the steps you would go through in considering various alternatives, or helping someone else to consider them, would be the same:

1. Identify alternatives;
2. Identify values/importances of self and others;
3. Weigh alternatives against values;
4. And get a more clear sense of which alternative course of action seems most desirable after careful assessment.

Now, evaluate your own ability to go through this same process of planning specific and appropriate actions to reach specified goals:

Action Planning
1 = Skill is new to me, cannot do it 2 = Understand it but cannot perform it 3 = Can begin to do it, but not naturally 4 = Can do it naturally in many situations 5 = Can do it well and teach others if I want

Implementing Action Plans: Increasing the Success Rate

The material to explain this skill will be longer than the other ones, because it is so important for leaders to consider. Helping self and others to reach goals and succeed in taking planned action steps is an important final step in the problem management process, perhaps ultimately the most important. If we do not succeed in counseling ourselves and others to accomplish worthwhile goals, then how effective is our helping or problem management?

Action plans tend not to get off the ground because people tend to cling to old, less functional patterns of behavior. It can be scary to give up familiar patterns of action in favor of more effective but foreign ones. If action plans do get implemented, they tend to fall apart over time, or fade in intensity, and quite often they are replaced by old patterns of behavior.

Leaders often get discouraged with how often people "fail" at living up to their expectations for improved performance. We find that we can get discouraged with ourselves in certain areas of our lives because we want change and it doesn't come easy. It would be good for us to accept that deeper changes often come about with great struggle, much encouragement, and often, quite a bit of time in the process. We have all seen that just because people set goals and plan to take new actions, that doesn't mean that the leader's task ends there, and the "follower" is now fully capable and responsible. There are some steps which leaders can take to help ensure that when they have spent time with people to help them specify problems, goals, and action plans, that they get the support and encouragement to carry them out to success.

A model for increasing the motivating power of agents of change has been developed by Janis (1982).[28] This model can be applied by leaders in a wide range of situations. This model also specifies actions which are required when exercising this skill of *action plan implementation*.

The Janis Model: Critical Phases and Key Variables Which Increase and Decrease the Motivating Power of Change Agents

Phase 1: Building Up Motivating Power

1. Encourage people to make self-disclosures versus not doing so.
2. Give positive feedback (acceptance and understanding) versus giving neutral or negative feedback in response to self-disclosure.
3. Use self-disclosures to give insight and cognitive restructuring versus giving little insight or cognitive restructuring.

Phase 2: Using Motivating Power

4. Make directive statements endorsing specific recommendations regarding needed behavior changes versus abstaining from any directive statements or endorsements.
5. Elicit commitment to the recommended course of action versus not eliciting commitment.
6. Attribute the norms being endorsed to a respected secondary group versus not doing so.
7. Give selective positive feedback versus giving non-contingent acceptance or predominantly neutral or negative feedback.

Phase 3: Retaining Motivating Power After a Contract Ends to Promote Internalization of New Learning

8. Give communications and training procedures that build up a sense of personal responsibility versus giving no such communications or training.
9. Give reassurances that you will continue to maintain an attitude of positive regard versus giving no such reassurances.

---

28 I. Janis, *Short-Term Counseling* (New Haven: Yale, 1983).

10. Make arrangements for phone calls, exchange of letters, or other forms of communication that foster hope for future contact, real or symbolic, at the time of terminating face-to-face meetings versus making no such arrangements.

11. Give reminders that continue to foster a sense of personal responsibility versus giving no such reminders.

12. Build up the other person's self-confidence about succeeding without the aid of the counselor versus not doing so.

When a leader engages in behaviors outlined above the likelihood of permanent behavior change is encouraged and increased, and the goal is more likely to e accomplished.

Marx's Relapse Prevention Theory: Further Steps Toward Getting New Behaviors to Stick

Marx (1986)[29] outlines a program for *self-managed skill retention* which can be used by or taught by leaders or trainers to others. In his work with managers who were involved with such persistent behavior problems as alcohol addiction and weight control, he found that the environment acted as a strong stimulant for the managers to return to the dysfunctional behavior patterns. In order to inoculate these managers against the environment and better enable them to succeed in their behavior change programs, they were taught the following relapse prevention process:

- ANTICIPATE AND MONITOR POTENTIAL DIFFICULTIES
  - Understand the relapse process
  - Observe differences between training and work settings
  - Create an effective support network
  - Expect subordinates' skepticism of new behaviors
  - Identify high-risk situations
  - Avoid implementing new skills in overwhelming situations
  - Recognize seemingly unimportant things that can lead to errors
- INCREASE RATIONAL THINKING
  - Reduce dysfunctional emotions
  - Retain self-confidence despite temporary errors

---

29 R. Marx, "Improving Management Development Through Relapse Prevention Strategies," *Journal of Management Development*, vol. 5, 2, 1986, 27–40.

- DIAGNOSE AND PRACTICE RELATED SUPPORT SKILLS
  - Diagnose necessary support skills
  - Review disruptive lifestyle patterns
  - Mix required and desirable activities
- PROVIDE APPROPRIATE CONSEQUENCES FOR BEHAVIOR
  - Assess organization support for skill retention
  - Create meaningful rewards and punishments where they otherwise don't exist

Although the relapse prevention process is more detailed than outlined here, we can see that behavior change in problem areas is often not an easy task for leaders or for those whom they lead.

Now that you have been introduced to this skill of program implementation, rate your own ability to perform it in the same way you rated other skills above:

Implementing Action Plans
1 = Skill is new to me, cannot do it
2 = Understand it but cannot perform it
3 = Can begin to do it, but not naturally
4 = Can do it naturally in many situations
5 = Can do it well and teach others if I want

Challenging Skills: The Advanced, Action-oriented Skills

Although these skills are presented as a cluster of related skills, you will be rating your ability to perform each skill within this cluster.

Challenging skills can be used at any of the three stages of the problem management process. They are especially potent skills which require quite a lot of trust in a relationship. There are several action-oriented skills which form the challenging skills battery below (adapted from Egan, 1986):[30]

---

30 G. Egan, *The Skilled Helper*, 3rd ed. (Monterey, California: Brooks/Cole Publishing Company, 1986), 241–245.

1. **Summarizing:** When you assist others to summarize what they have said, this challenges them to focus on central issues more clearly, and move them toward action. This skill softly challenges people to gain new perspective on their experiences and feelings.

Summarizing
1 = Skill is new to me, cannot do it 2 = Understand it but cannot perform it 3 = Can begin to do it, but not naturally 4 = Can do it naturally in many situations 5 = Can do it well and teach others if I want

2. **Information Gathering and Giving:** When you do your "homework" and give others information which they previously lacked (or correct information because what they are aware of is incorrect), you are also challenging them to view things from a new perspective. It is important not to overload people with our information, views, opinions or advice which makes us seem to be the "know-it-alls." Well timed, carefully selected information will be helpful to people when they are ready and willing to accept contradictory data.

Information Gathering and Giving
1 = Skill is new to me, cannot do it 2 = Understand it but cannot perform it 3 = Can begin to do it, but not naturally 4 = Can do it naturally in many situations 5 = Can do it well and teach others if I want

3. **Advanced Empathy:** Sharing your "hunches" with others about their experiences, behaviors or feelings can help them move beyond blind spots and develop needed new perspectives. In using the skills of advanced empathy, you can help others to express what they are implying, help them to identify themes in their stories, assist them to connect islands of experiences, behaviors or feelings, and help them to draw conclusions. This skill is critical to facilitating deeper under-

standing in others but must be approached with caution and respect because of the powerful and intensely personal nature of the material which is likely to emerge.

Advanced Empathy

1 = Skill is new to me, cannot do it
2 = Understand it but cannot perform it
3 = Can begin to do it, but not naturally
4 = Can do it naturally in many situations
5 = Can do it well and teach others if I want

---

4. **Confrontation:** You can challenge others' discrepancies, distortions, smoke screens, and games which they seem to use to keep themselves and others from seeing their problem situations and unused potentials; or you can use confrontation to challenge people to move beyond discussion to action.

This skill is the most risky of all of the other skills because it involves getting the other person to confront self directly. A great deal of trust is required in order for people to feel comfortable allowing you to challenge what you think may be self-deception, self-defeating behavior patterns, or destructive interpersonal "games." It would seem that we have to earn the right to confront by developing the relationship over time prior to engaging in a confrontation.

Strength Confrontation: You challenge others to focus on strengths which you observe are present, but ones which they tend to ignore or deny. Berenson and Mitchell (1974)[31] found that more facilitative helpers used strength confrontations significantly more often than less facilitative helpers. They also found that helpers overall used this type of confrontation least often!

Weakness Confrontation: You can challenge others to face their weak spots because they are tending not to see them. This is the more risky

---

31 B. Berenson and K. Mitchell, *Confrontation for Better or Worse!* (Amherst, Mass.: Human Resource Development Press, 1974).

type of confrontation because it requires that the other people have enough self-worth to face their deficits without feeling like losers. Many people cannot face weaknesses or faults directly without feeling shaky in the self-worth department. They can also feel threatened and fearful that others will judge them negatively and discriminate against them when it comes time for a promotion. In some environments this is probably a realistic fear. There are several kinds of confrontation which you can examine in Berenson's and Mitchell's book.

Now assess the extent to which you believe you can confront others effectively:

Confrontation
1 = Skill is new to me, cannot do it
2 = Understand it but cannot perform it
3 = Can begin to do it, but not naturally
4 = Can do it naturally in many situations
5 = Can do it well and teach others if I want

5. **Self-sharing**: You can share your own experience with others as a way of modeling non-defensive self-disclosure, or as a way of helping them move beyond blind spots, and as a way of seeing possibilities for problem-managing action.

This is perhaps the most encouraging of all the types of challenging. When you are genuine enough to share an experience which shows the other person that you have some true sympathy with theirs, there develops a sense of comraderie or mutuality. This is trust building and eliminates a tone of judgment so often feared by many.

It is important that your sharing of your experiences does not turn into a domination of the dialog, that it be well timed, *and most importantly useful* to facilitating further understanding or insight in the other person. It is an especially valuable skill to use when a person is stuck when attempting to specify their own part of a problem, or when attempting to come up with action alternatives.

Now rate your ability to use this skill of self-sharing:

Self-sharing
1 = Skill is new to me, cannot do it 2 = Understand it but cannot perform it 3 = Can begin to do it, but not naturally 4 = Can do it naturally in many situations 5 = Can do it well and teach others if I want

6. **Immediacy**: This is a very versatile and widely applicable skill which enables you to deal with issues which must be dealt with before other problems can be tackled. It could be considered a "process" skill that enables you to help yourself or others get "unstuck" when things aren't moving forward. This skill can assist you to improve your working alliance with others in two ways:

1. by using *relationship immediacy*, which focuses on your ability to discuss with another person your relationship with him or her with a view to managing whatever problems have existed, and maintaining strengths in the relationship; or,

2. by using *here-and-now immediacy*, which focuses on your ability to discuss with others whatever is standing in the way of working together right now.

Immediacy is a powerful skill in establishing your genuineness as a person and as a helpful leader. It expresses your concern that the relationship go well and your commitment that problems get solved. It is an excellent way to "cut through" tension and a stuck feeling in the relationship if the other person is the type who can handle direct, face-to-face honesty. If the other person is too intimidated to deal directly with such intensity and openness, then this could be a risky skill to use, especially in the beginning of a relationship.

Rate your ability to use the skill of immediacy effectively.

Immediacy
1 = Skill is new to me, cannot do it
2 = Understand it but cannot perform it
3 = Can begin to do it, but not naturally
4 = Can do it naturally in many situations
5 = Can do it well and teach others if I want

Making an Effective Referral to a Professional Helper

When you realize that the person with whom you are working is facing a personal problem which is over your head it is appropriate to make a smooth referral to a professional helper. In making an effective referral, it would be best to refer the person to someone who is already known and respected by your friend, associate or employee. However, when this is not possible, then it is ideal if you personally know some good helpers whom you can recommend to others when they are in need. The following steps could be followed when making a referral:

1. Gather as much information about the counselor or therapist to whom you might make a referral.

2. Make sure that the counselor is formally qualified (through university training and certification, as appropriate in certain states and provinces) and has had a track record of reputable practice whenever possible.

3. Meet this professional helper face-to-face so that you get a sense of who the person is and what approaches are preferred.

4. When you are satisfied that you have located a good counselor then suggest to the person needing assistance that you would like to make a personal introduction to a new helper who can help more effectively than you in this instance because of very specific reasons.

5. Personally introduce the two who may work together whenever possible and leave them alone to have their first session.

6. Follow-up with both parties to see how things went (you may have to make another referral if the first one doesn't click).

7. Make sure that agreements regarding confidentiality between you and the person and the therapist are specified and stuck to or you will lose trust and integrity in the eyes of others.

8. Continue supporting the person receiving help but do not enter into confidential conversations which could counter what work is being done by the therapist or you may get a frustrated therapist or counselor on the phone asking you to stay in your own territory.

Now rate your ability to make an effective referral.

Referral	
1 = Skill is new to me, cannot do it 2 = Understand it but cannot perform it 3 = Can begin to do it, but not naturally 4 = Can do it naturally in many situations 5 = Can do it well and teach others if I want	

Total for the Counseling Section	
Add all numbers in the boxes above.	

Conclusion

Now that you have completed this self-assessment on basic counseling skills, you may be feeling somewhat intimidated by the complexity and difficulty of the skills and the process or you may be saying to yourself that you have been doing these things all along but didn't have names for them. In either case, having gone through this assessment gives you the advantage of greater intentionality in the use of the skills, a perspective from which to evaluate your own counseling behavior and a model to plan for your own professional development.

In the next chapter (chapter 7) we will be examining how to build upon the interpersonal, counseling and problem management skills to intervene in a consultative mode in groups or organizations to make a transforming impact. This is the most cognitively complex mode in which to function because you are constantly and directly interfacing with dynamic human systems and organizations. Then in Chapter 8 we will examine the concepts of style, skill and role shifting for greater appropriateness and effectiveness. This will complete section 2 of the book, and we will then move into learning to use the tools of transforming leadership.

Research has established that basic counseling skills and core facilitative conditions are foundational to most successful relationships. Counseling roles and skills, as parts of a leader's transforming tools, are not ones to be taken lightly. Neither are they to be neglected or avoided.

Graphing Your Self-assessment Scores

Now that you have completed this section of the comprehensive self-assessment, graph in all of your individual scores so that you can get a visual summary of what skills you see are stronger and weaker. Graph in your self-rating scores on each skill using the "bar graph" method of drawing lines from left to right on each scale.

1 = Skill is new to me, cannot do it
2 = Understand it but cannot perform it
3 = Can begin to do it, but not naturally
4 = Can do it naturally in many situations
5 = Can do it well and teach others if I want

	1	2	3	4	5
Problem Exploration and Specification					
Goal Setting: Identifying Realistic and Motivating Targets					
Action Planning: Exploring and Evaluating Specific Pathways for Achievement					
Implementing Action Plans: Increasing the Success Rate					
Challenging Skills: The Advanced, Action-oriented Skills					
Summarizing					
Information Gathering and Giving					
Advanced Empathy					
Confrontation					
Self-sharing					
Immediacy					
Making an Effective Referral to a Professional Helper					

Knowledge and Skills which Develop and Transform People and Organizations

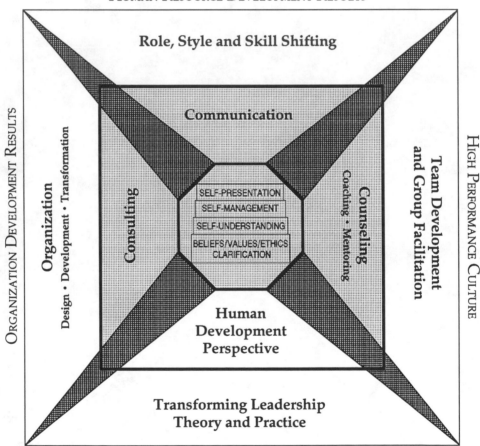

HUMAN RESOURCE DEVELOPMENT RESULTS

Role, Style and Skill Shifting

ORGANIZATION DEVELOPMENT RESULTS

HIGH PERFORMANCE CULTURE

Organization
Design • Development • Transformation

Communication

Consulting

SELF-PRESENTATION
SELF-MANAGEMENT
SELF-UNDERSTANDING
BELIEFS/VALUES/ETHICS
CLARIFICATION

Counseling
Coaching • Mentoring

Team Development
and Group Facilitation

Human
Development
Perspective

Transforming Leadership
Theory and Practice

EFFECTIVE PERSONNEL PRACTICES

Chapter 7

▼

CONSULTING SKILLS FOR DEVELOPING GROUPS AND ORGANIZATIONS

In the field of group endeavor,
you will see incredible events
in which the group performs far beyond
the sum of its individual talents.

Dee Hock, Former CEO at Visa International

It happens in the symphony, in the ballet, in the theater, in sports, and equally in business. It is easy to recognize and impossible to define. It is a mistique. It cannot be achieved without immense effort, training, and cooperation, but effort, training, and cooperation alone rarely create it. Some groups reach it consistently. Few can sustain it. (Schlesinger, Eccles, and Gabarro, 1983) .[1]

Introduction

This chapter, like previous ones, is presented in a developmental sequence. That is, you will be exposed to knowledge and a set of skills which are increasingly abstract and more difficult to learn and integrate into your work and life. They also build on the knowledge and skills which you assessed in previous chapters. By putting all these skills together into one process the

---

1   L. Schlesinger, R. Eccles, and J. Gabarro, *Managerial Behavior in Organizations: Texts, Cases, and Readings* (New York: McGraw-Hill, 1983), 486.

effect is that you will have the capacity to become a more effective *developmental change agent.*

A developmental change agent is another descriptive phrase for a transforming leader: it is a leader who has developed the awareness, knowledge, skills and care to exercise a catalytic impact on the development of individuals, groups and organizations in order to accomplish a premeditated purpose. Leaders who can act as *change agents* will be needed in the years ahead because in an increasingly competitive world great performances such as the ones alluded to in the preceding quote will be a requirement. The payoff for all the hard work of developing a group or organization to the point of high performance is described by Robert Quinn (1984):[2] "The interface of big dreams, hard work, and successful outcomes is potent. The sensation that accompanies the phenomenon is a feeling of exhilaration." It is important, therefore, that leaders light the way toward strategically managed change and innovation. When they are acting in the *consultative mode* they not only ardently practice experimentation and problem solving, but they also develop the tendency in others to be more explorative and prudently adventuresome.

This chapter is divided into two parts:

Part One: In the first part of this chapter we will first look at the **nature of the consulting process**.

Part Two: Then in the second part of this chapter (as in the previous two chapters which focused on **skill assessment** and attainment) you will assess the extent to which you have the various skills which are appropriate to the consultative mode.

In summary, although more difficult and abstract in nature, the knowledge and skills presented and assessed in this chapter are more powerful and far-reaching in their implications. As a *communicator* (Chapter five) you saw that you have significant impact on the quality of relationships with others in an organization; in the role of *counselor and problem manager* (Chapter six) you recognized that you can have specific preventative and remedial capabilities, but as a *consultant* (the focus of the role in this chapter) you will gain awareness and ability as a *change agent* to increase your effectiveness

---

2   R. Quinn, *Beyond Rational Management: Mastering the Paradoxes and Competing Demands of High Performance* (San Francisco: Jossey-Bass, 1988), 14.

and impact with individuals, groups and organizations. Then in Chapter eight we will explore applications of the various skills to a wide range of settings and review the advantages of learning to style, skill and role shift. Now we will examine the importance of intentionality in effecting a significant developmental impact on groups and organizations.

Intentionality: A Cornerstone of Transformation

Although exploration and experimentation are both important characteristics of transforming leaders and excellent organizations, conscious competency and technical know-how are also important factors to include in the recipe for success in managing and innovating change. The main difference between a professional and an amateur is that an amateur is often using the trial and error method, and the professional has a backlog of knowledge and experience as an inner guidance system: the professional "knows" what he or she is doing. The example of the brain surgeon who has specifically analyzed the exact part of the brain which must receive a keenly refined surgical intervention is a good one. The surgeon does not touch a surgical instrument to that exact part of a person's brain unless established procedures are being followed, unless there is a skilled and experienced hand which has been trained by others who have been trained, and unless there is constant monitoring of the physical system of the patient during the surgery. In many cases, the patient remains awake to report to the surgeon. Hopefully, this analogy has meaning for leaders who intervene in the lives of groups and organizations because it is possible that the impact of these interventions can be even more far-reaching than that of the brain surgeon. Acting intentionally and purposefully is critical to success. For a further exploration of intentionality, I refer you to the Center for Constructive Change (1984).[3]

Building the Consultant Inside of the Manager

As a manager (or other person in a position of leadership responsibility) becomes increasingly capable of being more objective by seeing an overarching view of things, there is greater opportunity for the strategic kind of intervention which we see in the example of a brain surgeon. The manager

---

3   Center for Constructive Change, "How Intentional is Your Life?" *Journal for Constructive Change*, 6(1), 16–17.

then becomes a leader with an objective perspective, able to "touch" groups or organizations with more precise effects to achieve agreed upon and justifiable ends. Oddly enough, like a successful brain surgery, a good consultative leadership intervention is very impersonal, removed, objective, aloof, and yet at the same time intimately personal, getting at the very nerve roots of groups and organizations and producing healing effects with developmental impact; or alternatively, it is possible to exert a destructive or neutral effect.

Consultative interventions can also impact individuals in personal and powerful ways. A clear example of this is when, in the role of consultant, one change agent shifted into providing personal counseling with a senior executive of a company which resulted in his treating most people in his life with greater respect, understanding and communication skill. This intervention had a far-reaching positive ripple effect throughout the whole organization and in his family relationships.

As can be readily seen, the consultative role can have many functions and "hats" and each of these "hats," which can be put on or taken off, has its own requisite set of skills. The consultative role may include such functions as: catalyst, developer, researcher, strategizer, trainer, analyst, motivator, group or team facilitator, problem-solver, organizational auditor, mentor and coach. The range of consultative functions which leaders can play in organizations is as varied as the organizations in which consultants find themselves. In many instances several roles at the same time are being played. The skills involved in fulfilling these functions are the skills of transforming leadership which have been outlined in previous chapters and which will be outlined in this chapter, and the one to follow. These skills are generic in that they are basic to and flexible enough to fulfill the demands of the various consultative roles and functions. For a more in-depth analysis of the various roles and skills which consultants can use see Menzel (1975).[4]

---

4   Robert K. Menzel, "A Taxonomy of Change Agent Skills," *Journal of European Training*, 1975, 4(5), 289–291.

The Importance of Consultative Roles and Skills in Transforming Leadership

The following example will illustrate the diversity of roles and stages which naturally occur in the course of a consultative intervention. Either a leader from outside an organization or group, or someone on the inside could perform the duties outlined below.

During the initial assessment phase of a consulting contract, a vice-president and general manager of a manufacturing firm confided in me that he had "tried everything" to increase employee productivity. He had put pressure on managers and supervisors to up the production quotas, threatened layoffs if production did not go up, and tried to "pump" all the managers with "excellence" audio and video tape programs. He even instituted a *Quality is Free* program. But in my interviews with his managers, supervisors and front line workers it became clear that the company was experiencing what I call "excellence burn-out:" The workers were pushed to the limit of what they believed was reasonable for what they were receiving in return— and they weren't *willing* to give any more unless they could see there would be "something in it for me." However, as a team they were, according to industry standards, functioning at only about 60% of the real potential of the equipment which they had to work with—and the vice-president made sure that they knew this fact on a daily basis. The more he pushed, the more they complained about being overworked and underpaid.

Upon further investigation in interviews with front line staff (the ones who directly control productivity) it became clear that they were *angry*. This anger came across in nearly every interview. I listened carefully and for many hours without turning my interviews with them into sessions which might be seen as "encouraging whiners to whine," as the vice-president put it. I made a list of complaints **and** a list of what they appreciated about working for this company during each of my 30 interviews with them, which included a random cross section of 30% of the front line staff. Here, in order of priority of importance as perceived by front line workers, is the list of complaints:

1.   Nobody cares about us around here, why should we put out for them— they won't even fix up the *rest rooms* and lunch room around here. They treat us like migrant workers. (This one complaint about the restrooms and lunch room was the *most* frequently mentioned of all complaints!)

2. They (management) say they care about us "people" and that "people are important to the company" but really they just talk the talk, but don't walk the walk. When Bill got seriously injured on the job, they just called the ambulance. Not one supervisor, manager or executive in this place even visited him in the hospital for 2 weeks. That's sick. (The fact was that management did make the call, then had to go out of town for a week. Not all 197 staff members knew this.)

3. Some low performers who are connected to the president's family get to stick around and continue to sluff off their responsibilities on the job, and we have to pick up the slack. The boss plays favorites, and we aren't his favorites. (From the boss's view, this one person was an old time friend of the family, and out of kindness and respect for this person's age, he decided not to fire him.)

4. Good performance is not even noticed or rewarded around here. Why should I put out my best when we don't get raises even when production does go up for a whole month? If I put out more on the job, then I get pressure from most other workers to fall back into line so they don't have to work harder.

5. People can get fired at any time around here, and without enough of a chance to better their job performance. They fired three receptionists in the head office without even giving them any training to do the job. Other people have just disappeared around here and no one knows why. You wonder if you are next! (The boss didn't fire the receptionists, they just couldn't do the job so he released them at the end of their probationary period. They couldn't keep up with a position around which we later had to build two positions due to the complexity of that job role.)

6. I've been here for 4 years and I still don't know if I will ever get a promotion. I don't know if I'm being seen as "just another worker" or not. I think I could do a good job as a supervisor, and I have taken the training, but no one will tell me if I should have any hope or not. I'm looking for another place to work where there is more opportunity. (This is something which has been remedied by including the issue of career path planning in the performance review process.)

7. Management keep changing their minds about how things should be done and they don't involve any of us in making changes, and they don't even ask us how the changes are working! (This is another

problem area which has been remedied through more effective team meetings.)

From these complaints, which I collated and summarized into a brief report, the vice-president and I arrived at the following understandings:

1. Managers who aren't listened to and shown respect by the V.P. often do not listen to and show basic human decency and respect for their workers.

2. Managers demonstrated role, skill and style rigidity in the traditional manner rather than in the transformative leadership fashion.

3. People won't work over the long haul for people they don't like.

4. The president of the company had set the "impersonal tone" of the corporate culture by treating previous executive and management staff with a "transistor" approach to management: "If it doesn't work, unplug it, throw it away and get another one in there." There had been a 35% turnover in managers and supervisors during the past three years since the company really got off the ground, and a corresponding 40% (per year!) turnover in front line staff.

5. No one in management acted as an internal consultant to the organization, reading the "arational" factors in the workplace in order to respond to things like fixing up the rest rooms and lunch rooms (at least), which were considered to be the major sign of disrespect by management toward the employees (who were 65% women)!

It is clear from this list of complaints that I had discovered (in my role as external consultant) a series of problems which could be remedied if I could get the understanding and cooperation of the vice-president and the president. In a series of meetings and planning sessions, we came to the conclusion that there needed to be some changes in the way people treated people in this organization. Changes were made to address the specific complaints of the workers and the results have been that the company has increased it's productivity, that the employees who have stayed on have accepted the *Quality is Free* program with the resultant effects of decreased turnover, decreased absenteeism, increased performance and higher morale.

Leaders are often expected by those "below" them to act in a traditionally independent and decisive manner, but as we can see in the above example, in day-to-day affairs they are more likely to need the skills of consulting with others in a collaborative manner. It is ideal when all people involved can arrive at decisions for which there is team or group commitment and consensus. If the vice-president could have been the internal consultant this could have been ideal! "Participative management" is becoming even more popular because of the results which have been achieved through team efforts in many business environments (Peters and Austin, 1985).[5] Many Japanese companies have demonstrated the effectiveness of well functioning teams, and some North American companies find themselves attempting to emulate their efforts.

In another important and innovative work, which is referred to above, Philip Crosby (Crosby, 1979)[6] has developed a book and training program for managers called, *Quality is Free*. This program outlines many of the critical factors which appear to be required for organizational success. However, although Crosby places importance on the role of managers as internal quality consultants to the organization (calling them "quality managers"), he does not provide a means for training those managers into becoming skilled transforming leaders. The success of his program rests on the competencies of those who implement it.

Crosby's focus on developing "management participation and attitude" is a good start, but if we want to go the full length we will provide a means to develop the manager into a skilled and competent internal consultant to the organization who can do more than manage a good system for quality or productivity improvement. It would be preferable to develop the capacity within each manager to set up, monitor and develop people, morale and unique systems to facilitate an organization's success. But let's not sell Crosby short—he himself is an example of a transforming leader and does provide a tested system for improving quality and productivity.

Interpersonal communication, counseling and problem management, and consultative skills are required in order to do successful participative management. Even though it is important for those who are exerting leadership influence to shift at times from a mutually communicative to a helpful counseling mode, it is perhaps even more important that they be able to shift from the communicative and counseling modes to the *consultative mode*.

---

5 T. Peters and N. Austin, *A Passion for Excellence* (New York: Random House, 1985).

6 P.B. Crosby, *Quality Is Free: The Art of Making Quality Certain* (New York: McGraw Hill, 1979).

The Nature of the Consultative Mode

The consultative manner of dealing with people and problems is an innovative and creative one, a more "global" one—characterized by careful assessment, planned action and combined with empathy toward others. The consultative mode also requires pronounced detachment and objectivity about the group and/or organizational context in which a person's or group's problem is occurring. The strong leader is capable of transforming people and organizations by moving from a mutual communication mode to a counseling and problem management one, and then shifting to a consultative mode when the situation requires this type of "skill and role shifting."

Many leaders demonstrate role, skill and style rigidity, and this lack of receptivity and responsiveness to change and to people limits their potential to function effectively. Developing consultative awareness (objective awareness of the process and the context of people and events) and skills will assist you to be more effective in the consulting process cycle:

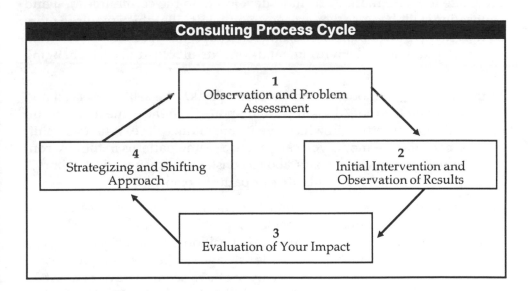

The multi-faceted and flexible leader functions in this "fluid" manner, not closing down options or opportunities, but using both intuition and rational calculation, theorizing, strategizing and then taking action—only to re-evaluate the impact and shift again.

This type of circular "modus operandi" is similar to what has been called "MBWA," or Management By Wandering Around, by Tom Peters. There is a certain informal quality, a genuine and mutual (but expert) quality of leading in this manner. This type of leader, while having the ultimate authority to make final decisions, can be more of a humble "servant," attempting to discover and meet needs in order to facilitate the accomplishment of agreed upon goals while keeping the "big picture" in mind at the same time.

This image of leading while wandering around talking with people for a purpose captures the spirit of the "hi-touch," but objective and result-oriented leader who can function in the consultative mode, and the other two modes (communicating and counseling) alternatively or in a blended fashion at the same time.

Difficulties in Developing Consultative Skills

As mentioned above, the consultative mode, and the skills which are appropriate to it, are more difficult to develop than the communication and counseling skills because they are more complex skills which require a more comprehensive awareness of self, others, groups, technical know-how, and the organizational and environmental contexts involved in each changing situation.

In the consultative mode, it is as though a part of the self is reserved and "perched upon the roof," looking down upon self in the context of a group or organizational setting in which events are taking place. When you shift into the consultative mode, you can practice seeing patterns in the environment, much as the eagle soars above constantly "casing the territory," looking for movement, irregularities or patterns below.

The consultative skills also require that you have a strong base of communication and personal/interpersonal problem management skills in order to be most effective. Many people in positions of authority over others have very few skills which they consciously and deliberately employ. Some people in positions of responsibility over others seem to have one or two sets of skills. Few managers seem to have developed all three sets of skills, and integrated them into practice.

Even though the consultative level of awareness and the skills which accompany it are the most difficult to develop, they are perhaps the most influential and impact-producing, and therefore are potentially the most rewarding. It is the challenge for the transforming leader, functioning in the role of consultant, to stay open, to deal with complexity and to be at least as complex as the complexity of the situation at hand. The capacity to be complex and versatile is vital to both effective processing of information, and creativity.

The consultative mode includes such roles as listener, interviewer, observer, data collector, reporter, teacher, trainer, coach, educator, sponsor, support giver, advisor, challenger, mediator, mentor, advisor, advocate, researcher, problem solver, entrepreneur and creator. All of these roles capture the complexity of leadership and require all three sets of skills in transformative leadership. With this complexity in mind, you now have an opportunity to familiarize yourself with a range of consultative skills, and assess the extent to which you see that you have developed the various skills.

In this next section below you will use the same self-rating scale from 1–5 which you used in the communication and counseling chapters of this book.

The Consulting Process

Outlined below is my summary of the consulting process so that you can gain better perspective on the steps involved. You will then rate your ability to go through these steps.

Step 1: Assessment of Needs, Wants and Problems

During this first step some kind of organizational needs assessment or organizational audit can fruitfully be undertaken. This needs, strengths, or problems audit can take the form of administering standardized question-naires for organizational assessment, interviews can be conducted with key people in the organization, or a systems effectiveness analysis can be con-ducted by an outside specialist (i.e., an accountant, engineer, etc.). Although the identification of problems and unmet needs is important, the *pinpointing of strengths and unrealized potential is also important* to discover and communi-cate to all members of the organization. Assessing both the technical and relationship aspects of a problem are equally important.

Step 2: Clarify the Need for Change in a Language Which Others Will Understand and Accept

The consulting process is very similar to the problem management process in this respect: Problem identification and specification is a most critical phase of the process. The more specific and careful the definition of the problem or need, the greater the likelihood of a successful intervention. There are both informal and formal ways of defining problems and assessing needs. Some informal ways include small group interviews with representatives from various parts of an organization, small group simulations of problem situations which are perceived to be occurring frequently in the organization, or anonymous surveys with key work groups, supervisors and managers. More formal methods of data collection will be specifically explored below. The problem must be communicated to the group in such a way that both leaders and members will be able to usefully identify it as a valid problem or need.

Step 3: Exploring the Readiness for Change

In each endeavor of a group or organization to make a positive difference, both the change agent and the individuals involved must assess one another's willingness and ability to make the change happen successfully. There are many obstacles to effective change, and many forces which can promote change effectively. Personal insecurity, interpersonal or intergroup conflict, financial pressures, political forces, and timing can all affect a change attempt adversely. When intervening in a consultative mode, regardless of your role, it is good to do a "force field analysis" and identify all the possible blocks and test to see if there are ways to remove some of the blocks before they hamper the effectiveness of your efforts.

For example, a principal of a large elementary school called me to assist her in the planning of some professional development activities for her teaching staff. During my interviews with some of the teachers (which I insisted upon), a few of them confided in me that nothing would likely be well received because the principal was not consulting with the teachers about what they felt was needed in the coming year, but was just planning to "lay on" some training. The resentment was so great that I confronted the principal with this perception. We thought through how we could overcome this block, and the principal decided to hold a meeting to specify the teachers' areas of need, using me as a planning facilitator.

The teachers appreciated the principal's using an outsider to facilitate staff consensus on training events because her communication and leadership styles were autocratic and authoritarian in nature, and she did not want to change her management style because she feared losing some of the authority and control she thought she had established. This principal was also able to get many of the things she wanted into the program, because she was participating in the planning process as a mutual leader/member of the group, instead of the "boss." People in her group who perceived themselves as mature, or as deserving more respect, resented being "bossed around" by her in the past, so we had to overcome this block before a positive difference could be made. She had to develop some additional style versatility in dealing with these followers or delegate some leadership to one of them in order to get the results she wanted.

She subsequently used the same consultative mode of operating she saw me use to solve two other problems which arose in her teaching team with good results; and because her performance was under review that year by her school district's Director of Instruction, she was greatly relieved at the increasingly positive evaluations she received from her teachers. Her readiness for change, inspired by her observations of how the consultative process can solve problems *without losing authority*, increased as time went by—this resulted in the teachers changing their perceptions and approaches with her.

Step 4: Exploring the Potential for Working In Concert

A good working relationship is imperative if we are to make the positive difference we would like to make. Establishing some bonds of common values, beliefs, or approaches can help in developing trust with those with whom you work. Being open about differences can also be important when it can prevent future expectation gaps and clashes in values or styles, and allow you an opportunity to work through agreements about how you will deal with problems and resolve conflicts which will inevitably emerge.

When expectations are not clear, anxiety levels often escalate, and arational, or even irrational behavior can be the result. One of the ways of managing non-rationality is to be clear about what you will not do and what you can be expected to do. Then see how much support you can get from the people you are working with on key issues. Not only can you test to see how much potential compatibility or conflict there is between various people, but you can communicate a certain degree of willingness to respect the values and approaches of others who are involved in the change effort. Establishing clear and agreed upon values and procedures in any group can help to create compatibility in your work relationships with others.

For example, while I was working as an organization development consultant on an 8-month contract with a juvenile correctional facility, I became aware that the administrator was perceived by most supervisors and workers as a "spineless jelly fish." Prior to my beginning this extended contract, I confronted the administrator with the fact that there was a lot of evidence from initial surveys and interviews that his behavior was being perceived as inconsistent, and that he was easily pressured by various kids or staff to change his mind on key issues. I informed him that this behavior caused specific problems such as: an undermining of the behavior modification reward system; staff and "kid" morale problems due to his being seen as "playing favorites"; and financial problems because he had approved spending by one department and left little money in the bank for some of the other programs.

I decided to try and get a commitment from him that he would meet weekly with his senior staff and consult with them about the likely consequences of various actions before he made major decisions which would affect them. I told him that otherwise I doubted that there could be a positive difference made in this situation. He agreed to the consultative sessions (because he hated saying no?). Actually, he was greatly relieved to get some assistance in making some of the more difficult management decisions, had never had training in leadership or management before, and as a result of our having several subsequent meetings together he decided to quit his position in order to do counseling in an alcohol and drug treatment program. He realized that administrative roles really weren't for him. We developed a good working relationship over the 8 months of the contract. Without developing these clear working agreements with he and his staff, my efforts at unblocking and developing this organization would likely have been entirely foiled.

Step 5: Setting General Goals

A parallel to this phase in the problem management model outlined in the previous chapter would be the goal setting phase. In this phase, agreements are made with others about what achievements or accomplishments are being attempted. These goals need to be stated concretely enough (and usually in writing, as much as most people resist doing this!) so that their attainment can actually be observed and measured. General goals are stated as what we hope for: "We want to improve our hiring process"; or "We want to use time more wisely in our meetings." It is important to come to consensus about general goals before moving on to seek consensus between members of a work group or team. Otherwise, you may be attempting to set more specific objectives to be achieved when there is no real commitment to do so. These goals can become an important part of a written contract, if this more formal type of agreement is appropriate.

Step 6: Specifying Objectives to Be Achieved

For most people who are busy doing the "job," whether that job is leadership in a home, a classroom, a school, a hospital ward, a company, or an army, there is some reluctance to take the time to do careful planning. It takes time and a stretching of the imagination. *It is hard work to be specific with language!* It is risky to announce to others that you have a plan because then you will be asked by them whether or not your plan worked! So quite often people just keep going along with the status quo, and don't rock the boat or set even slightly risky goals which could later prove to be embarrassing.

The director of a large church youth group called me and asked me if I could assist him to develop the team of people who were involved in working with about 150 of the youth in the church. On this staff there was one full time director, three paid part-time staff and 25 volunteer adult staff. The youth program has been going along steadily for 7 years or so with the same director, but no long range planning or annual goal setting had taken place at the team level. It was "top down" leadership where the director to this point had taken most of the responsibility for structuring activities and motivating the youth, with other volunteer leaders following along whether they liked how things were going or not. They did not want to confront the leader's authority because they valued showing respect to their leaders by not "disagreeing" with them. As the church became larger, the need for more staff and more diverse programs became evident.

One primary problem became clear. No one had systematically determined what the needs and wants were from the points of view of the youth, and no one had assessed the needs, skills and abilities of the staff or 25 volunteers. They were hired or accepted as volunteers based upon their personal qualities and their willingness to serve. This scenario is typical of most volunteer groups and committees where there is one leader taking most of the responsibility, and the followers are not specifically qualified for the roles they are vaguely assuming. I spent one day with the four leaders and their spouses (since they worked together as couples) to decide what they would like to do to strengthen their team effectiveness and the impact of their work with the youth in their church and in their community. With my assistance in wording their objective statements, they wrote out the following:

1. We will conduct an informal needs assessment (personal interviews) of the youth in our church and community, and also use a more formal questionnaire approach to see how much the two match.

2. We will create a comprehensive mission, goals, and programs statement based upon the above needs assessment of youth in our church and community.

3. We will write a proposal to the board which will include an outline of our departmental statements and a budget which will outline the financial requirements to achieve our goals; and this proposal will be given to them on May 1st for their consideration.

4. We will involve youth in the decision making process about programs we are planning for them in the future by getting their ideas and input at planning meetings we schedule each month.

5. We will engage in staff training for ourselves when we determine areas of need, assess the training needs of our 25 volunteer staff, and provide training for them, and begin both training programs in June.

6. We will discover and appreciate one another's strengths and create job descriptions for ourselves which reflect our individual abilities. We will communicate these job descriptions to one another and review their appropriateness every 6 months.

7. We will bring in people external to our church to assist in meeting needs which we don't have the expertise to meet (i.e., career and life planning seminar for senior high and college age youth, self-esteem seminar for junior and senior high youth, pre-marriage and marriage seminars for those who marry young, and provide longer term professional counseling for youth who have emotional and family problems).

This group needed assistance in specifying their objectives because they clearly would not have put them together in this more complete and specific way without external assistance. However, it would have been best if someone *within* the church organization had consultative knowledge and skills. The board was so impressed with the clarity of this department's plans that they funded all of their proposals without reservation and gave the youth pastor a promotion to Assistant Pastor.

Step 7: Setting Up Programs to Achieve Objectives

After objectives have been set and agreed upon, then you will be in a much better position to plan and implement them in a step by step fashion. It is also more likely that you will assign the most appropriate person to do various parts of the task or program if you have specified exactly what needs to be done in terms of action which needs to be taken and accomplishments which need to be reached in order for the group to achieve its goals and purpose.

For example, if we were to take objective number 6 above and develop a program to achieve it, such a program might look like this:

Example of a Simple Program of Steps

Step A: Two Hours — We will meet for a day on June 5th to do the Personal Style Indicator and specify our strengths, difficult areas, how we each react to stress, how we function on a team, how we tend to lead or follow, how we function with other styles, and what we could do to develop.

Step B: Two Hours — We will then share all this information about ourselves with one another. We will each have a summary of the above information about one another for later reference.

Step C: Four Hours — We will put up on the wall (using three-by-five inch note cards) all of the tasks which we can think of which we have to get done. Then we will negotiate who takes each card off the wall based on who is really best at achieving each task. From the list of tasks we collect on the cards we will each write a job description we will live with (for the most part) for 6 months, when we will review our job descriptions again.

These steps make the achievement of the objective come alive and be far more exciting than if everyone were to just have agreed that generally it is important to have job descriptions. Programs of steps for the accomplishment of other objectives could be delineated in similar fashion and with a similar level of specificity.

Step 8: Evaluating and Reporting the Impact of Your Intervention

It is important to assess the impact of your interventions as you intervene and at set time intervals during a project. Normally, you would do some type of assessment after the first session, another a third of the way through, another at two thirds of the way and a last at the end. This more or less regular evaluation will assist you to set a new course as you will likely see that your planned intervention did not hit the mark.

When you have evaluated that there is a problem you will need to communicate it to the group with which you are working and perhaps give them an opportunity to suggest alternative solutions, which you can integrate into an overall plan for improving your approach, or their strategies. You will win the respect of group members when you can "head problems off at the pass" rather than ignoring them or avoiding any awareness of them altogether.

An example of this type of evaluation and reporting is in my own teaching of courses at the college or university level. At the beginning of each session I hand out a three-by-five inch file card to all students and ask them to jot down on one side what "worked" and what didn't work that class, with suggestions for improvements. When I read all 30 or 40 cards, I know how to better approach the class next session. I have prevented many problems from developing and received may exciting ideas from students by opening up this simple channel of evaluative communication between the students in my classes and me. Teaching evaluations have gone up over the years as a result of this practice, and so has my teaching effectiveness.

Now you can rate your ability to use the eight steps in the consulting process.

Consultative Skills

Assessment Skills: Researching, Gathering, Interpreting and Reporting Information

This skill area is critical to the success of the change process because without careful and accurate assessment of needs, wants and problems in a group or organization there can be little or no effective intervention. In order to make a positive difference, goals have to be accurately and specifically stated and programs implemented so that targeted problems are solved and felt needs are met. Examples of such information gathering are:

1. A leader does a survey of what work group or team members would most like to do during a given session;

2. A teacher assesses the reading levels of students in order to plan individually tailored reading programs;

3. A manager or supervisor does a job satisfaction survey each week to determine problem areas and takes appropriate action based upon feedback;

4. A salesman reviews monthly data by geographic sales areas to better target for the achievement of next month's sales objectives;

5. A consultant assesses the factors related to absenteeism in a large company in an attempt to alleviate the absenteeism problem, and increase overall productivity;

6. A university president conducts an institutional self-study to determine areas of effectiveness and potential problems, or to identify unmet needs;

7. A parent has a family meeting to determine needs, problems and wants, and creates some strategies for meeting these;

8.   A consulting accountant provides cash flow or sales projections in order to plan effectively for future capital expenditures or project sales results needed to achieve the desired business goals.

Egan (1988)[7] outlines a practical model for changing and developing organizations which results in action which leads to valued outcomes:

1.   **Current Scenario.** Find out what is not going right or what's going wrong in terms of problems, unmet needs, unused resources, unmet challenges, and so forth.

2.   **Preferred Scenario.** Determine what the organization, organization unit, or project would look like if it were in better shape. A preferred scenario deals with what an organization needs and wants, not with how it is to be achieved.

3.   **Plan for Getting There.** Develop an action program or strategy for moving the current scenario to the preferred scenario. This stage deals with how results are to be accomplished. It projects action plans which lead to valued outcomes.

In Egan's model above there is a systematic and objective attempt to gather and interpret relevant information for the purpose of gaining insight about the nature of a need, problem or overlooked strength. This "diagnosis" provides the consultant with the information needed to design interventions which will more likely result in improvement of performance, morale and/or climate of a particular person, group or organization.

The information gathering and interpreting process has a number of steps which have been adapted from Kilburg (1978)[8] and are outlined below:

1.   **Clarify the purpose** of gathering information so that the information will assist in making better decisions in specific areas.

2.   **Formulate expected results** so that you can compare the real results with the expected results.

3.   **Use proper assessment tools**, surveys, interviews, questionnaires, or tests so that the information you collect will be focused and useful.

---

7   G. Egan, *Change Agent Skills*(B): *Managing Innovation & Change* (San Diego, California: University Associates, Inc., 1988).

8   G.R. Kilmer, "Consumer Survey as Needs Assessment Method: A Case Study." *Evaluation and Program Planning,* 1978, I, 286–292.

4. **Sample all or a representative selection of the members** of a group or organization so that you can have confidence that your results reflect the needs or problems of the whole group.

5. **Analyze and interpret the information** so that the results can be used to make better decisions about solving problems or meeting needs.

6. **Summarize and present the results** of the information gathering in a way others can understand and use it.

7. **Make decisions based on careful assessments** instead of "hunches," intuitions, "gut feeling," group member opinion, or "revelation" alone.

The data gathering process can be assisted by using already validated instruments or questionnaires which are appropriate to your environment. Specific ones which meet your exact needs may not be easy to come by, and you may have to create your own. Quite often it is more effective to design what are the key questions to ask in an interview or on a questionnaire because then you can be somewhat more assured that the questions you ask are appropriately focused and address real concerns.

A cautionary note is warranted about administering questionnaires or doing surveys in a particular organization. Before designing or administering various measures first find out if the people responding to the questionnaire or survey will perceive it worthy of responding to. Sometimes, people are "surveyed out," or they have no confidence that spending their time responding to one will result in any change which they view as positive. I remember an example my professor used when I took my first research methods class: The U.S. Army tried questionnaire after survey to assess the morale level of a certain division, but they couldn't get any clear sense that their information was representative or even accurate. Finally, the research team simply went around and asked people how their morale was and they gave them some incredibly personal and valuable information which enabled them to make much-needed changes. Selecting the appropriate way to gather information is important.

Here are some general guidelines to use when considering the various approaches to gathering information:

In Small Groups (4–15 or so): Where the members are relatively mature, simply ask the members what you want to know (by using direct and pointed questions), or ask open ended-questions to gather information (by using general questions which can be answered in any way respondents might like). If you have a group of shy teenagers, however, you might ask them to write down their concerns anonymously and place their notes in a "hat" for later reading and response.

In Larger Groups (16–60): You may consider using a simple questionnaire which was developed with the assistance of a few key members who are in touch with the general concerns of the group. Keep the size of the questionnaire down to one or two pages each time you administer it, and make the response time no more than just a few minutes in order to increase the response rate—ask both closed and open questions as appropriate. Alternatively, have key people in the group each approach five members with the same questions, have them record or write down the answers and report back to the group leader when the interviews are complete.

In Large Groups (60–200): Groups of this size can be approached in a similar manner as above but can often be more effectively assessed by using a more involved and carefully designed questionnaire which ideally can be computer scored. As soon as the group gets to be this large, the time involved in getting the data and collating it into some kind of meaningful interpretation is unruly, unless you have access to a computerized organizational assessment program—of which there are many. (See Gale Research's directory of computer programs, 1-800-877-GALE.)

Groups Larger Than 200: These groups will require some kind of more formal research or the time and expense of distribution, collection, collation, interpretation and presentation of the data can become unwieldy.

As a part of the assessment skill area, in more advanced assessment projects you may need to develop these research and statistical skills yourself. There are questionnaire generation and scoring software programs which make many of these more difficult tasks quite "user friendly," but a working knowledge of the research process and statistical analysis would be an asset in providing you with a greater sense of confidence that the information you have collected is representative of your total population, and not a biased sample. You can take a course in measurements, statistics, or you can also call on those who are more experienced in this area if you need assistance in developing these skills. You could also delegate this task to others if you are in a position to do so.

Rate your ability to successfully engage in the assessment process as generally outlined above:

Using Assessment Skills Effectively	
1 = Skill is new to me, cannot do it 2 = Understand it but cannot perform it 3 = Can begin to do it, but not naturally 4 = Can do it naturally in many situations 5 = Can do it well and teach others if I want	

Educating/training Skills: Leading Others Toward Greater Understanding and Effective Action

Leaders are often called upon as consultants in the role of educators, trainers or presenters to explain new concepts, to help others "buy into" them, and to assist people to attain higher levels of understanding and skill. In this section, we will not be going into great depth because there are a number of excellent books which cover the subject, and certainly being a competent communicator of information and knowledge is one of the skill areas which is desirable when you are functioning as a leader in an organization. For an expanded skills battery and elucidation of the training process see the American Society of Training and Development Competencies List by contacting them in Alexandria, Virginia.

Generally, the skills required in this area of competency include (adapted from Menzel, 1975):[9]

1. *Writing and speaking* skills, to communicate clearly and persuasively;
2. *Design* skills, to structure educational workshops, experiential learning exercises, and training events, and the materials which enrich them;
3. *Training, teaching, coaching or instructing* skills, to shape new understandings and behaviors in others, assisting them to develop knowledge or skills in needed areas;
4. *Evaluation skills*, to determine the effectiveness of a teaching, presentation or training endeavor;
5. *Contracting skills*, to arrange for appropriate facilitators to enter an organization or group in order to accomplish specific objectives.

---

9   R. Menzel, "A Taxonomy of Change Agent Skills." *The Journal of European Training*, 1975, 4(5), 289–291.

Whatever training or education interventions you decide to implement there are several criteria which, if met, will increase the effectiveness of any training you implement or arrange for others to implement. These criteria are outlined below:

1.   The training event will ideally meet needs or wants which are consciously felt by the recipients (a needs assessment of some kind should be conducted).
2.   The recipients will perceive that what you have to present to them is organized, up-to-date and credible.
3.   The recipients will perceive that you are more informed than they.
4.   The recipients will perceive that what you are presenting is relevant (both personally and professionally whenever possible).
5.   The recipients will perceive that you are involving them in such a way that they will be able to internalize what you present and use it in their own life and work settings.

These same points apply when you bring in outside trainers to accomplish specific training or educational objectives.

Rate your overall ability in education and training.

Education and Training
1 = Skill is new to me, cannot do it 2 = Understand it but cannot perform it 3 = Can begin to do it, but not naturally 4 = Can do it naturally in many situations 5 = Can do it well and teach others if I want

Empowering Others to Reach Goals

In addition to the communication and problem management skills, there are some specific group leadership skills which leaders engaging in the consulting mode need to use. These skills are important in a number of situations from board meetings to strategic planning sessions, team development sessions, regular staff meetings, family meetings and planning sessions, conflict resolution within or between groups, and in support groups.

If each group *member* has the basic awareness and skills of communication, then there is a decent chance of building an effective group or work team. If several members of a group are personally or interpersonally undeveloped or even resistant then this one factor can undermine the results you would want to achieve. If group members are less capable than others then the group has a difficult time moving in a specific direction and loses its energies by having to deal with irrelevant individual concerns or interpersonal conflicts. Personal maturity and a level of functioning well in interpersonal relationships is especially important in task-oriented work groups where the capacity to function on a team is imperative to the group's success in reaching goals.

The group-specific skills needed by leaders functioning in the consultative mode with more mature group members are delineated below.

Legitimizing Your Leadership in the Minds of Others

It is best for you to be seen as competent, informed, knowledgeable, capable, likeable, in a position of authority and trustworthy by group members if you are to be given the trust you need to unify and move a group in a particular direction. This can first be accomplished by making sure that you in fact are leading a group you have some real ability and knowledge to lead.

Sell yourself openly, but not boastfully. The group members need to know something about your background, how you deserve to be in this leadership position because of your confidence, experience, knowledge, or power due to your position. Kotter (1979)[10] studied many of the ways in which leaders gain credibility and power in groups and organizations. He illustrates how many of the "success" behaviors of influential leaders can be learned.

Your personal credibility will be established if you can follow the following general guidelines:

1. **State your own purpose** (based on your own inner clarity) for being in your role as leader. Let group members know that you are in harmony with and attempting to achieve your organization's purposes in ways which uphold the organization's values.

---

10 J. Kotter, *Power in Management* (New York: AMACOM, 1979).

2. **Communicate and check for the validity of the needs and wants you hope to meet**. In this way you will gain awareness of the degree of real or imagined consensus about these critical issues. This can save you the embarrassment of attempting to meet needs or solve problems which are only perceived as relevant by a few.

3. Communicate how you intend to **work in a respectful and helpful manner**. This is critical if you want people to feel comfortable and have a sense of trust in you. If they perceive you as a potential threat or a non-caring person, you won't get their support to accomplish goals.

4. **Value the worth and potential contributions of the other members** in the group. Look for opportunities when group members can gain various kinds of recognition or rewards for being involved in the work group's endeavors.

5. **Model good group member and leader behaviors**, which include all of the communication and problem management skills outlined in the previous two chapters. In this way, you will gain acceptance and trust more readily. There are a whole range of image management skills, also previously covered in Part One of this book, which can also assist you to refine your ability to assist others to see you as credible and thus follow your lead.

6. **Find out what is valued** and present the talents which you have if they match what the group needs. If the group members value experience, then share your experience; if they value academic qualifications, then share these.

You will need to be very open about your abilities and limitations, perhaps involve the expertise of others in areas in which you are not as competent, and not appear as the Jack of All Trades because you may be judged as the master of none. Know your strengths and talents, and develop a network of others who can assist in areas in which you have less interest or less ability.

Below is an example of when I was not skilled enough to solve one company's problem. I was involved in installing a personnel information system in a fast-growth textile processing company. At the beginning phase of my contract to install more effective personnel systems, I became aware that the work flow on the production line needed systems engineering attention. There were no systems for tracking or planning work flow, no time-and-motion studies and no performance standards. I knew a fine consultant who had 6 years experience implementing and overseeing exactly such systems and I introduced him to the general manager. This introduction resulted in his receiving a 2 year consulting contract to oversee the engineering aspects of the whole company. This strengthened my networking connection with my consultant friend, enhanced my reputation as a resourceful consultant, and this one intervention alone saved the company tens of thousands of dollars. This company calls me when they have a problem because of the results which have occurred in the past.

The same kind of events can occur within an organization or group, where internal (or external) expertise is recognized and capitalized upon in creative ways, especially when the leader, in a consultative fashion can empower others to achieve greater results than he or she could achieve alone.

Rate your ability to perform these skills in this area of creating and communicating credibility.

Creating and Communicating Credibility	
1 = Skill is new to me, cannot do it 2 = Understand it but cannot perform it 3 = Can begin to do it, but not naturally 4 = Can do it naturally in many situations 5 = Can do it well and teach others if I want	

Group Facilitation and Team Development Skills

Specifying and Clarifying Purpose and Vision

A leader needs to be able to communicate clearly with a group so that the group becomes unified, "of the same mind," about the purpose of that group. This could involve doing a needs/wants/problems assessment and reporting to the group the results of such a survey, or even involving the group members in such a consensus seeking activity. Sometimes surveys are too formal and time-consuming and either personal one-on-one dialog with individual group members or raising the issue at a group meeting is more appropriate and effective.

In various organizations a clear purpose statement is often written down as a charter, a terms of reference statement, purpose or mission. Sometimes, the leader has the original vision, and it is her or his job to find people who are already committed to it, or generate commitment in people who are new to the vision. In either case, this issue of *clarity of shared vision* is a critical foundational cornerstone upon which the success of all groups and organizations rest.

It is not enough to assume that everyone understands such statements of purpose. The leader's job is be assured that as many people as possible have *genuine psychological commitment and clear understanding* of the "vision" or it may never be communicated, internalized or achieved. Even in simple staff meetings or family meetings, quite often those in attendance lose sight of the real purpose for the meetings and the organizations of which they are members. All too often, the leaders of such important meetings are void of or lose sight of how to communicate a dynamic vision of possibilities which excites co-leaders and followers.

Framing the purpose and making it visible in a number of ways helps to "lock it in" to peoples' awareness. Using posters, flip charts, newsletters, slogan pins, stickers (without being "tacky"), or whatever is appropriate to your environment can be an important step in creating shared vision and commitment.

Mission statements must motivate to unleash human energy and power. Leaders, in a facilitative, consultative fashion, can help to create and weave a group's purpose or mission through each group member in the following ways:

1. Involve each group member in the clarification and even the creation of the purpose or mission statement by formulating the language for the statement while the group is together, using "flip chart" newsprint paper and felt pens or an overhead projector. Each person can give input, and have a turn to speak to this important issue.

    A recorder with a portable computer or shorthand skills (or a tape recorder, later to be transcribed) can input the final agreed upon purpose statement and print it out for final editing and viewing at or before a subsequent meeting. This statement becomes the first part of a staff manual, organization handbook, or association charter. Sometimes jointly creating a logo, coat of arms, or other symbolic representation of the organization's purpose can help to crystalize and seal a vision. The celebration of the achievement of the purpose is what seals the vision most effectively.

2. Ask each member to express reservations or confidences about the purpose statement, its clarity, completeness, specificity, adequacy, and its desirability.

3. Ask for a visible and verbal commitment, witnessed by all other members (if the group is smaller than 30 or so) to the final statement in written form. *This commitment phase is very important, and it is even more important that each group member observes and hears each of the other members make their commitments to the purpose*—this last step "seals" the vision into a mission with a collective thrust. Some kind of symbol, logo, coat of arms, celebration, "rite or ritual" often imbeds the vision even more deeply into the hearts and minds of those present.

Rate your ability to perform these skills in this area of creating and communicating vision and purpose.

Creating and Communicating Vision and Purpose
1 = Skill is new to me, cannot do it 2 = Understand it but cannot perform it 3 = Can begin to do it, but not naturally 4 = Can do it naturally in many situations 5 = Can do it well and teach others if I want

Specifying and Facilitating Consensus about Norms, Values and Beliefs

Groups must have some cohesion to exist over time. Cohesion is made up of good reasons to get together—to meet one another's needs, to solve problems and to reach goals. However, when group members are at odds with one another about how people should be treated, about how rules and regulations should be interpreted or followed, about how to conduct the meetings, about who has leadership and final decision making authority (when members cannot agree, etc.), then the group disintegrates, or perhaps worse it can exist in mediocrity for years. Therefore, it is of critical importance that these issues of group norms (rules, regulations, manners of treating people and solving problems), values (priorities, importances) and beliefs (assumptions about what is good, true, worthwhile, etc.) be addressed in the first stage of a group's development.

In the same manner as outlined above for specifying a purpose, a group can be facilitated to seek and arrive at some consensus about these issues. Where conflict is not resolvable, group members must compromise, follow the authority of a leader who is given ultimate decision making authority by the group or by a higher authority, or leave the group.

When this step is not attended to in the development of a group or organization, there is bound to be undue and ongoing conflict, strife and unresolved problems. I am not suggesting that people should all believe the same and have the same priorities or values, but I am asserting that when people don't agree that it is OK to disagree then there is often an intolerable clash of expectations and hard feelings coupled with people blaming one another for the demise of the organization or group.

An example of this is when a college faculty had a departmental meeting and sought consensus about and agreed upon written purpose, goals, norms, values and beliefs statements. However, one person only pretended to "buy into" the statements because to resist the group's momentum would have meant she was clearly out of line with the very basic human values prized by all the other group members. She was neither wanting to give up her values in favor of the group's nor be openly at odds with the other group members. So she just quietly operated from her own opposing values without the group's immediate knowledge.

However, over time, several of the group's members began to notice that students were being treated in an arbitrary fashion, without due respect and according to principles which the other members of the department did not value. This kind of internal sabotaging of a group's key values happens in other organizations where people are hired claiming they have a certain type of character and then turn out to be the exact opposite. These problems are the more difficult ones to solve.

Rate your ability to perform these skills in this area of assisting group members to seek consensus about these key issues of norms, values and beliefs.

Specifying Norms, Values and Beliefs

1 = Skill is new to me, cannot do it
2 = Understand it but cannot perform it
3 = Can begin to do it, but not naturally
4 = Can do it naturally in many situations
5 = Can do it well and teach others if I want

Specifying and Facilitating Consensus About Needs, Wants, Problems, Goals and Objectives

It is also important that the purpose be translated very concretely, in the form of goals. This is true especially with groups whose members are less mature, more stressed or where additional clarity of purpose needs to be stated in each session when the group meets. Often a group will need assistance in dealing with this task of specifying the *language* for goals to which group members can commit themselves.

One way to achieve this in small groups is to write the key needs, wants and problems on flip chart paper or a blackboard and beside each need, want or problem write in a specific goal, which when accomplished will meet the need or solve the problem. Your goal as group facilitator could be to assist group members to *specify realistic, achievable, believable and measurable* goal statements. The simpler the better as long as the language captures the essence of what needs to be done. From these "what needs to be done" general statements it is possible to state more specific objective statements about "how" each goal is to be achieved. These objectives get broken down into realistic steps. Each group member can leave the meeting with a written "to do" list or "minutes" which summarize what he or she will accomplish, and by what date this achievement will be completed.

Another way to achieve desired clarity about needs, wants, problems and goals could be as simple as to hand out a three-by-five inch note card to each group member at the beginning of each group session and ask members to anonymously write down their wants, needs, problems or expectations for this session. Then collect the cards, shuffle them for anonymity if group members prefer, read these comments out to the group and mutually decide on the agenda and goals for that group session.

In this way, group members would be encouraged to come to some degree of consensus about what are the concrete expectations of *their* group for that session. This step is important because often the well laid plans of leaders do not fit the real needs of their group. When this process is followed, members own the group as their own, feel that they belong in it, and make a personal investment in reaching the stated goals of the group. In areas of disagreement, compromises can be made unless a decisive leader finds it necessary to "call the shots" as a last resort.

Being specific and concrete in your goal setting language is a skill which is very important. It is not enough to say that we want to improve the quality of production. We have to quantify—for example, what "acceptable numbers of defects" means in terms of units which are "scrapped" per week.

Rate your ability to perform these skills in this area of assisting group members to specify needs, wants, problems and goals.

Specifying Needs, Wants, Problems and Goals	
1 = Skill is new to me, cannot do it 2 = Understand it but cannot perform it 3 = Can begin to do it, but not naturally 4 = Can do it naturally in many situations 5 = Can do it well and teach others if I want	

Developing and Implementing Programs Which Expedite the Achievement of Objectives

In the same way that it is important in the counseling process to help clients or workers to formulate program steps which will make the achievement of goals more realistic and motivating, it is also important to formulate a set of steps which translate goals and objectives into language and visual plans to make them more achievable and exciting. Being as specific as possible about these steps can bring group members together and cause a synergistic, energy-releasing effect. The increased energy which is released by careful program planning is well worth the trouble and time it takes to formulate such plans. A thorough plan makes it possible for you to clarify in the minds of team members who will do what, why they will do it, and how they will do it. A brainstorming approach is often most effective in stimulating a consideration of a wide range of options for possible implementation. A closer look at how this set of skills can be effectively implemented is outlined in the following chapter.

An example of a very effective goals, objectives and program planning sheet is presented below for your examination. This sheet can be blown up, taped onto a wall, and movable "post-it notes" can be put into the squares. The concept of this sheet came from Walt Disney, and many others before him. Walt Disney used a wall-sized version of this sheet to create each segment of a cartoon! If we so carefully plan our interventions we will create more effective scenarios.

Specifying and Facilitating Consensus Regarding Objectives

1 = Skill is new to me, cannot do it
2 = Understand it but cannot perform it
3 = Can begin to do it, but not naturally
4 = Can do it naturally in many situations
5 = Can do it well and teach others if I want

Dealing With the Detracting or Interruptive Member

Sometimes you will have one or two people in a group of 20 or so who seem to have their own "axes to grind." It is important that you use your communication and problem management skills to confront this group member on a one-to-one basis, and then later in the group if necessary. You can invite group feedback if the offending person is willing to solicit this kind of group member feedback, either in writing or verbally. Sometimes you can get a person who has a tendency to compete for leadership power to cooperate if they can just have some responsibility, recognition or respect. Some people settle into a group only after they have tested the limits of the leader and the group. It is important for you to know, or at least negotiate with the group, what those limits are.

Rate your ability to perform these skills in this area of dealing with difficult group members.

Dealing With the Detracting or Interruptive Member

1 = Skill is new to me, cannot do it
2 = Understand it but cannot perform it
3 = Can begin to do it, but not naturally
4 = Can do it naturally in many situations
5 = Can do it well and teach others if I want

Style, Role and Skill Shifting Has a Transforming Effect

Style shifting is an important concept which will be explored in the following chapter. The consultative mode is important and often one which is curiously absent in the behavior of many managers. It is especially important when we realize that the skills appropriate to the consultative mode are so important in facilitating the effective and creative functioning of groups and organizations as a whole. Burns (1978)[11] points out that transformational leaders do more than reach performance standards and reward employees when he reminds us that they raise the awareness of others, they inspire people to transcend their self-interests for the sake of the larger good, and they stimulate higher level needs that people might have. Bass (1985)[12] reminds us of the complexity and openness required by the transformational leader.

To further enhance our understanding of the importance of an objective and consultative awareness, Morgan (1988)[13] suggests that if we wish to be successful in managing the turbulence of the modern world, we must develop the following transformative type skills:

1. *Read the environment, fracture analysis, scenario building*, and other methods to identify the changes relevant to their organizations;

2. Manage their organizations from the *outside in* to sustain an ongoing environmental focus, and use *positioning* and *repositioning* skills to adjust to new opportunities;

3. Recognize the importance of *leadership and vision* at all levels of organization, and build direction and commitment around key values and shared understandings;

4. View *people as a key resource* and value knowledge, information, creativity, interpersonal skills, and entrepreneurship as much as land, labor, and capital have been valued in the past; reorient the economics of organizations so that human potential is not unduly constrained by short-term financial considerations;

5. Develop *corporate cultures that encourage creativity, learning and innovation*, and develop managerial structures, skills and processes that promote intelligence and creativity as the life blood of an organization;

6. Replace organizational hierarchies with *flatter, decentralized, self-organizing structures*, in which *facilitation, networking, and remote management* are crucial;

---

11 J.M. Burns, *Leadership* (New York: Harper & Row, 1978).

12 B.M. Bass, *Leadership Beyond Performance Expectations* (New York: Free Press, 1985).

13 G. Morgan, *Riding The Waves of Change: Devloping Managerial Competencies for a Turbulent World* (San Francisco: Jossey-Bass Publishers, 1988).

7. Use *information technology as a transformative force*, to create new products and services and to support the decentralized, flatter structures required in flexible, innovative organizations;

8. Develop the skills to *manage complexity*, especially the demands of multiple stakeholders, multiple performance objectives, and transition and change;

9. Reshape the environment through development of *contextual competencies* that help to mobilize key factors from different sectors of society in common attacks on shared problems. Networking, creation of alliances, and new methods of tackling old problems will become central concern.

The next chapter attempts to elucidate how the knowledge and skills presented in this book can be applied in a creative, flexible and responsive manner through "style, role, and skill shifting." The next chapter will assist you to become more aware of and to develop the contextual competencies which are so important for success.

Total for the Consulting Section

Add all numbers in the boxes in this section.

Graphing Your Self-assessment Scores

Now that you have completed this section of the comprehensive self-assessment, graph in all of your individual scores so that you can get a visual summary of what skills you see are stronger and weaker. Graph in your self-rating scores on each skill using the "bar graph" method of drawing lines from left to right on each scale.

1 = Skill is new to me, cannot do it
2 = Understand it but cannot perform it
3 = Can begin to do it, but not naturally
4 = Can do it naturally in many situations
5 = Can do it well and teach others if I want

	1	2	3	4	5
Understand the nature and functions of the consultative role and process.					
Apply the consulting process: 8 steps.					
Use assessment skills effectively.					
Plan and implement training sessions or make convincing presentations.					
Legitimize your leadership in the minds of others.					
Specify and facilitate consensus about a group's or organization's purpose.					
Specify and facilitate consensus about norms, values and beliefs.					
Specify and facilitate consensus about needs, wants, problems and goals.					
Specify and facilitate consensus regarding objectives, action-program planning and implementation.					
Deal with the detracting or interruptive member.					

Knowledge and Skills which Develop and Transform People and Organizations

HUMAN RESOURCE DEVELOPMENT RESULTS

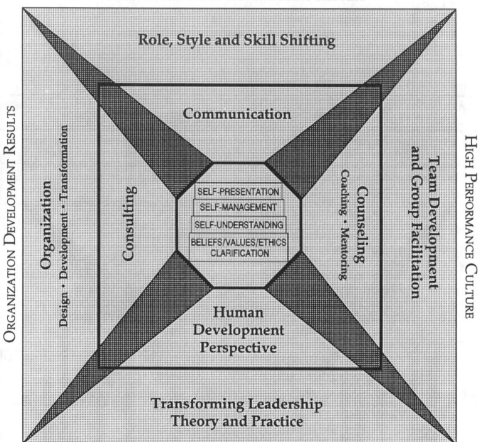

ORGANIZATION DEVELOPMENT RESULTS

HIGH PERFORMANCE CULTURE

Role, Style and Skill Shifting

Communication

Organization
Design • Development • Transformation

Consulting

SELF-PRESENTATION
SELF-MANAGEMENT
SELF-UNDERSTANDING
BELIEFS/VALUES/ETHICS
CLARIFICATION

Counseling
Coaching • Mentoring

Team Development
and Group Facilitation

Human
Development
Perspective

Transforming Leadership
Theory and Practice

EFFECTIVE PERSONNEL PRACTICES

Chapter 8

▼

STYLE, ROLE AND SKILL SHIFTING: DEVELOPING VERSATILITY

Think about the productivity of employees
who bring motivation, imagination
and energy to their work—who have spirit.
If you wish all your employees
were that way, you know that work
spirit is a serious, not soft, subject.

Sharon L. Connelly

Introduction

It is one thing to compose or begin to play a piece of music, it is quite another to practice and develop one's potential enough to play well. Quality, productivity, motivation, imagination, the willingness to sweat and persist in the face of stress and occasional exhaustion—all these factors when blended together can produce unforgettable performances. People who are willing to "go all out" are doing so for good reasons. Someone has impelled them with hopes, ideals, expectations of rewards, and instilled in them some enthusiasm. Star athletes are another example of those who train until their maximum potential is unleashed.

In a similar way, transforming leadership has the potential to empower leaders and followers to achieve higher levels of impact to motivate and move people to take new action, reach for new levels of achievement and reward, and simultaneously facilitate the development of all those involved together in an endeavor.

In order to achieve these heights, leaders do not necessarily have to be charismatic. But they do have to be effective in shifting to meet the needs of people and the changing demands of fast-moving surroundings.

Max DePree (1989),[1] in his fascinating book titled, *Leadership Is An Art*, states:

> *...it is fundamental that leaders endorse a concept of persons. This begins with an understanding of the diversity of people's gifts and talents and skills. Understanding and accepting diversity enables us to see that each of us is needed. It also enables us to begin to think about being abandoned to the strengths of others, of admitting that we cannot know or do everything. The simple act of recognizing diversity in corporate life helps us to connect the great variety of gifts that people bring to the work and service of the organization. Diversity allows each of us to contribute in a special way, to make our special talents a part of the corporate effort.*

Essential to the *Transforming Leadership* approach are concepts which relate to the acceptance and integration of diversity in others: the concepts of "style shifting", "role shifting" and "skill shifting". Learning to recognize different personal styles in others' behaviors can lead to more appropriate leadership responses, and can bring forth the best in others. Moreover, trying to shift roles appropriately (which also involves shifting sets of skills) to respond accurately to individual differences and preferences can improve communication, problem-management and leadership effectiveness. Thus, **style, role and skill "shifting"** are presented together to provide a more comprehensive and versatile model to subtly capture many of the important aspects of leadership complexity—yet the model is presented so that it will be practical and applicable in a wide range of settings.

Therefore, with the new understanding in this chapter you will eventually find yourself responding to others and to situations more flexibly and therefore more appropriately. This chapter builds upon the knowledge and skills in previous chapters so you can develop expertise and even finesse in expressing your own individual approach to leadership, especially when your goal is to facilitate group and organization development. A final thrust

---

1   Max DePree, *Leadership Is An Art* (New York: Dell Publishing, 1989).

of this chapter will be to examine how to do more than just develop a group or organization—it presents some direction on how to transform a well-functioning group or organization into a dynamic one.

The objectives of this chapter can be summarized in the following specific objective statements below—when you complete this chapter you will:

1. Learn about transforming leadership's facilitative "style, role and skill-shifting" approach which leaders can use to facilitate individual, group or organization development.

2. Evaluate the extent to which you believe you can perform the "style, role and skill-shifting" approaches outlined in this chapter.

3. Learn about the stages of development of a group or organization so you can assess what interventions are appropriate in each stage and thereby intervene more effectively.

4. Learn the steps and processes to design and set up a group or organization.

5. Explore the future of transforming leadership as a new practice of designing and managing change.

In Chapter Nine we will examine The Comprehensive Personnel System as a tool for assessing, facilitating and managing the development and performance of any organization's most important resource: people. You will also be introduced to a new personnel performance software concept: *People-Systems SoftInfo*. This new software program performs various performance-related assessments, and records, tracks and reports all non-financial personnel information.

Finally, at the end of this book is an Afterword by William Gray, Ph.D., President of The Mentoring Institute, who will clarify how developing the skills in this book can prepare people to engage in more effective mentoring relationships. Perhaps the most complex and powerful for transforming leaders is mentoring. Mentoring is such an important role because it is the vehicle for transferring the knowledge, perspective and wisdom of experience to others who will replace us as we move into new stages of our lives.

The Impact of Leadership in Organizations and Groups

Organizations do not have a life of their own separate from the individuals in them. Wittingly or unwittingly, leaders especially shape the climate which influences performance and morale. They can and do have a tremendous influence on how people think, feel and behave. If you look back into the history of your own life in the context of the social systems which have surrounded you, you will become more aware of how many social factors, and certain leaders, have had profound effects on your own development. When we consider the staggering impact that all social systems (and especially the leaders in these systems) can potentially have on the development or destruction of the morale and fabric of people, the need to develop innovative approaches to design and to develop positive organizational spirit becomes evident. As Bass (1985)[2] has concluded from his research:

> ...*transformational leadership will contribute in an incremental way to extra effort, effectiveness, and satisfaction with the leader as well as to appraised subordinate performance beyond expectations....*

Transforming Leadership moves the development of a leader one step further toward effectiveness and competency by going beyond communicating the important quality of charisma, the kindness of empathy, the insight of intellectual stimulation, and the benefits of providing rewards. *Transforming Leadership* proposes to develop the core of a leader into a more versatile and creative master of positive change. This leader will then design and manage the quality, health and performance of an organization or group.

Style, Role and Skill Shifting: Versatile Wisdom for Inducing Positive Change

It is of prime importance in the development of such mastery as suggested above that leaders develop not only skills, but versatility as well. The fluid concept of **"shifting" styles, roles and skills** was adopted to capture the essence of the artistry and intelligence-in-action which *Transforming Leadership* asserts is so vital. As we move into examining the complexity of effective leadership you will learn to see your own behavior more keenly within the context of the overall environment. Further definition of terms for each of the three aspects of style-shifting will assist you to understand some of the basic ideas which underlie the notion of *"shifting"*:

---

2   B. Bass, *Leadership and Performance Beyond Expectations* (New York: The Free Press, 1985), 201.

Style shifting is the ability to assess the personal style of another person and adjust your responses to better fit what is most effective in achieving your purposes, and to do this genuinely, without manipulation, while meeting the needs of the other person.

Role shifting is the ability to recognize which of three major roles is most appropriate in any given moment and thereby alternate between communication, counseling and consulting interventions as the situation or person requires.

Skill shifting is the ability to move gracefully between three different sets of skills to accomplish various tasks depending upon the circumstance or the developmental level of a person, group or organization. As you "skill-shift" more appropriately, you will subtly increase your effectiveness in each of the three major roles.

It is important to develop the ability to act consciously and intentionally but also to spontaneously "oscillate" between and within each of the three roles and sets of skills. This could seem to make the process of leadership complex and difficult. Of course, it is complex, but the **style-shift** approach breaks down some of the complex reality of leadership behaviors into small enough "chunks" so that we can learn each part before integrating it into a more fluid practice.

Effective leadership requires the ability to deal with complexity, break it into manageable pieces, and intervene with a continuous alertness to the impact we are making. This continuous vigilance to the impact of your interventions will better enable you to shift styles, roles or skills again and again as it becomes appropriate to do so.

The first skill required to do this style-shifting is thought to be a cognitive skill. Lombardo (1978)[3] summarizes some important research findings on the relationship between the ability to be complex and leader effectiveness.

Complexity and effectiveness: Complex leaders are indeed more effective under certain conditions. A summary of the major findings follows:

---

3 M. Lombardo, *Looking At Leadership: Some Neglected Issues*, Center for Creative Leadership, Technical Report Number 6, January, 1978. Research Sponsored By: Organizational Effectiveness Research Program, Office of Naval Research (Code 452), under contract No. N00014-76-C-0870;NR 170-825.

1. Suedfeld and Rank (1976) found that successful revolutionary leaders were those who were able to shift gears from the single-minded dedication needed to foment revolution to the subtle complexities of negotiation and tightrope-walking once power has been attained. Examples of leaders who successfully made the transition—Jefferson, Lenin, Washington; failures—Trotsky, Hamilton, Guevara.

2. Mitchell (1972) found that complex leaders have a higher performance on lab tasks than simple leaders. Simple leaders think they have more influence and control, the opposite of the way their subordinates see them. What differentiates them is that the complex vary their behavior more. It is not what the leader does (being considerate), rather it is his or her ability to change "mindset."

3. Psychologically distant leaders may do better because they individuate (Ziller, 1964). A leader who individuates is able to differentiate sharply between more and less competent subordinates and between self and others. Those who fail to individuate (make a lot of group decisions, diffuse responsibility widely) suffer a loss in group productivity (Fiedler, 1964).

4. Those who reward more productive behaviors will be more complex because they are better able to spot organizational incongruities (Kerr, 1975). Those who are more simple will reward A when hoping for B.

5. Schroeder, Driver, and Streufert (1967) found dramatic differences between cognitively simple and complex individuals. They found that the following characteristics differentiate complex from simple individuals. Complex individuals:

   a. Give more information in decisions.

   b. Qualify their decisions with remarks indicating doubt.

   c. Use more dimensions.

   d. Track information not immediately available.

   e. Spend more time processing information.

   f. Increase searching and processing as uncertainty increases.

   g. Perform better in public.

   h. Use more complex decision-making strategies.

i. Have fewer overgeneralized strategies.

j. Use less retaliation under stress.

k. Don't differ from simple if both environment and criterion are simple.

l. Persist in face of failure.

m. Are more open to attitude change.

n. Formulate long-term strategies.

o. Show more understanding of the "other side."

In summary, complex individuals are more effective in many leadership situations because they are more versatile in their capacity to be objective in their assessments and interventions. They shift gears better, are more flexible, and individuate more sharply than concrete individuals.

It is this complex manner of thinking which keeps leaders open, prevents premature decision making, characterizes a tentative, open manner of functioning, and provides enough awareness for shifting—as circumstances and people change. But the ability to think in a complex manner is not enough when we face the complexities of life in the 1990s and beyond. We need to develop the capacity to not only react and adapt to change but to design and create changes which build new and more effective relationships, groups and organizations. Developing the capacity to do this "shifting" is at the heart of a leader's ability to react to the environment (and the people in it) in somewhat the same manner as the skilled martial artist or jazz musician.

Transforming Leadership's Style, Role and Skill Shifting Model

Transforming Leadership is built upon a meta-model for lifelong personal and professional development that consists of several skills training modules, the skills for which were outlined in the previous chapters. A new and practical synthesis of the various areas of skill is what the Style-Shift model attempts to present.

The remainder of this chapter is divided into three sections. The first section focuses on introducing you to Personal Style Theory and its application to transforming leadership in the form of "style shifting." The second section focuses on "role shifting" to increase your effectiveness in recognizing and shifting into appropriate role behaviors. The third section emphasizes your applying these various skills to develop and even transform a group or organization into one which functions and performs more dynamically and successfully.

The "shifting" model, in its most basic form can be expressed visually in the following way:

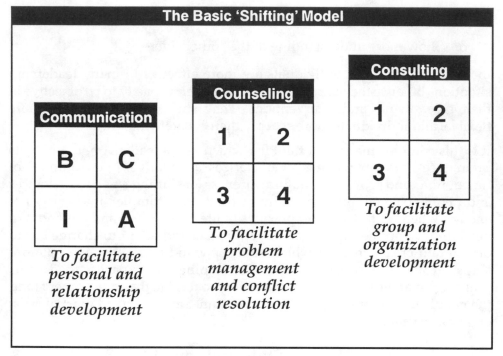

Further Explanation

In the communication section of the model above, the B,C,I and A letters represent different quadrants of personal style (to be explained further below) which, if we are aware of them, will tend to influence how we approach an individual person or even how we approach a group or organization.

In the counseling section of the model the numbers 1,2,3, and 4 represent levels of task-specific functioning or development of the individual, which provide indications of how you might best approach that particular person for optimum appropriateness and effectiveness (as indicated in the chapter on counseling skills).

In the consulting section of the model, the numbers 1,2,3, and 4 represent stages of group or organization development which require different approaches and skills in order to optimize the results you desire.

Therefore, when utilizing the model above to plan for more effective interventions, we can take into consideration:

1. The factor of individual style;
2. The appropriate role we should be playing in the situation we are in;
3. And an individual's, group's or organization's stage of development and functioning.

Now we will examine the issue of personal style assessment and "style-shifting" into various types of behavioral responses in order to match the needs and preferences of others. This matching will increase your effectiveness when relating with others or attempting to solve problems with them. It should be pointed out that style shifting can also be used with groups and organizations as well as with individuals.

What Personal Style Means

People tend to approach and interact with their surroundings (i.e., people, things, situations, and time) based upon their perceptions of them. This part of the personality superstructure is believed by both Anderson and Robinson (1988)[4] to be largely predisposed from birth and tends to strongly influence individual perception of and response to the environment throughout life. If this kind of natural "filter" through which each individual perceives the environment does exist, then it is important to identify and specify what it is. Personal Style Theory asserts such a filter does indeed exist and attempts to provide theoretical constructs which delineate and

4   T. Anderson and E. Robinson, *The Leader's Manual for the Personal Style Indicator and Job Style Indicator: A Guide to Their Significance, Development, Administration, and Practical Applications* (Abbotsford, B.C. Canada: Consulting Resource Group International, Inc., 1988).

explain such a phenomenon. Without "pigeonholing" people, the term "personal style" reflects each individual's predisposed and preferred way of behaving.

Personal style is defined by Anderson in the preceding referenced manual as "a person's habitual way of behaving, or predisposition to act, in everyday situations with most people." Robinson further defined it as "a person's natural predisposition to perceive, approach, and interact with the environment." Thus, personal style includes characteristics of personality and behavior such as a person's:

1.   Preferred manner of accomplishing a task;
2.   Preferred manner of reacting to individuals;
3.   Strengths and difficulties characteristic of his or her unique style;
4.   Natural reaction to stressful events;
5.   Preferred manner of functioning in a group;
6.   Propensity to lead or follow;
7.   Predisposition to be extroverted or introverted;
8.   Predisposition to be task vs. relationship oriented;
9.   Predisposition to be right or left brain oriented.

When we can understand others in such a detailed and specific manner, we are in a better position to respond to them in ways which lead them in directions in which they are more likely to go, and assign tasks to them at which they are more likely to succeed.

Personal Style Assessment

People who are versatile in their approaches to others will consider the individual style preferences of others and tend therefore to be more versatile and effective than those who do not.

In order to accurately assess another person's style, you need to be able to observe and predict how a person (or a group) will tend to act on a fairly regular basis. If you have a model for style assessment, you can observe and listen to a person and thereby determine which two or three quadrants of personal style are preferred by that individual.

Since it is a critical factor in the practice of transforming leadership to appreciate the unique tendencies, needs and preferences of other people, groups or organizations, it is important that we become more proficient in

Understanding the Four Personal Style Dimensions

Behavioral   *ACTION*

This style dimension is characterized by a strong tendency toward altering the environment in a way which will achieve well thought-out goals. Therefore, people who naturally operate mainly from this quadrant of style are likely to seem self-assured and driven, many times oblivious to other people's feelings and on a track of their own. When their vision is shared by a group, then they are often seen as heroes and leaders because they tend to forge ahead to meet challenges with unusual fearlessness. This style position by itself is extroverted and can withstand greater stress. It does not favor artistic, aesthetic or emotional modes of operating, but prefers a planned method by which previously defined goals and results are achieved. In this style there is a clear sense of acting upon the environment to achieve these results.

Cognitive   *ANALYSIS*

This style dimension is characterized by a strong tendency to avoid being influenced negatively by people or environmental influences. This type moves toward goals which are often perceived as requirements of others in positions of authority. Attention to details and being on the alert for potential dangers or inconsistencies enable people with this style to maintain a better position of security and control. People with this style tend to avoid emotional intensity and unpredictability; and they may especially need intimacy because they find that trust in others is not easily attained. This style position by itself is introverted, being more sensitive to stimulation. It does not prefer the sensory, emotional modes of operating, but tends toward logical analysis and correct performance of tasks, with an additional interest in the fine arts.

Affective   *EXPRESSION*

This style dimension is characterized by a strong tendency to intuitively explore the environment and interact with it to assess the outcome. Spontaneous exploration and expression of ideas and feelings mark the natural tendencies of this style. People with a natural tendency toward this dimension of style are often attempting to influence others through the creative media of speaking, writing, dance, art or music. They would like to sell others on themselves, and ideas or products which they believe will be helpful. They will go out of their way to help others, even if it inconveniences them because often they believe in the value of people. By itself, this style is extroverted, not being easily overstimulated by the environment. It does not favor the analytical modes of operating, but is more intuitive and creative in its way of functioning.

Interpersonal   *HARMONY*

This style dimension is characterized by a strong tendency to adapt to people and surroundings in order to promote harmony and comfort for self and others. The approach to life and people in a practical, friendly and naturally warm manner is typical of this style dimension. Adaptation to all other styles is a way of life, providing the desired security and balance needed and preferred by those who score higher in this style dimension. A desire to support others in order to gain a sense of validation and approval is a natural tendency. This style position by itself is introverted, being more sensitive to stimulation. It favors a practical balance of both the logical and intuitive modes of functioning, thereby avoiding extremes. In this style there can also be a tendency toward stubbornness, especially if others are being overbearing.

assessing others' style tendencies so our responses will be so much more appropriate and well-received.

In order for you to gain a general assessment of your own style you will see descriptions of four general quadrants of personal style which are extracted from a more extensive instrument developed by Anderson and Robinson (1988).[5] When you have read these descriptions of the four style tendencies, you will be able to gain a general picture of your own style tendencies which have an impact on how you tend to approach others.

Now that you have read through the four personal style dimension descriptions above, you will next do a general assessment of your personal style. After reading the following instructions, read through the next page titled, "Understanding Your General Style Tendencies." This page will assist you to become more familiar with your own and others' general style tendencies.

Instructions for General Style Assessment:

1. Place the number "1" in the quadrant (where you see the word "score") which you believe best describes you;
2. Place the number "2" in the quadrant which describes the style behaviors you would likely shift into next;
3. Place the number "3" in the quadrant which describes behaviors which are less typical of you;
4. And place the number "4" in the quadrant which least describes how you would act.

Now that you have reviewed your general style tendencies and have become more familiar with the four quadrants of style, you can begin to explore the value of assessing the styles of others and shifting into various style behaviors which they would likely prefer. Keep in mind that you have done only a general estimate of your personal style. You could do a more in-depth assessment of your own personal style and learn greater detail about style assessment using the Personal Style Indicator which is available for you to order from the publisher (see reference on p. 283). Also available for further reading is Robinson's (1990)[6] book on personal style.

---

5   T.D. Anderson and E.T. Robinson, *The Personal Style Indicator*, 3rd ed. (Abbotsford, B.C., Canada: Consulting Resource Group, Inc., 1988), 4, 6, 14–15.

6   E. Robinson, *Why Aren't You More Like Me?* (Dubuque, Iowa: Kendall-Hunt), 1990.

Understanding Your General Style Tendencies

B	Behavioral	SCORE
	ACTION	

General Orientation:

To tasks:	wants results now
To people:	seeks authority
To problems:	tactical, strategic
To stress:	doubles efforts
To time:	future and present

Typical Strengths:

Acts rapidly to get results
Is inventive and productive
Shows endurance under stress
Is driven to achieve goals
Can take authority boldly

Common Difficulties:

Can be too forceful or impatient
Can often think their way is best
Can be insensitive to others
Can be manipulative or coercive
Can be lonely or fatigued

C	Cognitive	SCORE
	ANALYSIS	

General Orientation:

To tasks:	wants quality
To people:	seeks security
To problems:	analyzes data
To stress:	withdraws
To time:	past and future

Typical Strengths:

Acts cautiously to avoid errors
Engages in critical analysis
Seeks to create a low-stress climate
Wants to ensure quality-control
Can follow directives and standards

Common Difficulties:

Can bog down in details and lose time
Can be too critical or finicky
Can be overly sensitive to feedback
Can seem to be lacking in courage
Can be too self-sufficient, alone

A	Affective	SCORE
	EXPRESSION	

General Orientation:

To tasks:	people come first
To people:	seeks to influence
To problems:	intuitive and creative
To stress:	escapes from it
To time:	present and future

Typical Strengths:

Acts creatively on intuition
Is sensitive to others' feelings
Is resilient in times of stress
Develops a network of contacts
Is often willing to help others

Common Difficulties:

Can lose track of time
Can "overburn" and over-indulge
Can be too talkative
Can lose objectivity, be emotional
Can be self-oriented, self-assured

I	Interpersonal	SCORE
	HARMONY	

General Orientation:

To tasks:	reliable performance
To people:	seeks to help others
To problems:	practical solutions
To stress:	adjusts to it
To time:	present

Typical Strengths:

Promotes harmony and balance
Is reliable and consistent
Tries to adapt to stress
Sees the obvious that others miss
Is often easygoing and warm

Common Difficulties:

Can be too easygoing and accepting
Can allow others to take advantage of them
Can become bitter if unappreciated
Can be low in self-worth
Can be too dependent on others

Assessing Others' Styles, and Style Shifting

According to the field research of Anderson and Robinson (1988) and the experimental investigations of Merrill and Reid (1981)[7] learning to assess the personal styles of others, and shift into an interpersonal style which best allows others to receive and understand your messages is an often overlooked and effective skill which can be learned in a relatively short period of time.

In order to learn some basics of how to assess others' styles and practice this style shifting skill, there is on the next page a four quadrant grid—titled "Style shifting Guidelines"—which offers general direction and hints for style shifting effectively with the four style types.

Instructions: Place a person's name who you know well in the quadrant or two near the guidelines which you believe could assist you to approach that person more effectively.

The process of assessing style and shifting into various behavioral approaches involves five main steps. These steps may seem mechanical at first, but with practice can become an automatic part of your approach to interacting with other people. By using the five step process outlined below, the transforming leader thus becomes his or her own observer, critic, feedback-coach and planner of the next response.

General Style-shifting Considerations

If we examine the various needs and preferences of each style type, we can see why it is so easy to make mistakes out of ignorance of such individual differences between people. Below are some general considerations which can act as guidelines for planning a response to the four types of people.

Behavioral Action-Oriented: If you assess that a person is mainly action-oriented in style, then you would: give this person "bottom line" facts in summary fashion, assign challenging assignments and opportunities, not distract with too many details or personal issues, expect him or her to get on with the "task" or job at hand, not challenge personally but provide brief evidence to support your challenge, and respect this person's high need for

---

7   D. Merrill and R. Reid, *Personal Styles and Effective Performance* (Radnor, Pennsylvania: Chilton Book Company, 1981).

Style Shifting Guidelines	
BEHAVIORAL *ACTION* STYLES	**C**OGNITIVE *ANALYSIS* STYLES
### Want others to: Give them summarized facts Respect their judgments Support them to reach goals Cope with unwanted details Cooperate with them	### Want others to: Give them detailed information Ask for their opinions Not interrupt their work Treat them with respect Do quality work the first time
### Get most upset when others: Are too slow Get in their way Talk too much Try to be in control Waste time	### Get most upset when others: Move ahead too quickly Don't give them enough time Are vague in their communications Don't appreciate their efforts Are too personal or emotional
### Respond best to: Direct, honest confrontations Logical, rational arguments Fair, open competition An impersonal approach Getting results quickly	### Respond best to: Diplomatic, factual, challenges Arguments based on known facts Freedom from competitive strain Friendliness, not personal contact Doing tasks well and completely
AFFECTIVE STYLES *EXPRESSION*	**I**NTERPERSONAL STYLES *HARMONY*
### Want others to: Give them opportunity to speak Admire their achievements Be influenced in some ways Take care of details for them Value their opinions	### Want others to: Make them feel like they belong Appreciate them for their efforts Be kind, considerate, thoughtful Trust them with important tasks Value them as persons
### Get most upset when others: Are too task orientated Confine them to one place Are not interested in them Compete for and win attention Seem judgemental of them	### Get most upset when others: Get angry, blow up, or are mean Demand that they be too mobile Take advantage of their goodness Are manipulative or unfair Are judgmental of others
### Respond best to: Being challenged in a kind way An influencing, sales approach Enjoyable competitions Affection and personal contact Having a good time	### Respond best to: A gradual approach to challenging A factual, practical approach Comfortable, friendly times Respecting their boundaries Conventional, established ways

cooperation from others—these interpersonal behaviors appear especially important to these types of people.

Cognitive, Analytical: If you assess a person has mainly an analytical, introverted style, then you would: provide detailed and comprehensive factual information, give ample time for decision making, announce changes in advance, respect any areas of special competency, and show appreciation for efforts and accomplishments—these things appear to be especially important to people with this style.

Interpersonal, Harmonious: If you assess that a person has mainly a need for a harmonious approach to people and the environment, you would: shift into providing social behaviors which show recognition and appreciation of services and efforts provided, offer a safe relationship climate relatively free of judgments and high pressures to perform, and provide opportunities for success by service to others instead of achievement of results—people with this style seem to appreciate and respond well to this approach.

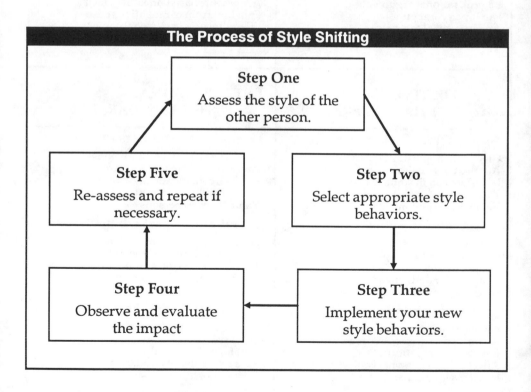

The Process of Style Shifting

Step One
Assess the style of the other person.

Step Five
Re-assess and repeat if necessary.

Step Two
Select appropriate style behaviors.

Step Four
Observe and evaluate the impact

Step Three
Implement your new style behaviors.

Affective, Expressive: If you assess that a person has mainly this type of outgoing style orientation, then you could best relate by: giving recognition for achievements and self-presentations (performances, clothes, successes); listening more than you speak; providing opportunity for promotions, to earn money, travel and mobility; and not supervising too closely or you could kill creativity in this type of person.

Developing Style Versatility: A Case Study

The case of Sandy: General Manager for a West Coast paper distribution company which sells and delivers paper to printing companies.

Sandy's Profile: High Behavioral (Action) and Cognitive (Analysis). Low Interpersonal (Harmony) and Affective (Expressive).

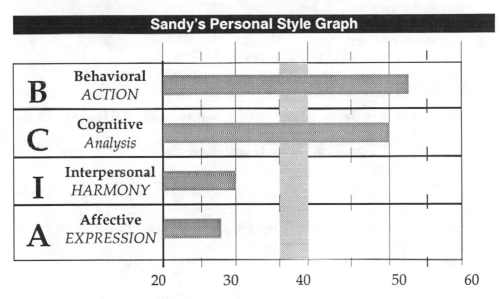

Sandy's Strengths:

- Often gets quality results the first time
- Can process large volumes of information
- Can make objective decisions using a large data base of information from many sources

---

- Challenges others toward excellence
- Acts as a model for others
- Is inventive and original
- Is careful to avoid pitfalls
- Provides guidelines others can use
- Ensures quality control
- Endures and persists when under stress

Sandy's Difficult Areas:

- Is impatient with lower performers
- Can appear smug and "know-it-all-ish"
- Can be insensitive to others' feelings
- Can be lonely and fatigued
- Can be too critical
- Can be "touchy" with critical feedback
- Can be too self-sufficient
- Can lack in courage to face emotions
- Can get lost in details before deciding
- Can seem to be manipulative or coercive

Upon reading his in-depth interpretation, Sandy laughed. He said that the description of him was better than 90% accurate and that he became more aware of some things about himself which he figured were often "blind spots."

The Problem: Sandy is in charge of a sales force of 9 people who tend to be predominantly high in the AFFECTIVE Expressive and INTERPERSONAL Harmony dimensions of style. They resent Sandy's air of superiority and demands of high performance without any promises of rewards. They need recognition and appreciation from Sandy but he rarely has time to give such "soft" rewards. He has only rewarded people for sales results which affect the "bottom line." He has, over the years, demonstrated inflexibility in his approach to others and gets really irritable at people who don't accept his domineering approach, putting them down in front of others. The increases in company profitability were 3 and 5% during the past 2 years, not enough to keep up with inflation. The turnover rate in the sales division and in the secretary and receptionist positions have been over 34% per year primarily because these employees have had frequent contact with Sandy—and as a result had reported that their primary reason for seeking work elsewhere was to avoid working for him. Sandy's wife had left him 3 months ago.

The Intervention: Sandy took a 1-day Personal Style Indicator workshop, and learned that his relationships with all those in his life had been characterized by a rather self-oriented and caustic approach, because he often got short-term results by intimidating people in subtle ways. As a result of the workshop, and the feedback Sandy got from his wife and other managers just below him, he decided to change how he treated the high A and I sales and support staff (and his A-I marriage partner) to eliminate "put-down" statements and behaviors from his management style, add more interpersonal behaviors such as expressing appreciation for a job well done, host an awards ceremony every 6 months for all those in the company who achieved agreed-upon reasonable levels of performance, institute an employee-of-the month recognition program for exceptional performance beyond what is expected, and institute interpersonal skills training and team building sessions for him and his management staff.

The Results: After 1 year, the turnover rate had decreased to 7% instead of the previous 34%. Two-way communication improved between Sandy and all levels of employees. Problems got solved which previously were "swept under the carpet" because most people avoided Sandy altogether. Overall profitability of the company increased 14%. Sandy's wife decided to come back and try to re-establish their marriage relationship.

This is a dramatic example of how Sandy's having developed some interpersonal skills and developing versatility in his approach to people with styles which were opposite to his had a dramatic effect on the performance of his subordinates.

Quinn (1988)[8] proposes that there are values and cultural differences within organizations. Personal Style Theory draws a parallel between these values and cultural differences and style variations. To illustrate this relationship I have superimposed the PSI (B,C,I, and A) style designations on Quinn's framework for competing values. You can see below the parallels in the relationship between style and organizational values and culture. The figure can be seen on the next page.

It is important to realize that style shows up in organizational orientations, government leaders' approaches to politics and international relations, and

---

8   R.E. Quinn, *Beyond Rational Management: Mastering the Paradoxes and Competing Demands of High Performance* (San Francisco: Jossey-Bass, 1988), 51.

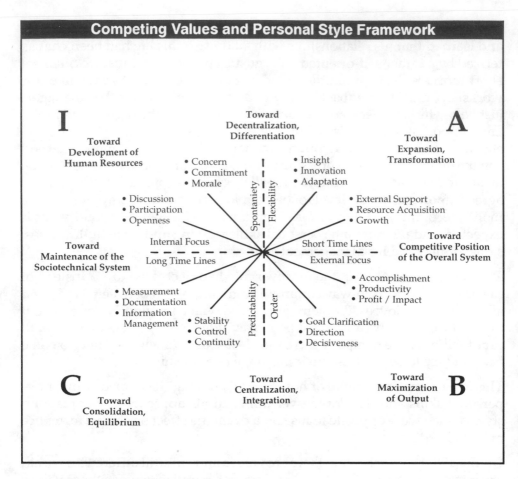

that certain style tendencies can pervade whole societies. For example, Reagan and Thatcher are often perceived as demonstrating a Behavioral Action orientation, acting upon the environment in an aggressive manner. The United States and Great Britain, as cultures, are often perceived quite differently from one another. However, the English people have described the U.S. as appearing to be more "bizarre" (expressive) than the U.K.; and the U.K. is described by Americans to tend toward an analytical approach, being more reserved and "stuffy." The English can be heard saying that the Americans are too impulsive and run headlong into situations without first thinking through the consequences. Of course, England and France have been experiencing "clashes" of style for centuries, in the same way that English speaking and French speaking Canada have (although, in general,

Canada could be seen, like Switzerland, as having an Interpersonal Harmony orientation). The English find the free expressiveness of the French to be overwhelming and even revolting (in the extreme) and the stuffiness and formality of the English make the French feel restricted—giving them the impression that the English are "phony." Modern Japan could be seen as having a more complex combination of action, analytical and interpersonal orientations.

Style assessment is complex and difficult, but that there are significant differences which cause difficulties between people cannot be denied. Learning to shift approaches to people can increase our effectiveness with them, limit conflict and facilitate relationship development.

In the next section of this chapter we will examine the nature of the three major roles (and the tasks which are appropriate to accomplish in each role) which the transforming leader fulfills. It is important to keep in mind that a continuing awareness of "style" has a catalytic effect when functioning in all three of the major roles of communicator, counselor and consultant.

Self-evaluation

Now rate your ability to accurately assess others' styles and shift your own style appropriately, depending upon the situations or individuals you face.

Style Assessment and Style Shifting
1 = Skill is new to me, cannot do it
2 = Understand it but cannot perform it
3 = Can begin to do it, but not naturally
4 = Can do it naturally in many situations
5 = Can do it well and teach others if I want

Role Shifting for Greater Effectiveness and Appropriateness

Appropriate role shifting makes the leader's responses more effective, and in turn, a follower's response is often more favorable. Proper role shifting as a foundation of appropriateness is needed in order to build the base of influence and trust leaders need to help develop both people and organizations in a positive manner. It is quite ineffective for a leader to attempt to function in a mutual-communicative or advisory-consultative manner with a resistant employee who clearly needs to be responded to with a problem management approach in the counseling role. It is likewise counter-productive to "counsel" with people who need either to first develop a mutual open communicative relationship or see that they can work as an effective team member with the leader as consultant and group facilitator.

What Is Role Shifting?

Role shifting is the ability to shift moment-to-moment between three different sets of skills depending upon the situations or people which are encountered. It is important that you become able to shift between these three sets of skills when interacting with colleagues or followers, so that your interventions will have a greater likelihood of meeting expectations, needs and preferences. This could seem to make the process of leadership very complex and difficult. It is complex but a style-shift model breaks down reality into small enough "chunks" that we can learn each part of it before integrating it into a larger picture. Effective leadership requires the ability to deal with complexity, break it into manageable pieces, and intervene with a continuous alertness to the impact we are making.

In keeping with the evidence that effectiveness is related to complexity and versatility of leader behavior it would assist leaders to be more effective if they could discern which of the three modes are appropriate with each individual, group or organization in each moment. A further delineation of the three modes involved in role-shifting are:

1. **In the Communication Mode** — Positive interpersonal communication is the appropriate mode to be functioning in when you want to develop a mutual relationship with a person. It is appropriate with co-workers, family, friends, and even acquaintances on a day-to-day basis. It forms the foundation of all relationships, and is usually ap-

propriate at the beginning of a relationship and for maintaining and building relationships. It is the informal "glue" that bonds any relationship, and without it there can be a kind of robotic formality which can interfere with the fostering of easy-going and effective relating with others. This mode can also include the more difficult aspects of interpersonal communication such as giving and receiving feedback, assertiveness and confrontation.

2. **In the Counseling Mode** — Effective counseling and coaching, which involve personal and interpersonal problem management and personal problem solving, are most appropriate when co-workers, colleagues or subordinates are having personal difficulties which are interfering with their performance or relationships with others. Your acting as a facilitator of their personal and interpersonal development by assisting them to specify their own problems in relation to a problem situation (and then take effective action) can be a great impetus in keeping people, groups, and organizations "unblocked." Coaching is related to counseling in that it is a process by which a manager guides the development of a subordinate by continuous observation and assessment, discussion, guidance and encouragement so the subordinate learns more from completing the task and the manager's own expertise is passed on.

3. **In the Consultative Mode** — It is appropriate to shift into the consultative mode or role when the person, group or organization you are interacting with requires and expects you to do some kind of assessment, intervention, evaluation and ongoing monitoring. Sometimes you may find yourself under pressure to respond authoritatively or even sternly, perhaps because your position as leader causes others to expect you to be decisive and resolute, especially when time is limited for key decisions. However, when you have to make decisions which require an overall awareness of organizational factors which others may not be aware of, then it is especially important to act cautiously using this consultative mode. Even if you are not in a leadership position, it can be appropriate at times to act in this mode, especially if your action can be seen as effective and appreciated by those in positions "above" and "below" you.

Blending Modes to Increase Effectiveness

Sometimes, situations occur where it is important to accomplish the goals of two or three of the modes of functioning. These interchanges are more complex. For example, suppose you have an employee named Manuel who has recently lost his brother in an automobile accident. In some situations like this, which require greater complexity on your part, you may find that it is more effective to begin your conversation with a mutuality mode (role free) communication response such as—

1. "Is it possible that you might join us for that round of golf on Saturday we have been meaning to have?"

    Then, as the conversation progresses to more personal material, you could appropriately intervene with a counseling response—

2. "I can understand how you are finding it difficult to get into traveling on your sales route this next week because of the recent loss you have experienced in your family."

    Then, intervene with a consultative response as you get into exploring options with Manuel about how to deal with the grief problem—

3. "I think I can arrange for Bill and Sue to take your sales route next week if you would like that. The company would cover your time off."

Manuel needs time off work to spend with his family and your caring about his pain by giving him time off will likely be of great value to him. He is an employee who will likely never steal from you, will likely defend you when others may be unfairly critical, and is likely to find working for you and with you a refreshing change from what he would receive from many other employers.

The creative combining of the three modes of leading can provide you with greater freedom of choice in how you will respond to another person. Role shifting, by changing modes allows you to communicate the value you place on people.

How Role Shifting Communicates Your Valuing of Others, and Builds Positive Culture

The critical difference in transforming leadership is that it attempts to meet organizational objectives and at the same time communicates the value of persons in each interchange. In fact, one of the organizational objectives in an organization led by a transforming leader is to communicate the value of persons to co-workers and followers, and encourage them to understand and communicate that same value to others. In this way you can better create a value-driven organization which lives and breathes what it believes. This positive culture encourages and nurtures the development of people, which in turn can promote well being, creativity and productivity of work groups and organizations.

Compare this vision with the one of the rigid, role-bound bureaucratic manager who responds mainly by the "book," and does not "flex" self or procedures for the sake of people. Demoralization occurs when people are treated in this depersonalizing manner. Leading others the way we would like to be led, by considering them and even asking them how we can respond in order to meet needs is leading by the "golden rule." Using the communication mode to make friends and develop relationships, the counseling mode to resolve personal and interpersonal problems, and the consultative mode to implement group or organizational interventions will increase the complexity and therefore the effectiveness of your responses.

The Importance of Being Genuine and Respectful When Acting in Various Roles

Most people prefer a leader who is a genuine person at all times, and treats them as individuals. Sincerity and respect are key qualities to communicate in all three roles. If I am myself when I attempt to communicate with, counsel, or lead someone, my credibility will increase nearly automatically. Making statements which clearly identify your personal opinions and feelings can encourage others to see that you aren't "role bound," that you are approachable, and that you too are a person who can also make mistakes, learn and develop.

This genuine and respectful attitude and approach communicates the qualities of honesty and humility. Even when you have to exercise sometimes difficult leadership authority in difficult situations you can still communicate this kind of humility, a willingness to serve, and a willingness to be wrong. By communicating these qualities in your language, tone of voice and actions, others will feel more respected and will have a greater sense of trust in and respect for you.

There are specific tasks which are appropriate in each role. These tasks are typical of the kinds of things which you would normally discover need to be attended to in each role. The achievement of these three sets of tasks requires the three sets of skills for their accomplishment. We will summarize these tasks in the next section to further elucidate the complexity and potential in style, role and skill shifting.

Role Shifting: The Tasks Inherent in the Three Roles

The relationship between the three roles (or modes of functioning) and the tasks in each of the three modes is illustrated in the chart on page 239.

The tasks outlined above are typical of each role, the achievement of which require the practice of the three sets of skills appropriate to each of the three modes. Understanding that these tasks are a part of what is often required to facilitate development of people and organizations is another step toward exerting a transforming effect wherever you go.

Role Rigidity Obstructs Leadership Effectiveness

A parent who cannot become a friend to his or her child, is all too common. An overly friendly boss can lose credibility and clout when it comes time for confrontation. Trying to act in the consultative role when others are not asking for it or expecting it can cause others to see you as overly-officious or "high-minded." However, with practice, your increased ability to shift roles gracefully and appropriately will assist you to meet the challenge of constant change and complexity in your organization, with groups and with individuals at work or at home.

In addition to more appropriate interventions with individuals, groups and organizations can be better understood by using Personal Style Theory. Once you internalize a clear understanding of the Theory you can learn to better "read" the style tendencies of groups and organizations.

Appropriate Shifting of Roles and Typical Tasks

Communication

B	C
I	A

FOUR STYLES

Counseling

1	2
3	4

FOUR D-LEVELS

Consulting

1	2
3	4

FOUR STAGES

To facilitate personal & relationship development

- Developing trust
- Sharing fun times
- Relaxing together
- Appreciating and attending
- Facilitating two-way, mutual listening
- Showing interest and understanding
- Getting agreements about how to communicate better
- Being assertive and respectful at the same time
- Encouraging, validating and rewarding others
- Making the work more meaningful and less lonely
- Understanding personal styles of others
- Shifting your style to develop versatility
- Solving simple, external problems
- Challenging others to develop

To facilitate problem management & conflict resolution

- Problem management and solving
- Specifying internal problems
- Developing deeper trust
- Specifying personal problems of followers
- Setting goals
- Exploring alternate strategies
- Action planning for problem management
- Confronting low performance
- Giving direction when appropriate
- Mediating interpersonal disputes
- Negotiating interpersonal contracts
- Understanding the developmental levels of others
- Adjusting helping approach based on these levels

To facilitate group &organization development

- Developing more credibility and organization-wide trust
- Specifying internal problems of the organization
- Specifying the vision and purpose
- Communicating organizational goals, values and norms
- Building organizational culture
- Selecting and training appropriate people
- Building effective work teams
- Evaluating and researching
- Forecasting changes required for success
- Adjusting course based on these forecasts
- Being open to innovations and opportunities
- Understanding the stage of the group/organization
- Adjusting approach based on stage of development

Now rate your ability to appropriately shift roles and tasks depending upon the circumstances you face.

Appropriate Shifting of Roles and Tasks
1 = Skill is new to me, cannot do it
2 = Understand it but cannot perform it
3 = Can begin to do it, but not naturally
4 = Can do it naturally in many situations
5 = Can do it well and teach others if I want

In the next section of this chapter we will examine the stages of a group or organization and the skills which are appropriate to each stage. You will have an opportunity to assess the extent to which you believe you possess the knowledge and ability to evaluate the stage of development of a group or organization and address the demands of each stage.

Four Stages of Development in a Group or Organization

Understanding stages of development is beneficial to a leader because it enables accurate assessment of the stage at which a group or organization is presently functioning and facilitates clear planning for the next steps of development which need attention. Without the ability to assess stages of development you could commit often-made mistakes such as: trying to build teams before goals are clarified; setting goals and attempting strategic planning before a clear purpose is in the minds of the people involved; or specifying programs to achieve goals before specific objectives to be accomplished are identified. In order to develop greater leadership effectiveness it is important to avoid the typical difficulties mentioned above and proceed in a step-by-step fashion toward the formation of groups and organizations which can be winners.

The stages of group and organization development can be graphically represented in cyclical fashion. The cycle needs to be repeated as frequently as the group or organization can benefit from such feedback and planning sessions without overburdening it with formality.

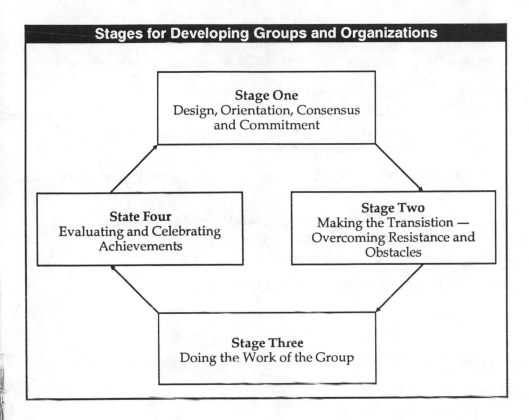

Stages for Developing Groups and Organizations

Stage One
Design, Orientation, Consensus
and Commitment

State Four
Evaluating and Celebrating
Achievements

Stage Two
Making the Transistion —
Overcoming Resistance and
Obstacles

Stage Three
Doing the Work of the Group

A more detailed view of the steps and stages for designing and developing a group or organization are presented on the following page.

As a leader who can demonstrate versatility it is useful to understand the development of groups and organizations using some kind of model. There are various models for assessing the levels of development of a group or organization. Some are complex and others are relatively simple. The model outlined below corresponds in some ways to the four quadrant approaches outlined in previous sections of this chapter and in previous chapters because this has been demonstrated to be a practical way to describe, remember and intervene appropriately. Of course, in reality there is some overlapping of events in each stage, but the details of the four-stage model presented below will be useful in assisting you to map the territory of group and organization development and thereby respond more effectively as a leader.

The Steps and Stages of Group and Organization Development

Stage One — Design, Orientation, Consensus and Commitment

Step 1:   Solidifying and Communicating the Mandate

Step 2:   Clarifying Purpose, Mission or Vision

Step 3:   Specifying and Gaining Consensus about Philosophy —
            Values, Beliefs and Norms

Stage Two — Making the Transition: Overcoming Resistance and Obstacles

Step 4:   Formulating General Goals Which Meet Needs
            or Solve Problems

Step 5:   Specifying Objectives

Stage Three — Doing the Work of the Group

Step 6:   Planning Action Programs

Step 7:   Implementing Programs

Stage Four — Evaluating and Celebrating Achievements

Step 8:   Learning from the Past and
Planning for the Future

Step 9:   Celebrating and Enjoying the Rewards

Step 10:   Recycling the Ten Steps

First, we will define the four stages of development, each of which needs to be established in a group or organization prior to moving fully into the next. Although there is some overlap between the stages, the order of presentation is logical and can be validated through observation of how real groups and organizations are formed, and developed and transformed into dynamic entities.

Introduction to the Four Stages of Group and Organization Development

Stage One: Design, Orientation and Commitment

Orienting people to the basic vision, philosophy and goals of the organization so they are inspired to commit themselves to the task of achieving the vision are critical factors in transforming leadership. Informal introduction and orientation processes can be engaged in most successfully. These can involve retreats, the "whisper in the ear" approach where successful group members act as ongoing mentors in the orientation, coaching or training process. Usually people want to know how they can succeed in the organization or group when they first enter. Those who meet this prime need are likely to be heard most thoroughly. Often some kind of emotional experience needs to occur for an orientation to be effective. Some companies have effectively created corporate culture in their executives at retreats in remote places where the company's norms, values, beliefs and philosophy are introduced in both a formal and informal fashion.

Commitment by a member to a group or organization is achieved to the extent to which the neophyte "buys into" the stated purpose, philosophy and goals of the organization in a genuine way. The closer the new member's position is to the group's values and beliefs prior to joining, the more likely there will be a "locking in" or bonding effect. Just prior to commitment, there is often an experience on the part of the new member of, "I feel like I belong here." This sense of belonging would appear to be a critical factor in achieving the level of commitment required for the achievement of highly developed corporate culture which leads to exceptional achievements.

Normally steps 1-3 have to be achieved before it is possible to effectively move members into stage two which involves the fourth and fifth steps of specifying general goals and articulating objectives.

Stage Two: Making the Transition — Overcoming Resistance and Obstacles

Even though a person has psychologically "bought into" the group or organization at the end of stage one, there has not yet been a real investment of self, time, energy, planning, envisioning of achievements, and sweat to match dreams. In making the transition to full involvement, group members need to be personally involved in formulating some of the general goals and action plans which will later result in programs to be implemented and evaluated. They need to be recognized and rewarded in ways which are personally meaningful.

It is during this transition stage, where general goal setting and specific objectives are committed to by each member, that resistance and obstacles often rear their heads. Many people will commit themselves to lofty goals and agree to achieve objectives but when they show up to the next meeting, they often have not achieved what they intended. How people are handled by leaders during this critical stage can set the tone for failure or success of a group.

It is also at this stage that the distracting or withdrawn group or team member will often rear his or her head. This is when some of those who said that they "bought in" to the purpose and philosophy of the group or organization often unwittingly reveal feathers of a different color. Conflict ensues, feet drag, and some members just can't seem to "get with it." Resentment can develop on the part of the group members who are with it. If the leader does not facilitate the group or organization through this stage then it is likely that it will never move onto accomplishments which fulfill the vision which was thought to be shared, but may limp along acceptably, minimally, for a time.

At this stage, when goals are being set and objectives are being committed to, leaders who facilitate further development will take actions such as confronting and coaching (or dismissing) poor performers, resolving group member conflict, working through intergroup clash or confusion, and refusing to tolerate opposition to or undermining of valued corporate culture. If the leader allows conflict and tension to continue to the point of undermining the potential effectiveness of the group or organization, then he or she is either knowingly or unwittingly participating in its demise. However, if leaders intervene swiftly and effectively at this time, great potential lies ahead in the working stage of the group.

Stage Three: Doing the Work of the Group

When individual resistance, group member conflict and intergroup clashes are for the most part dealt with then the group members can get on with the achievement of the vision with a simultaneous sense of relief and enthusiasm. When this stage begins, people often sense it! It is a pleasure to work at a place, with a group, in an organization where the "unfinished business" doesn't pile up under the carpet. Leaders are respected when things can move to this working stage, when energy is released, and learning and creativity are unleashed. When problems are encountered at this stage, the group or organization has already developed systems and approaches to dealing with many of them effectively.

In addition, several other important things occur during this stage. Members have become acquainted with one another, they are more familiar with one another's personal and work styles, strengths, difficult areas, reactions to stress and pressure, and tendencies to lead or follow, and this familiarity can breed performance and fine-tuning of the team's efforts. Job descriptions can also be re-negotiated and re-written based on expressed needs for change or newly recognized talents of group members in areas of specialty which were previously unknown in stage two.

Stage Four: Evaluating and Celebrating Achievements

In this stage, which can occur quite often or at scheduled intervals, people's achievements are often overlooked or recognized and rewarded in too formal a manner, especially in larger organizations. The need for most people to have honest, valid feedback about their performances, and to be recognized and rewarded for positive achievement is greater than most people may realize. We need only to look to ourselves to recall those times when we were keenly appreciated and honored for a contribution we have made to understand how much of a validating experience this can be. We also can recall how negative feedback can be devastating if delivered in an accusatory or devaluing fashion, or how constructive criticism from a respected team member or leader can be both a relief and an inspiration.

One company I consulted with to improve their hiring (and firing) practices had great service accomplishments and sales increases for 3 years in a row. The employees were rewarded only with increased pay, but without anyone directly telling them that the pay increases were in part due to their increased service and sales performances. They came to expect the pay increases every 6 months or so, even though the increases were significantly above the standard cost-of-living allowances most of their friends in other companies were receiving. Then, over a period of about 5 months, sales dropped and customer complaints increased significantly. During the next anticipated pay increase period, there was no raise. The staff threatened to form a union until the president of the company told them in a general meeting why they were not getting a pay increase. They told him that if they had known for sure that their pay raises were tied to their performance that they would have continued to increase their performance. He decided to give them the raise he previously withheld, but did so at the first annual recognition and awards ceremony. It was fun, funny, jubilant and expensive. Company performance continued to climb to an all time high in the coming months. The president later instituted a profit sharing program which gave further incentive for increased performance and satisfaction.

Learning from feedback, both positive and negative, celebrating success, and planning for new levels of achievement can all have a powerful impact on how people experience their membership in organizations and groups.

Ten Steps in The Process of Developing a Group or Organization

In this next section of this chapter we will examine each of the first nine steps in more detail so you can gain further insight into the nature of the process of how groups and organizations develop, and how you can act as a catalytic agent to make this development occur.

Stage One: Design, Orientation and Commitment

Step One: Solidifying and Communicating the Mandate — Step one of a group's or organization's development requires that the leader have a mandate or some authority to proceed with a position of power to decide, power to move in certain directions and not others, or a vision or mission which has the sanction of an official body. For example, only when a college president has a mandate from its Board or other governing agency to provide a certain level of quality and scope of instruction may he or she proceed with clarity. Furthermore, if an entrepreneur were to start his or her own company, then the government of most free-world states would give that person the right to exercise a self-decreed mandate: to make money by engaging in free enterprise.

It is often necessary and many times desirable for there to be a clear mandate (from "on high" as it were) in order to proceed without coming into conflict with the purpose of the organization or authorities in charge of the overall direction or operation of it. Volunteer organizations are famous for "splintering" when a "leader" decides that he or she needs to achieve a personal purpose which is not in harmony with the larger (officially) "mandated" vision of the organization, which is often spelled out in it's constitution. It is desirable to prevent this splintering effect whenever possible by making the mandate clear in the minds of all those in a group or organization.

Clarity is made possible by publishing the mandate in writing and by initiating an orientation process whereby people understand that going against the mandate will result in their losing membership in the group or organization. One delivery company has issued a mandate of safety at all levels of the organization. Irresponsibility toward the safety of anyone is not tolerated. If, for example, an employee of the company is caught speeding while driving a company delivery vehicle on the freeway the result is known in advance to be immediate dismissal.

In summary, the mandate delimits what the purpose of an organization or group can and cannot be. It specifies what is acceptable and what is not. It spells out in no uncertain terms how things will be and often remains quite stable and inflexible throughout the life of the organization, like the constitutions of various government bodies. It comprises the assumptions, fundamental definitions and rules which everyone is required to begin with and follow when dealing with one another and with the organization. Some organizations or groups call the mandate its "terms of reference."

Many people resist creating, publishing, communicating or standing up for a mandate because it can seem to some people to be "authoritarian" or rigid. It does not have to be, however, as in the case of a constitution founded upon democratic principles of freedom of speech, freedom of worship, freedom from discrimination, etc. A humane mandate, which is built upon the assumption that people are valuable, will be a solid foundation on which to build a group or organization.

Example Mandate Statement of A to Z Community Services Agency: "Our Mandate is to provide support and develop community based social services mostly to needy members of the community. We cannot compete with existing government or private agencies, but will supplement their services to fulfill unmet needs where such government services fall short due to funding, staff shortages or people's inabilities to pay for such services."

If you can assist a group or organization to clarify and communicate its mandate effectively to its members, you will likely prevent all sorts of misunderstandings, misdirection and conflict from emerging to destroy the integrity and cohesion which is needed for further development. After achieving this first step, the next one is assisting in the clarification of the organization's purpose, vision or mission.

Step Two: Clarifying Purpose, Mission or Vision — As a next step in this first stage, a purpose statement is a further specification and extension of the mandate statement. The terms purpose, mission and vision are used synonymously to refer to a group's or organization's reason for being. Some leaders, like Dr. Martin Luther King, Jr., have a "dream" (which in his case was an inner vision driven with passion and commitment) which they communicate to their group members. Others have a purpose statement which is perhaps less fiery, but nevertheless provides overall direction and reason for being to the members of a group or organization.

Assisting group members to achieve understanding of and consensus around a purpose statement, and what the statement means is a critical prerequisite to "gelling" the group into one functional entity. If you can get people to "buy in" to the organization's reason for existence as a part of their own reason for being, then you have instant commitment! For example, it wasn't hard for Douglas Aircraft plant workers to arrive at work group consensus about what their purpose was at the beginning of WW2! The employees realized that they were an absolutely necessary part of a war machine which, if they built it fast and well, had the potential to save their own lives and the lives of their children as well.

Example Purpose Statement of A to Z Community Services Agency:

Our purpose is to enrich the lives of community members, especially the poor, provide for their basic material needs and offer them personal development opportunities which they otherwise would not receive, and provide training and avenues for the expression of volunteer services and financial contributions.

Step Three: Specifying and Gaining Consensus about Philosophy — Values, Beliefs and Norms — This next step in the first stage of developing a group or organization is also very important. Without a similar philosophical orientation there really cannot be a cohesive group or organization. A group's philosophy is comprised of values (priorities and importances) and beliefs (assumptions about what is true, good, false, bad, etc.). In addition, without agreed upon norms (extension of values and beliefs, which are agreements about ways of treating people and solving problems), people may find they have frequent clashes with one another and the group or organization will likely either live in disharmony and lose productive energies or fall apart.

In one organization where I was acting as an external consultant, there were staff who were working with a base of conflicting values, beliefs and assumptions. They certainly were at odds with one another and there was resultant harm to young people in the organization where there was a mandate to rehabilitate them. In this example, about half of the correctional officers in a juvenile correctional facility honestly believed that their purpose was to attempt to facilitate the development of juveniles with the eventual hope of rehabilitating them as self-respecting citizens of the community. The other half of the staff referred to the residents as "slugs who'll never amount to anything" and treated them with strong disrespect. The staff fought bitterly with one another and were in conflict daily about this issue of the worth of the offenders in custody, and turnover was high as management was blamed by both sides (!) for "hiring a bunch of idiots." The leaders of the juvenile facility did not attend to this issue of specifying and communicating purpose when they hired the correctional officers. They didn't even ask them or their previous employers what their purpose was for working with juveniles! The juveniles got these two conflicting messages communicated to them on a daily basis, and as a result program efforts were undermined and discipline procedures were implemented with entirely opposite spirits—one with a spirit of discipline and the other with a spirit of punishment. The end results were disastrously in favor of the punishing officers' predictions.

At a point of crisis when there had been a very expensive riot during which the youth damaged the facilities extensively, management called me in to do a team development process with the management group first, then with the whole staff. We started with an examination of the mandate which was in the contract the agency had signed with the government funding body. Then we moved on to creating purpose statements on "flip-charts" on the walls until we had as much consensus as possible among the group of 28 staff. It became clear that it was going to be difficult to move ahead with the next step of specifying philosophy because the conflict in the air was so thick it could have been cut with a knife. When we moved into clarifying the organization's philosophy about how to treat kids and staff, the worth of kids, the approach to discipline and control, etc., 8 of the "old school, old guard" staff quit the next week. New staff were hired within a month who "bought in" to the juvenile center's philosophy, and stress and conflict levels decreased immediately. The organization began to "gel" into a cohesive group of people who were "of the same mind." Within a few weeks they observed consistent evidence of positive impact on the juveniles who were in their care. They were then in a position to re-evaluate the general goals of their organization.

Stage Two: Making the Transition — Overcoming Resistance and Obstacles

Step Four: Formulating General Goals Which Meet Needs or Solve Problems — Motivating goals can be effectively formulated only upon a foundation of clear and agreed-upon mandate, purpose and philosophy statements which are real to those in a group or organization. Perhaps it is true that a band is no better than its worst player, and that a band which has a drummer who plays to a different beat should suggest that the drummer go play jazz fusion somewhere else (unless the band's purpose is to play jazz fusion). If there is no agreement on the general direction and hoped for accomplishments of a group then it will not achieve much that it intends to achieve. If there is agreement on general goals it will be possible to achieve higher levels of success. The transforming leader's job is to assist in the consulting mode to articulate and translate the aspirations of group members or needs of a group they serve (or sell) into goal statements which are motivating, realistic, achievable, worthwhile and adequate to solve problems or meet needs.

In the case of the juvenile correctional facility, a subsequent consulting intervention resulted in the writing down and implementing of the following goal and objectives statements:

Goal #1.   We will provide a clean, colorful and socially supportive environment which will encourage the development of residents at the spiritual, intellectual, physical, social, emotional and creative arts levels.

Objective A: Staff Team E (educators) will implement the Skills for Living Program for life skills development from January through April of this year.

Objective B: Staff Team P (physical plant maintenance staff) will paint this ugly place during the next month in colors which the kids have a say in choosing.

You can see from the above that from the general goal flow specific objectives. Clear general goal statements are the soil out of which grow specific implementation plans and commitments.

Step Five: Specifying Objectives — Objectives are statements of commitment which have a name and a date attached to them. They are highly specific in terms of defining what will be accomplished by a certain date. They are based on general goals which reflect known and felt needs or problems.

In order to facilitate the achievement of objectives which are specified, each objective can be recorded on simple sheets during staff or planning meetings. These sheets can become the "minutes" for any meeting, which can in turn be reviewed and evaluated at the next scheduled meeting. Each team member who has an objective to achieve can set up a program of steps to achieve it and can get ideas from team members for effective implementation of the program plan. An example format of a sheet we used to hold objective setting meetings with the correctional staff is outlined on the following page.

As you can see from the format of the above overly-simplified version of the staff meeting minutes, all those at the meeting eventually committed themselves to accomplishing a specific objective by a specific date, and agreed to give a report on that date about the results which occurred from his or her effort. This kind of specific planning and recording by each member of a group or organization has the effect of enlivening meetings, setting up achievable targets and meeting the needs of staff members for being recognized for their acccomplishments. It also allows them to gain assistance and support when their efforts fail.

Stage Three: Doing the Work of the Group

Step 6: Planning Action Programs — Programs are objectives translated into the smaller, logical, more realistic steps which are required to achieve the desired objectives within certain time-frames. Program planning requires experience in the area of expertise which is being exercised. This is true because if the steps are too large to be achieved people will become discouraged by failure. If the steps are too small, they will become bored or fatigued with meaningless repetition. Steps in programs need to be large enough to be challenging but small enough to be realistically achieved. Failing to plan realistic but challenging program steps is the main reason

---

XYZ Juvenile Rehabilitation Center Staff Planning Meeting				

Date: _____

Staff Present: _____

Staff Absent: _____

Team Leader: _____

AGENDA ITEM	OBJECTIVE	ACTION BY WHOM	ACTION BY DATE	RESULTS
Inconsistent discipline practices between staff	Develop plan for new discipline system	Ted	05/02	
	Schedule team development session: problem solving — discipline issue	Gil	05/15	
Staff shift schedule undermines relationship development with kids	Develop new shift schedule which matches programs	Marg	05/01	
	Schedule staff vactions to match program dates	Art	06/01	

many objectives fail to materialize into action. Unless this step is attended to thoroughly and carefully, an individual's or group's objectives may never be translated into achievements.

Step 7: Implementing Programs — Effective program implementation by a group or organization requires a follow-through on the leader's part to monitor, recognize achievement, encourage commitment and reward performance in both formal and informal ways. The consistently successful implementation of a sales program, for example, could likely depend upon the long-term follow-through of a good sales manager who realizes that the power of his sales force resides within the skills, attitudes and motivations of the people who sell. This sales manager will plan regular and meaningful sales feedback, training, motivational incentives and various types of ongoing recognition.

Stage Four: Evaluating and Celebrating Accomplishments

Step 8: Learning from the Past: Evaluation — Honest and valid feedback to members of a group or organization can be extremely valuable or destructive. Regular performance reviews can be conducted by leaders who are in touch enough to actually observe performance. Obtaining an agreement in advance of such an assessment that it will occur on a regular formal basis as well as on an ongoing informal basis can alleviate much anxiety which is often associated with such evaluations. One method of beginning the performance review process is to ask group members to critique the performance of their own work team during team development or planning sessions. People in leadership positions can also give and receive feedback about positive and negative impacts which occurred as a result of their actions or practices. One company gave weekly feedback to assembly-line employees about how their performance compared with the competition's performance. They were embarrassed to the point of increasing their productivity over 15% in the following weeks—6% on the average over the competition's.

Planning for improved future performance is another event which can occur on a regular basis as a part of step eight. This step is one which often has to be leader-induced because work teams often are resistant to improving their performance when it means they have to work harder. If planning for improved performance will result, however, in an increase in meaningful rewards and recognition, we can expect there will be more enthusiasm for such activities.

Step 9: Celebrating and Enjoying the Rewards — If genuine celebration can be fostered and allowed to occur it can seal a group together for long periods of time. Genuine celebration can only occur however, when there has been some kind of dramatic and hoped-for achievement beyond the commonplace. If leaders can challenge exceptional performance in only one area, and provide opportunity for valued recognition and rewards to come back to group members, then there will likely be further commitment to the achievement of other challenging objectives. Rewarding innovation and creativity is another way to promote celebration and recurring high performances.

Step 10: Recycling the Ten Steps — It is important to recycle group or organization members through any or all of the steps in the process of developing a group or organization as often as is needed. Sometimes it is critical to re-examine the mandate. It may need to be adjusted as a result of changing markets, changing needs of people being served, changing priorities or shifting values of those in positions to set the course or fate of an organization. However, mandates are perhaps the most stable of all the steps in the process. I have found it most useful to ensure that the value of the vision is renewed in the minds of group and organization members regularly. Also I have found it especially helpful to re-assess needs and problems to ensure that our goals are in line with what is truly important. When failure occurs, it is especially important to examine the appropriateness and workability of objectives and programs.

Now rate your ability to use the stages and steps outlined above to facilitate the development of the groups or organizations with whom you live or work.

Ability to Facilitate Group Development

1 = Skill is new to me, cannot do it
2 = Understand it but cannot perform it
3 = Can begin to do it, but not naturally
4 = Can do it naturally in many situations
5 = Can do it well and teach others if I want

"Well Functioning" Is Not Enough: Pressing Toward Transformation

Ackerman (1986)[9] describes the essence of what she calls "flow state leadership in action"—a non-traditional view of organizations as bundles of energy-in-motion.

> *In order to increase performance, leaders must be able to release energy that is blocked, to free untapped potential, and to organize in ways that facilitate rather than impede energy flow (p. 245).*

The basics of Flow State leadership are in sync with transforming leadership. The ideas that blocks must be removed, a vision created and communicated, people must be empowered and enlisted, and performance factors must be enhanced are key to transforming leadership.

Groups, companies or organizations which merely run smoothly often fail to grow and creatively adapt to changing demands and opportunities. They often become boring and generally lack an innovative spirit which, if its potential were released, could generate enthusiasm and energy capable of propelling even higher, more interesting and more rewarding achievements. Therefore, we will conclude this book with an examination of the nature of the transforming process and begin to explore this relatively new field of how we can transform organizations or groups into dynamic high-performers (such as Federal Express, People Express and Microsoft).

After you have practiced the skills and awareness you have assessed in this book as needing further development, you will have an opportunity to creatively apply the transforming leadership approaches in your own groups or organizations. Finally, you can benefit from the structured learning strategies (in the Leading Manager training modules) which will be available. Through these training modules, you will have an opportunity for more in-depth training.

The development and transformation of a group or organization into a dynamic and high-performance entity is an inspiring phenomenon to observe and participate in.

---

9   L. Ackerman, in *Transforming Leadership: From Vision to Results,* ed. by John D. Adams (Alexandria, Virginia: Miles River Press, 1986).

An Illustration of Organization Development and Transformation From My Past

There were five of us at Manuel's place on a hot July evening in Southern California practicing rock and roll numbers for a dance which was scheduled for the following Saturday night. We had only been playing for about 2 years, but we were good enough that we enjoyed playing about 25 different numbers (albeit somewhat mechanically). Our "organization" had developed to a point that we were a solid group of musicians who had enough talent developed to contract to play for pay at some local dances, schools and fairs. We had agreed together on a vision of becoming the best band in Southern California—and winning the upcoming "battle of the bands" at the San Bernardino County Fair (our competition, little did we know, would be The Beach Boys).

Then, that evening after about 2 hours of practice, something new happened which began the process of transforming our group into an exciting and dynamic performing group. We were competent enough at playing a particular song that we simultaneously forgot to "try"—there was a feeling of effortlessly "flowing," of "having it made," and mutual glances and grins spread from member to member, as a fine clean sound emerged which most other 16-year-old band members would have been "green with envy" to have achieved.

In jazz slang, we had finally started to "cook." Prior to that all we had been doing was cutting the tomatoes and the celery on the cutting board. It wasn't a bad salad, but boring after a while. But when our performance "heated up" to the point of excellence, over 20 of the neighborhood kids often dropped in to listen to our practices (about 18 of them were girls!)—then we knew we had transcended the "beginner" phase. Our band (organization) had become transformed to a new level of creativity and expression of "spirit"—a spirit of success and freedom which went beyond the commonplace novice performances of our past.

As a result of this new "flowing" sound, an unexpected mystique developed around our band and we were among the first to achieve enough recognition to have "groupies" follow us around to our dances (groups of girls who admired and wanted to date us). We used our profits to buy the best Fender guitars, Showman amplifiers, French Selmer Saxophones, a 55 Chevy, a T-Bird, a street rod, a 57 Chevy and a VW van. A "cool" young culture of dancers and other young musicians developed around us and regularly attended the dances where we played.

As our excitement and confidence continued to build we learned to trust that we could practice nearly any song and "glide" (or transcend) into that same clean, crisp competent sound that moved people to dance and even return to our next performances. As a result, bigger dance promoters began to book us for the dances where more than 1,000 kids, and on several occasions even over 2,000 kids would turn up. We added some rather simple choreography to our stage presentations (which was rare in 1963) and became one of Southern California's 5 most popular bands (known as Manuel and The Renegades).

As a result of all these factors, we got exciting new jobs at the Cinnamon Cinder Teen Nightclub, came in second at the "battle of the bands" at the San Bernardino County Fair (yes, the Beach Boys won!), and cut several "surfing" style records which unfortunately sold well only in Chicago.

Those of us who were in the "Renegades" went through the design, development and transformation stages of a group without any awareness of what was happening to us. Our experience was so rich and powerful that nearly all of the groups and organizations which we have encountered since those days have been pale (and some have been grim) by comparison. For years after we disbanded, there was a sense of disillusionment with the other groups and organizations we belonged to including some members' marriages, and certain colleges and universities because none of them ever "transcended" the ordinary, "heated up" or creatively "cooked" to the same extent that the Renegades did. However, to my great relief, I finally found another "hot" band to play music with (called The Reactions) during my college years, and to this day I still find myself playing the audio tape recordings which we made during the dances at Running Springs Lodge near Big Bear Lake, California.

The significant thing about this story is that at this time in my life I first realized that the same type of experiences and performances of being "on a roll," "really high," "on," or "in the groove" can be achieved inside of myself first, then to an increasing extent in family, group and other organizational settings.

Perhaps the "trick" of releasing the transforming "spirit" in other settings is to learn to transfer the same principles and practices learned in the "hotter" settings to the more mundane ones:

1. Set up the group or organization properly at its inception—with enthusiasm about a clear vision, a worthy purpose, adequate goals, and shared beliefs, values and norms.
2. Select competent members who genuinely share and "buy into" the above vision.
3. Gain a refined consensus and commitment between the members about the specific purpose, goals, values and norms of the group, company or organization.
4. Learn to play a series of "numbers" well together.
5. Practice until you begin to "cook" with spontaneous creativity.
6. Apply that creative "style-shifting" power and "flow" to any number of other emerging situations or problems.
7. Stay open to the potential of positive change and a diversity of approaches which demonstrate themselves as appropriately viable, so long as they are consistent with number 1, above.
8. Play "numbers" or create products or services which meet the emerging needs or challenges of the times.
9. Stay alert to changes in the environment which require a response so adjustments and developments can be made in a timely fashion.
10. Celebrate the achievement of goals, recognize the unique contributions of each member, share in the "take" so that each member receives a portion of the profits from the endeavor, and look to the future for new opportunities.

Conclusion

The endeavor of creating and managing positive change is really just emerging as a science and an art. This book has been a starting place from which to collect what in the past might be effectively transported into what I believe in the future will become a new kind of practice of leadership, a constantly adaptive and evolving sort of leadership.

Many books describe transformation in organizations and illustrate how excellence has been achieved. However, they do not offer a comprehensive, integrated competency-based working model which reveals and develops within you the knowledge, skills and tools for transforming yourself and your organization into a more powerful one—one which can produce both business and human development results simultaneously. However, there is a wealth of additional ideas regarding the nature of the transformation process and how leadership can have a positive impact (see Albrecht (1987)[10]; Bass (1985)[11]; Bennis (1966)[12]; Beckhard and Harris (1987)[13]; Brandt (1986)[14]; Kirkpatrick (1984)[15]; LeBoeuf (1980)[16]; Martel (1986)[17]; Tichy (1983)[18]; Tichy and Devanna (1986).[19] For those who are serious about reviewing some of the critical works which have come before this, you could review any one or all of these books.

To conclude this book, we turn to the words of John Kotter (1990),[20] Professor of Organizational Behavior at the Harvard Business School. He writes:

Some people have the capacity to become excellent managers but not very strong leaders. Others have great leadership potential but, for a variety of reasons, have great difficulty becoming strong managers. Smart companies value both kinds of individuals and work hard to make them a part of the overall team. But when it comes to grooming people for executive jobs, such

---

10 K. Albrecht, *The Creative Corporation* (Homewood, Ill.: Dow Jones-Irwin, 1987).

11 B .M. Bass, *Leadership and Performance Beyond Expectations* (New York: Free Press, 1985).

12 W.G. Bennis, *Changing Organizations.* (New York: McGraw-Hill, 1966).

13 R. Beckhard and R.T. Harris, *Organizational Transitions* 2nd ed. (Reading, Mass.: Addison-Wesley, 1987).

14 S.C. Brandt, *Entrepreneuring in Established Companies. Managing Toward the Year 2000* (New York: Mentor, 1986).

15 D.L. Kirkpatrick, *How to Manage Change Effectively: Approaches, Methods, and Case Examples* (San Francisco: Jossey-Bass, 1984).

16 M. LeBoeuf, *Imagineering: How to Profit from Your Creative Powers* (New York: Berkeley Book, 1980).

17 L. Martel, *Mastering Change: The Key to Business Success* (New York: Simon & Shuster, 1986).

18 N.M. Tichy, *Managing Strategic Change: Organization Development Redefined* (New York: Wiley, 1983).

19 N.M. Tichy and M.A. Devanna, *The Transformational Leader* (New York: Wiley, 1986).

20 J. Kotter, *A Force for Change: How Leadership Differs from Management* (New York: The Free Press, 1990), 125-126.

---

firms ignore the recent literature that says people cannot manage and lead, and focus their efforts on indivduals that seem to have the potential to do both. That is, they try to develop more leader-managers than managers and leaders, and for one very important reason.

Leadership and management are sufficiently different that they can easily conflict. A firm made up mostly of leaders and managers often polarizes into two warring camps, eventually resulting in one side winning (usually the managerial camp because it is bigger) and then in the purging of the other side. In firms with a large contingent of leader-managers, this rarely happens.

Developing enough leader-managers to help run the huge number of complex organizations that dominate our society today is a great challenge. But it is a challenge we must accept. The more pessimistic among us think this is hopeless. Some even argue that there is no such thing as a leader-manager. They are clearly wrong; most of the individuals discussed in the book both lead and manage. At this point, it is simply not clear how many more of these peole would emerge if circumstances were right. The only way to find out—is to try.

The *Transforming Leadership* approach asserts confidently that *any manager who wants to become a better leader can learn to do so! Transforming Leadership* is an attempt to provide these "right circumstances" which Kotter suggests. This book, and The Leading Manager Program, combined with a program of formalized mentoring could be a next step for many who would stretch themselves from the limitations of management into the exciting challenges of leadership which lie ahead of us. This new development and growth can have positive impact at every level of society: at home, at work and in our other systems.

Being versatile is important. Using this talent to hire, train and keep key people is the focus of our final topic. Effective personnel practices are a foundational building block of the *Transforming Leadership* approach. The next chapter leads us to a practical application of the principles, steps and tools which can be implemented to increase the effectiveness of personnel screening, assessment, selection, placement, orientation, person-job match, performance review, performance enhancement planning, career path planning, and research.

Total for the Style, Role and Skill Shifting Section

Add all numbers in the boxes above from this chapter.

Graphing Your Self-assessment Scores

Now that you have completed this section of the comprehensive self-assessment, graph in all of your individual scores so that you can get a visual summary of what skills you see are stronger and weaker. Graph in your self-rating scores on each skill using the "bar graph" method of drawing lines from left to right on each scale.

1 = Skill is new to me, cannot do it
2 = Understand it but cannot perform it
3 = Can begin to do it, but not naturally
4 = Can do it naturally in many situations
5 = Can do it well and teach others if I want

	1	2	3	4	5
Present style-shifting self-assessment					
Present role-shifting self-assessment					
Present assessed ability to develop and transform groups and organizations					

Professional Development Planning Summary

Now that you have completed all sections of the comprehensive self-assessment, graph total score from each section so that you can get a visual summary of what skills you see are stronger and weaker. Graph in your self-rating scores using the "bar graph" method of drawing lines from left to right on each scale. These scores can be compared with others who have completed this self-assessment program. This will assist in planning for group training programs.

Skill Levels		1	2	3	4	5
Chapter 4 Total from p. 105		10	20	30	40	50
Awareness and Self-Management Skills						
Chapter 5 Total from p. 123		12	24	36	48	60
Interpersonal Communication Skills						
Chapter 6 Total from p. 170		14	28	42	56	70
Counseling and Problem Management Skills						
Chapter 7 Total from p. 210		10	20	30	40	50
Consulting Skills for Developing Groups and Organizations						
Chapter 8 Total from p. 261		3	6	9	12	15
Style, Role, and Skill Shifting for Developing Versatility						

Note: Training or coaching would be indicated if any skill area is 3 ("can begin to do it, but not naturally") or less. Mentoring would be indicated if any skill area is at level 4.

Chapter 9

Transformation Through Personnel Systems

If organizations wish to be successful
in managing the turbulence of the modern world
...they will view their people as a key resource
and value knowledge, information, creativity,
interpersonal skills, and entrepreneurship
as much as land, labor, and capital
have been valued in the past.

Gareth Morgan

Introduction

One of the most important aspects of leadership where a transformative effect can be realized is in the careful assessment, selection and development of people. Finding and retaining high quality, committed employees or followers is absolutely critical to the success of any leader and any organization.

This book has to this point introduced you to knowledge and skills which can assist you to improve your effectiveness as a leader. But tools are important as well. I could not fulfill my original vision for this book without including a system and some tools which can be implemented to improve the quality, productivity and profitability of organizations.

Therefore, this chapter will introduce you to the concepts, steps and practices which were originally introduced in the *Comprehensive Personnel System*

(CPS) (Anderson and Zeiner, 1989).[1] But it will introduce them by acquainting you with a new software technology, *PeopleSystems SoftInfo (PSSI)* (Anderson and Stanley-Jones, 1992)[2] which is an expanded development of the CPS.

First, a brief history of the CPS: it was originally designed in 1986 as a paper-based introductory seminar program titled: *Selecting and Developing Exceptional Employees.* It was field tested between 1987 and 1991 with over 400 small-to-medium sized companies. The program was evaluated very positively, and many of the companies have implemented parts or all of the CPS in their day-to-day operations. They did so in some cases on their own, and in other cases with the assistance of CRG Associate Company Principals who are business consultants. Most of the company owners and personnel managers who attended the one or two day sessions had either not had a course in personnel management, or had not implemented the principles they were introduced to in such courses. Therefore, to their satisfaction, many of the staff problems they encountered on a day-to-day basis were addressed in the seminar.

As a group, they reported that the following fifteen of their most frequently encountered problems were causing them moderate to serious concern from time to time:

1. Not hiring the right person for a job.

2. Failing to communicate clear performance expectations.

3. Fear of telling employees what they honestly think.

4. Forgetting to reward or recognize positive performance.

5. Losing track of personnel information.

6. Failing to collect personnel information.

7. Employees make the same mistakes repeatedly.

8. Fear legal repercussions when firing low-performers.

---

1   T. Anderson and B. Zeiner, *Selecting and Developing Exceptional Employees with the Comprehensive Personnel System* (Abbotsford, B.C. Canada: Consulting Resource Group International, Inc.: 1989).

2   T. Anderson and Stanley-Jones, *PeopleSystems SoftInfo* (Abbotsford, B.C. Canada: Consulting Resource Group International, Inc.: 1989).

9. Misplacing files or information in files.

10. People aren't motivated to perform well.

11. Employees don't do what I want them to.

12. Failing to capitalize on strengths and talents.

13. Absenteeism rates are too high.

14. Employees don't know how to solve problems on their own.

15. Training takes too much time, or is ineffective.

The PSSI contains information services which can help solve many of these problems, and save time and money in the management of all non-financial personnel information. It also includes a variety of employee assessment tools which focus on issues of employee work style, job style assessment, employee-job compatibility, employee-team compatibility, performance enhancement, motivation and morale, performance evaluation, training needs identification, career planning, and research.

Unlike most existing human resource information systems, *PeopleSystems* does not address the issues of benefits, labor relations, human resource planning or compensation. There are a number of human resource information systems (HRIS) software programs which perform these functions (the management of "hard, numbers-related information" very well. However, PSSI can "clip on" to most of these HRIS's quite readily to provide additional capabilities for managing the non-financial aspects of personnel information (what I have termed *SoftInfo*).

What is *SoftInfo*?

SoftInfo is systematically collected and reported personnel information which both employees and employers agree to share with one another for mutual benefit. *SoftInfo* is job-related information which is offered willingly by the employee in order to improve his or her communication with the employer about work preferences, stressful vs. productive work placements, deficient areas of performance which need improvement or require training, motivational information, and career plans with the organization. A primary goal of having updated and instant access to *SoftInfo* is to increase everyone's understanding of the strengths, preferences, goals and motivating needs of the person doing the job. It is also to clarify the nature and requirements of the job itself, and as a result increase the probability that it will be possible to match the nature of an employee with the nature of the job. Quite believably then, the quality, productivity and profitability of the organization would be the end result.

Access by each employee to his or her own *SoftInfo* is critical to the success of the system. Some legal jurisdictions in various countries, states, or provinces have laws which require employees to be cognizant of, or at least have access to, everything which has been placed into their personnel files. It is my belief that information such as employee strengths, weaknesses, training plans, self-assessment results, psychometric test results, career path plans, interest and personal style inventories (all *SoftInfo*), should go into a person's personnel file only with his or her consent and knowledge. Such information is open to such diverse interpretation that it is important that employees have the opportunity to formally comment in writing on what is being officially recorded about them on their files.

In many jurisdictions, such "access to information" policies are becoming law, and it appears that there is an increasing trend toward access to information by employees, and privacy by protection of such information by allowing only certain people to access it. The *PeopleSystems SoftInfo* software program can be programmed with various levels of security to prevent access to information by those who do not have clearance.

What is "Hard" Info?

Hard information is information about people which is external—their payroll and benefits administration, accident record, performance reviews based on measurable accomplishments, letters of reprimand and commendations, days absent, etc.—information which is quantifiable and not as subjective in nature.

Hard information can also be employee information which must be handled by professionals with specialized training such as the medical information which must be handled by certified doctors, and psychological and personality testing information which is often handled by qualified psychologists. Hard information is often not as interesting, accessible or relevant to employees as is soft information.

When employees want to be understood, it is often the softer side of issues which they wish to communicate—such as preferences for certain types of jobs, work environments or preferred placements with certain work team members. Hard information is often used to screen people in determining who should be interviewed for a particular job, but *SoftInfo* is the type of information which should be exchanged during the interview, at the time of hiring, and during orientation, performance review and career planning sessions. It is critical information about jobs and people which affects performance and morale.

Both hard and soft information are important. Most human resource information systems (HRIS) account for hard information but not *SoftInfo*. This is why *PSSI* is so significant. Now *PSSI* can be "clipped-on" to most HRIS systems, and in this way it is possible to have an integrated system with both types of information instantly on line, networked, and accessed by security codes.

Specifications and Applications for *PSSI*

PeopleSystems SoftInfo is a user-friendly human resource information system which can record, manage and track all non-financial information electronically on an IBM compatible computer with a minimum of 640k memory. It can be used by any organization, business, placement agency, educational or governmental agency. It contains only job-related information and does not discriminate against anyone in any way. In fact, the system prevents negative discrimination which can otherwise occur due to lack of information about employee work preferences, strengths, interests, career plans, motivational priorities, claimed competencies, and training needs.

PSSI can be used with both a keyboard and a mouse. Colors and data base fields can be customized by the user, and complete custom software designs and alterations can be developed through Consulting Resource Group's Software Associates. *PSSI* will also print a variety of dot matrix or laser printed reports in any specified order so that both employees and those who lead them can communicate more precisely and effectively about issues which affect individual, group and organizational performance, morale and health.

PSSI can be used in small, medium and large organizations, and is particularly effective in developing and managing high performance work teams where quality service and production are important, and where there is diversity in the work force. The various assessment and communication tools can be effective in assisting managers, supervisors and employees to appreciate individual differences, preferences, talents and strengths so that these can be fully utilized on the job.

PSSI is useful for tracking and communicating all non-financial job and employee information in a clear and trouble-free manner because it will enhance two-way communication in the personnel process. Finally, it provides some guidelines for what job-related questions you may want to ask applicants, and cautions about some you may not want to ask, depending upon the laws in your jurisdiction.

Tools in the PSSI Version 1.0

1. Job Analysis—Knowledge and Skills Inventory
2. Applicant Job Knowledge and Skills Inventory
3. Job Description Builder
4. Job Style Indicator
5. Personal Style Indicator
6. Performance Review System
7. Performance Enhancement Guidelines
8. Employee-Job Compatibility Report

Additional Assessments Planned for Version 2.0 of PSSI

1. Organizational Audit and Needs Assessment
2. Training Needs Assessment
3. The Stress Indicator and Health Planner
4. The Work Values Inventory
5. The Self-Worth Indicator
6. The Entrepreneurial Style and Success Indicator
7. The Sales Style Indicator
8. The Leadership Skills Inventory

What About Validity and Reliability?

You may examine the Leader's Manual for the *Personal Style Indicator* and the *Job Style Indicator* to see that there is no doubt that the *Personal Style Indicator* (PSI) has established itself as a valid self-assessment tool. Thousands of people have agreed or strongly agreed when asked that the In-depth Interpretations for the PSI are accurate or very accurate. On average, they have agreed that more than 90% of the comments describe them accurately. The test-retest reliability coefficient for each of the four scales yields better than +.86 in replicated studies with various sample groups conducted by the authors. Hundreds of companies and over 100,000 people have completed the PSI and less than 1 in 100 has disagreed or strongly disagreed with his or her overall results. As an ipsative (non-normative) self-assessment and performance planning tool not claiming to have predictive validity, this is more than satisfactory.

Although the *Personal Style Indicator* and other self-assessment tools in *PSSI* were not designed to be normative measures (the results from normative measures might allow you to compare one person with another and predict future performance in some settings) studies are currently being conducted to determine the relationship between the four scales on the PSI and the various scales on the *Myers-Briggs Type Indicator* and the *Cattell 16 PF* (which are normative psychometric tests). The results of these studies will be included in version 2.0 of the *PSSI* software manual.

Selecting and Developing Exceptional Employees

PeopleSystems SoftInfo (PSSI) is a time and cost effective communication system in which employers and applicants or employees share a common language to discuss performance expectations and review progress on the job with those who manage or supervise them. It is not a substitute for careful decision making or testing (when appropriate), but a vehicle for enhancing the specific description, communication and recording of information about jobs and people in the work place.

Often we are "caught" without a key person in a given position—and there is very little time to establish a comprehensive system that will fulfill our immediate needs. Therefore, in order to reduce frustration and save time and costs this system is presented in a practical and easy-to-use software format.

There are twelve key things you can do to select and develop the people who are critical to the performance and productivity of your organization—they are:

1. Screen applicants more accurately and efficiently.

2. Build a data base of applicant and employee information.

3. Create target interview questions and use them.

4. Assess work behavioral style of applicant or employee.

5. Assess work behavioral style of each job.

6. Assess past work performance history.

7. Match knowledge and skills of employees with jobs.

8. Contract for employee performance enhancement.

9. Conduct and record performance reviews.

10. Create and record an employee career plan.

11. Reward and recognize employee performance.

12. Communicate on a regular basis, using a shared language.

The *PSSI* can assist you to assess, record or report all these things in a time and cost effective manner.

Results You Can Expect When Using the PSSI

PeopleSystems SoftInfo adds productivity, efficiency and profits to your organization or company by assisting you to more carefully manage:

1. How you select, orient, place, train and evaluate people;

2. How you organize things and people in the work environment in order to make best use of people's talents;

3. How you record and track all personnel data; and,

4. How you use ideas to improve performance and morale on the job.

The primary aim of the *PSSI* is to provide you with the knowledge and tools needed to lead others effectively toward increased productivity, efficiency and profitability. Because employees differ in regard to motivation, age, maturity, experience, competence and styles of approaching people and tasks it is important to understand each employee or applicant on an individual basis. The *PSSI* will assist you, or those in your organization who are responsible for developing human resources, to get to know each applicant or employee more quickly and carefully, and have a record of this information which can be accessed instantly—thus, you will be able to make more effective personnel and leadership decisions.

Dispel Employee Fears, Suspicions and Anxieties

Clear expectations and feedback provided by the *PSSI* relieve anxiety and promote positive motivation. Once people understand the system and know that it will be used to help them do a better job they will see how they can benefit from it personally. It is relatively easy to dispel suspicions and fears which can crop up when managers attempt to be careful and accountable in personnel practices, if the information which goes into the system is understood by the employee. If your policy is to give employees access to viewing their own files, and gain their consent prior to adding "soft" information to their files, you will find that trust levels will increase between employees and management.

Nine Steps in the Personnel Assessment and Development Process

Some people may already be familiar with the personnel process, and the steps involved in it, but the following page titled *The Comprehensive Personnel Process* will assist you to do an assessment of what areas you think need attention in your organization by highlighting the area(s) which you would like to see developed further.

1. *Specify Knowledge and Skills Required in a Position*

Both skills and knowledge areas need to be delineated for each position. Relationship, task and leadership factors also need to be specified. The Job Knowledge and Skills Inventory is used to specify all of the skill areas required by an employee in order that he or she will be most effective in a given job. The more carefully the job analysis is done, the more accurately the requirements for that job will be understood and communicated to those doing the interviewing to select new personnel. Follow the instructions on screen in order to analyze a particular job—this analysis leads to the production of a job description which can be attached to each employee's file. This

The Comprehensive Personnel Process
Job Analysis – Job Specification – Screening

1. Job Analysis	2. Job Description	3. Screening Process
Identify Required:	*Specify in Writing*	*Rate Applicant's:*
· Results	· Results expected	· Skills
· Job tasks	· Specify tasks	· Knowledge
· Job skills	· Specify roles	· Work history
· Social skills	· Extent of authority	· Extent of training
· Behavioral styles	· Job style pattern	· Extent of education
· Difficulty level	· Performance criteria	· Application form
· Training requirements	· Progress evaluation date	· Decide on short list

Selection – Placement – Orientation

4. Applicant Interview	5. Applicant–Job Fit	6. Orientation Process
Assess Applicant's:	*Rate Applicant's:*	*Contract for, or Inform about:*
· Skills	· Skills	· Work tasks
· Knowledge	· Knowledge	· Expected results
· Work style (i.e., PSI)	· Training required	· Work behavioral style
· Perception of job (i.e., JSI)	· Work/job style fit (PSI/JSI)	· Appraisal criteria
· Past work experience	· Interview performance	· Appraisal dates
· Interview impressions	· Past work performance	· Work team placement
· Testing results	· General suitability	· Length of probation

Performance Appraisal – Career Path Planning – Research

7. Performance Review	8. Development Plans	9. Career Path Plan
Give Feedback About:	*Facilitate Agreement About:*	*Specify Agreements About:*
· Results achieved	· Present strengths	· Future job potentials
· Problem areas	· Past successes	· Plans for development
· Performance of tasks	· Areas to develop	· Competition dates
· Relationship factors	· Plans to develop	· Lateral transfer options
· Work style/job fit	· Plans for training	· Research to validate
· Performance goals	· On-the-job coaching	selection criteria
· Probationary status	· Date of next review	

job description can be easily edited as changes may be required from time to time.

2.   *Specify Appropriate Work Style Behaviors in Each Job*

By seeking agreement on a range of Job Style Indicator (JSI) scores on each style dimension of the JSI, managers and supervisors can agree upon an appropriate work style for each position in the organization. Asking employees who do a particular job to complete the Job Style Indicator is also useful in arriving at their understanding of the job they do.

This style (or range of acceptable behaviors) can be included as a part of each job description, if you want to print or view the JSI scores for a job role. This agreement can be achieved by using the Job Style Indicator to define the appropriate work style for each position in the organization, as above. Those employees who are assessed as being very successful in their positions should have input into describing the requirements of each position so that managers who have never done the job can appreciate and consider their successful workers' points of view.

Doing a good job analysis requires a careful assessment of all of the dimensions of the job, and an annual (or even more frequent) review of the job requirements often reveals that jobs, in fact, change over time.

3.   *Specify a Job Description*

Each position needs to have a clear job description, which attaches all of the above information plus:

a.   Any objectives and time-line performance requirements;

b.   A clarification description of roles in relation to other positions—how this job fits in with other jobs;

c.   A clarification of extent and limits of authority in the position;

d.   A clear line of authority (who is above and below);

e.   Information on how problems can best get solved;

f.   Progress evaluation criteria (how the employee will be evaluated);

g.   Incentives or rewards which will be given if goals and performance criteria are reached;

h. First and second performance evaluation dates, and who is to conduct them;

i. Terms of probationary appointment;

j. Conditions of termination (behaviors which will definitely cause the employee to be fired).

A good job description can be created from the information gathered from the above two steps. *PSSI* automatically prints all such information when you ask for a particular job description on file.

4. Screen Applicants on Paper Qualifications First

Using the Applicant Job Knowledge and Skills Inventory, evaluate each applicant's extent of training and experience. Arrive at a short-list based on close examination of paper applications, letters of reference and resumes.

5. Assess Work Styles and Prepare for the Interview

Use the Job Style Indicator and the Personal Style Indicator to arrive at a clear summary of an applicant's *perception* of his/her work style and his/her perception of the work style thought to be appropriate for the job. If an applicant is not familiar with computers, a receptionist can assist to get people started—the rest is easy! Sometimes, instead of using the computer, you may wish to use the paper-based response sheets which are available from Consulting Resource Group or a CRG Associate Company. In these cases, the PSI audio tape, *Living and Working with Style* (Anderson, Clark, & Clark)[3] administration program can save staff administrative time. Some employers simply give the paper-based PSI and JSI to an applicant and send it home, offering to answer questions about the instruments on the phone or in person if needed.

Assess Other Relevant Factors: various other factors can be assessed at this time and entered into the applicant's data base; such as typing speed, other task competencies, intellectual abilities, knowledge or personality tests, etc., which are appropriate and directly related to the requirements of the job.

Preparation for the Interview: applicants are instructed prior to the interview to come ready to talk openly about how they would personally

---

3 T. Anderson, J. Clark & S. Clark, *Living and Working with Style* (Consulting Resource Group International, Inc.: Abbotsford, B.C. Canada, 1987).

approach the tasks and the people in the job for which they are applying. Make sure they have completed the *Personal Style Indicator* and *Job Style Indicator* before the interview and have read the interpretive comments appropriate to their profile pattern. In this way applicants will be specifically prepared to answer the following eight (among other) key questions:

a. How do you treat people while you get your tasks done?

b. How much of a "fit" is there between how you see your own nature and the nature of the job?

c. How much style flexibility are you able and willing to demonstrate in your approach to tasks and people in this job?

d. What strengths would you bring to this job?

e. What difficulties might you have in this job?

f. How do you react under increased stress?

g. Do you have leadership inclinations or preferences? What kind of boss are you likely to follow?

h. What training do you think you might need in order to do the job better?

In the *PSSI* system, applicants are given a copy of the appropriate In-depth Interpretation from the PSI (and instructions about how to prepare for the interview) to take home with them. They are instructed to highlight those statements in the interpretation with which they agree, and expand upon the interpretation in their own words, in preparation for discussion during the interview. They are told that will be required to answer the above eight questions, as well as other questions which are deemed important enough to be asked.

It is made clear to all applicants in the instructions given them prior to the interview that neither the *Job Style Indicator* nor the *Personal Style Indicator* results will form the primary basis of any decision to hire them or to not hire them, but that their responses to the questions asked in the interview *will* partially determine the outcome. The instructions inform them that they are being assessed on a number of measures, all of which will be included in the final decision to hire, or not to hire. They are also informed prior to the interview that they will be encouraged to clarify their approach to the job in their own words during the interview.

Below is a sample of the one page letter from PSSI you could use to assist the applicant to understand the interview and selection process you will be implementing:

To the Applicant: Preparing For Your Job Interview

Congratulations! You are among several candidates being given a final interview for the position you are seeking. Before you show up for your interview, it is requested that you complete the *Personal Style Indicator* and the *Job Style Indicator*. Preparing to discuss your styles in the interview will take about one hour of your time at home, using the materials below.

These indicators are not tests, but tools we use to help us communicate about the requirements of the job, and to help you communicate clearly to us about your style of getting the job done. You will not be selected or rejected on the basis of your responses to these indicators, but only on the basis of your qualifications and your performance in the interview. The indicators are used as communication vehicles only.

You may take home the interpretation booklet or computer printout to assist you in understanding your work style and the style you think is appropriate on the job.

You will be asked to talk about your work style in the job interview. Your understanding of the attached materials will assist you in interpreting your style indicators and in speaking clearly about how you would react to certain people or certain situations on the job.

Be ready to answer the following eight questions:

1. How do you treat people while you get your tasks done?

2. How much of a "fit" is there between how you see your own nature and the nature of the job?

3. How much style flexibility are you able and willing to demonstrate in your approach to tasks and people in this job?

4. What strengths would you bring to this job?

5. What difficulties might you have in this job?

6. How do you react under increased stress?

7. Do you have leadership inclinations or preferences?

8. What training do you think you might need in order to do the job better?

General Instructions: With the *Personal Style Indicator* you will describe your work style; and with the *Job Style Indicator,* you will describe the style you think is important in the job for which you are applying. Follow the instructions in the *Personal Style Indicator* booklet and *Job Style Indicator* booklet. Complete both booklets. Please ask for assistance if you need further clarification, or use the Personal Style Indicator Audio Tape Seminar for clear instructions.

6. Interview Short-Listed Applicants

During this interview the interviewer would have a similar set of questions (prepared in advance) to ask each interviewee in order to have some continuity between each interview session. These questions can be generated or read from the Job Description. This makes it possible to compare how each applicant answers the same or similar questions. Mostly open questions should be asked (questions which require elaboration by the applicants, rather than closed questions which require a "yes" or "no" answer) so that there can be depth in key areas of focus.

7. Hire, Orient and Train New Employees

After hire, the new employee will likely have many questions about the manner in which they were hired, and will have a new appreciation for the issue of STYLE and its impact on job performance. Some companies have provided each new employee a copy of the *Personal Style Indicator* package to go through at home—most employees become extremely curious about such instruments and want to use them with their family members. This is a positive step because they are likely to learn to use the knowledge for their own personal development. When this occurs, they will bring this learning back into the work place.

If groups of employees are hired at the same time, then they could all take a *Personal Style Indicator* workshop to orient them to the whole area of personal style, understanding and working with other's styles, and developing style flexibility in order to build effective work teams and improve performance and harmony in the work place. For this, they could use the paper-based PSI rather than the computer-based assessment.

Most new employees will see quickly why you have used the *PSSI* in the process of your hiring them and will see the sense of it all in clarifying the requirements of their new jobs. Most of them will appreciate your taking the time to clarify how they can be more successful: How to be successful is often uppermost in the minds of new employees. They will also be able to understand the styles of their new supervisors, and how to work with them more effectively.

During the orientation process you can provide your new employees with the following information if you want to get maximum performance with a minimum of confusion:

a. The purpose, philosophy, and goals of your organization (you obviously want your new employees to "buy into" how and why you want them to accomplish things);

b. The policies, practices, and procedures which the new employees will need to know in order to be most effective and least confused (ideally you would already have prepared a staff manual with all this information in it);

c. The job descriptions of their new positions, which will include everything (mentioned above) needed to understand what is required of them;

d. A formal letter describing the terms of their appointments, including length of probationary periods, amounts of pay, etc;

e. How the performance review and promotion system works in your organization, and when the first performance review will occur;

f. Check to see that all new employees actually have opportunity to talk about each item on their job descriptions. New employees are often so disoriented that they tend to assume they understand everything in their job descriptions. They often do not.

All of this information can be included in the Personnel Manual contained in the *PSSI* which can be edited and tailored to fit nearly any organization. This manual could be given to all new and existing employees to help them understand and gain a sense of accord with your organization.

8. *Conduct Performance Reviews*

For Employees Who Are Being Taken Off Probation

We have found that employees will, when given a chance, do their own performance reviews. They can do this review on screen within *PSSI* themselves if you give them access to the computer and to the *PSSI* program for that purpose. If you do not want to do this, you can ask them to write one out which can later be inputted into *PSSI*.

In the performance review, make sure that feedback given is tied to some kind of (preferably recent) behaviors which the employee can recall. Give positive feedback first, then feedback regarding areas in need of improvement.

Respond to the employee with some understanding of how they are feeling and what they are thinking about the items in the appraisal, and about the appraisal process itself. It is important that two-way, encouraging communication take place, and that the interview is seen as focused on how you appreciate that the employee has done well, and secondarily, what the employee can do to improve. Get commitments on paper about improved performance in a maximum of three areas (a long list doesn't work as well). Then give the employee his/her copy of the performance review printout and Performance Enhancement Guidelines, and set a date for the next review.

Performance Review: For Employees Who Will Stay but Will Require Further Documentation

These employee appraisal interviews are more difficult because you are giving a double message: You are saying that their performance is not satisfactory, but you are going to continue employment anyway, at least for a specified period of time.

It is especially important with these employees that the positive things they have done be highlighted, and that agreements for specific changes be identified, written down, and committed to. Supervisors also need to commit to giving the necessary coaching and support in order to get the desired results. Then, later, if the employee meets the specified requirements he/she will have hope of being taken off probation.

In order to develop morale and encourage minimal performers, you have to communicate to them that you believe their developing into good employees is a real possibility, otherwise their next three to six months will be too stressful (or boring) and will add to their anxiety (or to their low performance, while they find another job at your expense). Give them support and feedback every week or two for awhile, until progress is sure.

If you have serious doubts, tell the employee this in no uncertain terms using the approach outlined below.

Exit Review: For Employees Who are Being Let Go

If during the specified probationary period the employee is identified as a high risk, low performer, you will find it necessary to inform him or her of your decision to terminate employment. You can explain that job performance has not been to the standard specified on their job description, and/or that the style of treating people (which you have described in the Performance Enhancement Guidelines: Performance Planning Agreement) while getting the job done is not acceptable. If all this information is specified on the job description and your warnings have been entered into *PSSI*, you have covered your bases and are increasing your insurance against wrongful dismissal charges.

A letter of dismissal is appropriate at this time, and some outplacement service and direction regarding where to go from here may be appropriate. This is an important service to provide to the work force and to society in general, particularly if you see strengths in the employee which might be better exercised in a different work environment.

You are unlikely to see grievances from legal or union sources when you have fairly told the employee ahead of time that certain tasks had to be performed to specific standards in order to remain in the position, and there is documentation on paper that he or she in fact did not do so. Most employees will not argue with facts stated in terms of behaviors, which they agree they have done, or failed to have done adequately. When in doubt, however, you should always refer to legal counsel and to the labor laws in your jurisdiction.

9. Career Path Planning

For those employees who are demonstrating leadership or managerial potential or some other needed expertise in the work place, a career path can be identified and discussed with them in advance of an opportunity or job opening. They still need to know that there will be a competition for the position, but that you see them as having some potential for gaining the position.

This must be sincere, and you can't do this with very many employees because usually only a few can move up the organization's ladder. But you can sometimes lose some really good employees with real potential because you fail to help them see that they have real possibilities for promotion or lateral transfer. Help them articulate what they would need to do to get ready for a competition they would want to win, and encourage them to take courses, do readings, take workshops, etc., which would increase their likelihood of being promoted.

Use the *Job Style Indicator* and *Personal Style Indicator* to help the employee understand the style behaviors which are appropriate for the position which is available. This can help the employee to formulate a motivating internal career plan and a personal development plan, feel more challenged by the work, and assume more responsibility. This combination of factors will likely motivate him or her to seek the position even more strongly.

People Information is Performance Information!

By using the *PSSI* I have come to know those who work for me better. I also work with over 200 university students each year. I have found that if I know them well enough, I come to understand what challenges them as individuals. If I can come to know what areas of responsibility they want to assume, then I have incredibly motivating information! People information is leadership information!

Frederick Herzberg (1989)[4]asserts that we cannot do it by improving work conditions, raising salaries, or shuffling tasks. He asserts:

> *KITA—the externally imposed attempt by management to "install generators" in employees—has been demonstrated to be a total failure. The absence of such "hygiene" factors as good supervisor-employee relations and liberal fringe benefits can make workers unhappy, but the presence of these factors will not make employees want to work harder. Essentially meaningless changes in the tasks that workers are assigned to do have not accomplished the desired objective either. The only way to motivate*

---

4   F. Herzberg, *One More Time: How do you motivate employees?* (Harvard Business Review, reprint #68108, Boston, 1989).

employees is to give them challenging work for which they can assume responsibility.

If we can communicate with followers clearly enough to understand and appreciate the desires of their hearts, and provide opportunities for them to find the realization of them to some extent, we will likely find increased performance, loyalty and longevity as a result. In achieving this result, we will have been transformative leaders.

Custom Design Options

The PSSI has been designed in a modular fashion and can be customized by CRG's software associates to fit a wide variety of needs including:

1. Adapt PSSI to a local area network;

2. Create unique applications to meet your objectives by customizing various screens and reports;

3. Clip on to existing HRIS systems;

4. Create, electronically score and save to a data base file any other questionnaire, test or inventory for later reference or research purposes.

5. Export data to other data bases or statistical packages.

For a test drive of PSSI, or for more information, contact Consulting Resource Group International, Inc. at (604) 852-0566 or FAX (604) 850-3003.

Afterword

The Role of Formalized Mentoring in Transforming Leadership

by William A. Gray, Ph.D., and Marilynne Miles Gray, M.A., M.Ed.
The Mentoring Institute, Vancouver, B.C., Canada

In *Transforming Leadership*, Terry Anderson aptly discusses the urgent need for experienced leaders to pass the torch of practical wisdom to those individuals who will become transforming leaders. These leaders will perform the important task of continuously developing themselves, then other individuals, then groups and organizations to handle the uncertainties of the 21st century. Anderson discusses the knowledge, skills and attitudes needed to become a transforming leader and then recommends that organizations establish formalized mentoring programs to facilitate their development. Why is this recommendation made? How can organizations implement it?

Since 1978, we have helped over 30 educational groups and over 30 companies and government agencies to custom-develop formalized mentoring programs. We have used Gray & Anderson's *MSI • Mentoring Style Indicator*™ to train over 6000 mentors and protégés to provide and access appropriate styles of mentoring so they will work together more compatibly. We helped some companies (e.g., Winthrop Pharmaceuticals, Pacific Bell, Litton, Hewlett-Packard, Dow Chemical) link formalized mentoring with formalized training courses to eliminate the widespread "transfer of training problem" by better understanding and applying content learned in courses.

At Heublein, Eastman Kodak and Hewlett-Packard, we trained mentors and protégés to use Anderson's *PSI • Personal Style Indicator*™ to identify their preferred personal style (behavioral, cognitive, affective, interpersonal) or relating to people and events, to develop style-shift versatility with each other, and then to apply this skill to work better with co-workers and customers having different personal styles. We also trained mentors to help their protégés reconcile differences between personal style preference and what the job requires for success, as measured by Anderson's *JSI • Job Style Indicator*™.

Over 80% of the formalized mentoring programs we've helped corporations and government groups custom-develop were started primarily, though not exclusively, to develop the diversified workforce to its fullest potential. Other major reasons include: assimilating new hires, reducing turnover, expanding technical competency, eliminating the transfer of learning problem, aiding career planning and development, implementing quality improvement initiatives, and developing transforming leaders who will lead their organizations with a new vision into the 21st century.

Two obvious questions arise: Why not rely on informal mentoring (which occurs naturally and spontaneously) to develop transforming leaders? Won't these leaders then informally mentor junior colleagues to develop their potential? Although informal mentoring does benefit those fortunate few who are lucky enough to "be in the right place at the right time to be noticed and helped by the right person," most individuals—especially women and minorities—do not receive such informal mentoring, and those individuals who do are often "cloned" in the mentor's image and style of thinking and operating. This happens because those individuals in positions of power and influence who provide informal mentoring, typically choose as protégés those persons with characteristics similar to their own. These practices may have been acceptable in the past as a means of grooming leaders for succession planning, but this surely dooms today's organizations (business, educational institutions, government agencies, etc.) to stagnation and noncompetitiveness in a rapidly changing world.

Informal mentoring cannot be relied upon for other reasons: It starts spontaneously and then "just evolves" (usually protégés do not know they are being mentored). It has no definite beginning or ending, and does not intentionally develop protégés in a systematic way. It is usually not provided when most needed by would-be protégés

In contrast, formalized mentoring can be designed to help protégés make important transitions in two ways: It helps protégés find out if they have what it takes to make a key transition (relocate, rise to a higher level, redeploy to a different function, develop into a transforming leader) or are willing to learn it; protégés can then make an informed, reality-based decision to proceed or not. If protégés decide to "go for it," formalized mentoring can help protégés make the transition smoothly and achieve initial success instead of falling victim to the well-known Peter Principle (rising to one's level of incompetence).

What are some characteristics of formalized mentoring programs? They begin for a definite reason (to assimilate new hires, reduce turnover, expand technical expertise, develop the diversified workforce, aid career planning and development, develop transforming leaders) and last long enough to achieve this purpose (4 months to 3 years). They must be custom-designed to fit the organizational mission, strategies, goals and culture as this exists or to facilitate fundamental changes in these components. Would-be participants need to have input into how much structure the formalized program will have, what mentors and protégés will do together, how the program will be monitored by a program coordinator and will later be evaluated to determine results. Mentors and protégés must be selected from informed volunteers, then carefully matched and trained so they know what to do to achieve intended goals. Such formalized mentoring is carefully planned to achieve intended, utilitarian outcomes that benefit mentors, protégés and their organization.

Like Terry Anderson, we believe formalized mentoring and transforming leadership are integrally related. Formalized mentoring develops transforming leaders and Anderson's program can be used to develop transforming leaders—leaders who bring new visions and paradigms for addressing today's and tomorrow's global problems, leaders who appreciate the unique potential of the diversified workforce and will develop it to make innovative contributions, both in the workplace and in society as a whole.

Formalized mentoring provided *on-the-job* enables white-collar workers to overcome the widespread "transfer of training problem" often produced by group training and self-directed courses. Formalized mentoring can help learners better understand new skills and concepts taught in the Transforming Leader Program, and then correctly apply this in real situations (similar to the way on-the-job mentoring facilitates the development of apprentices in blue-collar occupations). This approach is especially needed to learn the complex skills, knowledge and attitudes of the transforming leader that Anderson describes:

- designated mentors, who have the characteristics of transforming leaders, can explain how they personally developed, over time and through various experiences, the inner skills of awareness and self-management described in Chapter 4;
- mentors, who are skillful in using 12 interpersonal communication skills described in Chapter 5, can demonstrate and coach these skills and give candid feedback to transforming leaders as they practice these skills and employ them in real situations (via on-the-job coaching);
- mentors, who are both person- and results-oriented, can help transforming leaders learn which counseling and problem management skills described in Chapter 6 are appropriate for assisting fellow employees who are having problems, and when to refer severely troubled employees to professional counselors;
- mentors in positions of power and influence can share their practical wisdom to help transforming leaders learn the consulting skills described in Chapter 7 so that they, in turn, can develop "intra-preneurs" and foster innovative vision and goals which cause an organization to develop instead of becoming stagnant.

Besides helping transforming leaders learn these complex skills, formalized mentoring can aid the more difficult task of developing role-shifting versatility and style-shifting versatility (described in Chapter 8). As mentors share their practical wisdom and teach the "tricks of the trade," transforming leaders develop role-shifting versatility to appropriately employ interpersonal communication skills, counseling skills or consulting skills to help less-experienced colleagues handle varied situations. Transforming leaders develop style-shifting versatility so they appropriately employ a personal style which better matches what other people need in order to communicate and work together effectively.

Just as transforming leadership is the missing ingredient needed to lead individuals, groups and organizations into the unpredictable 21st century, formalized mentoring is the systematic, yet personalized, mechanism for developing transforming leaders and for enabling them, in turn, to develop their colleagues and institutions to handle these uncertainties.

References

Ackerman, L. In *Transforming Leadership: From Vision to Results,* ed. John D. Adams. Alexandria, Virginia: Miles River Press, 1986.

Albrecht, K. *The Creative Corporation.* Homewood, Ill.: Dow Jones-Irwin, 1987.

Alderson, W. *Value of the Person: Theory R Concept.* Pittsburgh: University of Pittsburgh Press, 1985.

Anderson, T. and E. Robinson. *The Leader's Manual for the Personal Style Indicator and Job Style Indicator: A Guide to Their Significance, Development, Administration, and Practical Applications.* Abbotsford, B.C., Canada: Consulting Resource Group International, Inc., 1988.

Anderson, T. and B. Zeiner. *Selecting and Developing Exceptional Employees with the Comprehensive Personnel System..* Abbotsford, B.C., Canada: Consulting Resource Group International, Inc., 1989.

Anderson, T. *Leader's Manual for the Therapeutic Style Indicator.* Amherst, Mass.: Microtraining Associates, 1987.

———. *The Therapeutic Style Indicator.* Amherst, Mass.: Microtraining Associates, 1987.

Anderson, T.D. and E.T. Robinson. *The Personal Style Indicator.* 3rd ed. Abbotsford, B.C., Canada: Consulting Resource Group, Inc., 1988.

Argyris, C. *Integrating the Individual and the Organization.* New York: Wiley, 1964.

———. *Reasoning, Learning and Action: Individual and Organizational.* San Francisco: Jossey-Bass, 1982.

Bass, B.M. *Leadership and Performance Beyond Expectations.* New York: Free Press, 1985.

Beckhard, R., and R.T. Harris. *Organizational Transitions.* (2nd ed.) Reading, Mass.: Addison-Wesley, 1987.

Bennis, W. and B. Nanus. *Leaders: The Strategies for Taking Charge.* New York: Harper and Row, 1985.

Bennis, W. *The Unconscious Conspiracy—Why Leaders Can't Lead.* New York: AMACOM, 1976.

Bennis, W.G. "Revisionist Theory of Leadership." *Harvard Business Review,* 1961, 39 (1), 26–36, 146–150.

Bennis, W.G. *Changing Organizations.* New York: McGraw-Hill, 1966.

Berenson, B. and K. Mitchell. *Confrontation for Better or Worse!* Amherst, Mass.: Human Resource Development Press, 1974.

Bergin, A.E. "Negative Effects Revisited: A Reply." *Professional Psychology,* 1980, 11, 93–100.

Bergin, A.E. "The Evaluating of Therapeutic Outcomes," In *Handbook of Psychotherapy and Behavior Change,* A.E. Begin and S.L. Garfield, eds. New York: Wiley, 1971.

Bernard, L.L. *An Introduction to Social Psychology,* New York: Holt, 1926.

Biggs, B. "The Dangerous Folly Called Theory Z." *Fortune* (17 May, 1982): 48–53.

Bingham, W.V. "Leadership." In *The Psychological Foundations of Management,* H.C. Metcalf. New York: Shaw, 1927.

Blake, R.R. and Jane S. Mouton. *The Managerial Grid.* Houston: Gulf, 1964.

Blanchard, K. and P. Hersey. *Management of Organizational Behavior: Utilizing Human Resources.* New Jersey: Prentice-Hall, 1982.

Bogardus, E.S. *Essentials of Social Psychology.* Los Angeles: University of Southern California Press, 1918.

Brandt, S.C. *Entrepreneuring in Established Companies. Managing Toward the Year 2000.* New York: Mentor, 1986.

Brown A., and E. Wiener. *Supermanaging: How to Harness Change for Personal and Organizational Success.* New York: Mentor Books, 1985.

Brown, A. and E. Weiner. *Supermanaging.* New York: New American Library, 1984.

Burke, R. "Methods of Resolving Superior-Subordinate Conflict: The Constructive Use of Subordinate Differences and Disagreements." In *Readings in Interpersonal and Organizational Communication,* eds. R.C. Huseman, C.M. Logue, and D.L. Freshley, 3rd ed. Boston: Holbrook Press, 1977.

Burns, J.M. *Leadership.* New York: Harper & Row, 1978.

Carkhuff, R.R. *Helping and Human Relations. Vols. I and II.* New York: Holt, Rinehart, & Winston, 1969.

———. *The Development of Human Resources.* New York: Holt, Rinehart & Winston, 1971.

Carkhuff, R.R. and B. Berenson. *Beyond Counseling and Therapy.* New York: Holt, Rinehart & Winston, 1967.

Carnevale, Anthony P., Leila J. Gainer, Ann S. Meltzer, and Shari L. Holland. "Workplace Basics: The Skills Employers Want." *Training and Development Journal,* Oct. 1988.

Center for Constructive Change. "How Intentional Is Your Life?" *Journal for Constructive Change,* 6 (1), 16–17.

Crosby, P.B. *Quality Is Free: The Art of Making Quality Certain.* New York: McGraw Hill, 1979.

DePree, Max. *Leadership Is An Art.* New York: Dell Publishing, 1989.

Egan, G. *Change Agent Skills.* Monterey, California: Brooks/Cole Publishing Co., 1985.

———. *The Skilled Helper.* 2nd ed. Monterey, CA: Brooks/Cole, 1977.

———. *The Skilled Helper.* 3rd ed. Monterey, California: Brooks/Cole Publishing Company, 1986.

———. *The Skilled Helper.* 4th ed. Monterey, California. Brooks/Cole Publishing Company: 1990.

———. *Change Agent Skills (B): Managing Innovation and Change.* San Diego, California: University Associates, Inc., 1988.

Ellis, A. *A New Guide to Rational Living.* Hollywood: Wilshire Book Company, 1976.

Emrick, C.D. "A Review of Psychologically Oriented Treatment in Alcoholism." *Journal of Studies of Alcohol,* 1975, 36, 88–108.

Feather, F. *G-Forces. Re-Inventing the World: The 35 Global Forces Restructuring Our Future.* Summerhill Press Ltd., Toronto: 1989.

Fiedler, F. "How Do You Make Leaders More Effective: New Answers to an Old Puzzle," *Organizational Dynamics* (Autumn, 1972): 3–18.

Fiedler, F.E. *A Theory of Leadership Effectiveness.* New York: McGraw-Hill, 1967.

Fowler, J. *Stages of Faith: Psychology of Human Development and the Quest for Meaning.* New York: Harper and Row, 1981.

Gardner, J. *On Leadership.* New York: The Free Press, 1990.

Garfield, C. *Peak Performers: The New Heroes of American Business.* New York: William Morrow and Company, 1986.

Glasser, W. *Taking Effective Control of Your Life.* New York: Harper and Row, 1984.

Gray, W. and T. Anderson. *The Mentoring Style Indicator.* Vancouver, B.C., Canada: The International Centre for Mentoring, 1990.

Gray, W. *International Journal of Mentoring,* Vancouver, B.C. Vol. 1, No. 1, 1987.

Greenleaf, R. *Servant Leadership, A Journey in to the Nature of Legitimate Power and Greatness.* New York: Paulist Press, 1977.

Guralnik, D. (ed.) *Webster's New World Dictionary.* New York: Simon and Schuster, 1984.

Hickman, C. and M. Silva. *Creating Excellence: Managing Corporate Culture, Strategy, and Change in the New Age.* New York: New American Library, 1984.

Hickman, C. *Mind of a Manager, Soul of a Leader.* New York: John Wiley and Sons, 1990.

Homans, G.C. *The Human Group.* New York: Harcourt, Brace, 1950.

House, R. "A Path-Goal Model of Leader Effectiveness," *Administrative Science Quarterly* 16 (September, 1971): 312–338.

Ivey, A. *Developmental Therapy.* San Francisco: Jossey-Bass, 1986.

———. *Intentional Interviewing and Counseling.* 2nd ed. Monterey, California: Brooks/Cole, 1987.

———. *Intentional Interviewing and Counseling.* Pacific Grove, CA: Brooks/Cole, 1983.

Ivey, A. and J. Authier. *Microcounseling: Innovations in Interviewing, Counseling, Psychotherapy, and Psychoeducation.* (2nd. ed.) Springfield, Ill.: Charles C. Thomas, 1978.

Janis, I. *Short-Term Counseling.* New Haven: Yale, 1983.

Jennings, E.E. *An Anatomy of Leadership: Princes, Heroes, and Supermen.* New York: Harper, 1960.

Kanter, R. "Power and Entrepreneurship in Action: Corporate Middle Managers," *Varieties of Work,* Beverly Hills: Sage, 1982.

Kanter, R.M. *The Change Masters.* New York: Simon and Schuster, 1983.

Kilbourne, C.E. "The Elements of Leadership." *Journal of Applied Psychology,* 1959, 43, 209–211.

Kilmer, G.R. "Consumer Survey as Needs Assessment Method: A Case Study." *Evaluation and Program Planning,* 1978, I, 286–292.

Kirkpatrick, D.L. *How to Manage Change Effectively: Approaches, Methods, and Case Examples..* San Francisco: Jossey-Bass, 1984.

Kotter, J. *A Force for Change: How Leadership Differs from Management.* New York: The Free Press, 1990.

Kotter, J. *Power in Management.* New York: AMACOM, 1979.

Kouzes, J. and B. Posner. *The Leadership Challenge, How to Get Extraordinary Things Done in Organizations.* San Francisco: Jossey-Bass, 1987.

Kravetz, D. *The Human Resources Revolution.* San Francisco: Jossey-Bass, 1988.

Landman, J.T. and R.M. Dawes. "Psychotherapy Outcome: Smith and Glass' Conclusions Stand Up Under Scrutiny." *American Psychologist,* 1982, 37, 504–516.

Larson, Dale, ed. *Teaching Psychological Skills, Models for Giving Psychology Away.* Monterey, California: Brooks/Cole Publishing Company, 1984.,

LeBoeuf, M. *Imagineering: How to Profit From Your Creative Powers.* New York: Berkeley Book, 1980.

Levinson, D., C.N. Darrow, E.G. Klein, M.H. Levinson, and B. McKee. *The Seasons of a Man's Life.* New York: Knopf, 1978.

Levitt, E.E. "Psychotherapy With Children: A Further Evaluation." *Behavior Research and Therapy,* 1963, 1, 45–51.

Likert, R. *The Human Organization.* New York: McGraw-Hill, 1967.

Lombardo, M. "Looking at Leadership: Some Neglected Issues." Center for Creative Leadership, Technical Report Number 6, January, 1978. Research sponsored by: Organizational Effectiveness Research Program, Office of Naval Research (Code 452), under contract No. N00014-76-C-0870; NR 170-825.

Martel, L. *Mastering Change: The Key to Business Success.* New York: Simon & Schuster, 1986.

Marx, R. "Improving Management Development Through Relapse Prevention Strategies." *Journal of Management Development,* Vol. 5, (2), 1986, 27–40.

Mayeroff, M. *On Caring.* New York: Perennial Library (Harper and Row), 1971.

Mays, D.T. and C.M. Franks. "Getting Worse: Psychotherapy or No Treatment—The Jury Should Still Be Out." *Professional Psychology,* 1980, 11, 78–92.

McGregor, D. *Leadership and Motivation.* Cambridge, Mass.: MIT Press, 1967.

McGregor, D. *The Human Side of Enterprise.* New York: McGraw-Hill, 1960.

Menzel, R. "A Taxonomy of Change Agent Skills." *The Journal of European Training,* 1975, 4 (5), 289–291.

Merrill, D. and R. Reid. *Personal Styles and Effective Performance.* Radnor, Pennsylvania: Chilton Book Company, 1981.

Mintzberg, H. *The Nature of Managerial Work.* New York: Harper and Row, 1973.

Naisbitt, J. and P. Aburdene. *Megatrends 2000. Ten New Directions for the 1990's.* New York: William Morrow and Company, 1990.

Naisbitt, J. and P. Aburdene. *Re-inventing the Corporation.* New York: Warner Books. 1986.

Naisbitt, J. *Megatrends.* New York: Warner, 1982.

Orwin, R.G. and D.S. Cordray. "Smith and Glass' Psychotherapy Conclusions Need Further Probing: On Landman and Dawes' Re-analysis." *American Psychologist,* 1984, 39, 71–72.

Ouchi, W. *Theory Z: How American Business Can Meet the Japanese Challenge.* Reading, Mass.: Addison-Wesley, 1981.

Peters, T. and N. Austin. *A Passion for Excellence: The Leadership Difference.* New York: Random House, 1985.

Pietrofesa, J.J., A. Hoffman and H.H. Splete. *Counseling, An Introduction.* 2nd ed. Boston: Houghton Mifflin Company, 1984.

Quinn, R. *Beyond Rational Management: Mastering the Paradoxes and Competing Demands of High Performance.* San Francisco: Jossey-Bass, 1988.

Robinson, E. *The Values Preference Inventory.* Abbotsford, B.C., Canada. Consulting Resource Group International, Inc.: 1990.

Robinson, E. *Why Aren't You More Like Me?* Kendall-Hunt, Dubuque, Iowa: 1990.

Roglieri, J.L. *Odds On Your Life.* New York: Seaview, 1980.

Schafer, W. *Stress Management for Wellness.* New York: Holt, Rinehart and Winston, 1987.

Schlenker, B. *Impression Management.* Monterey, California: Brooks/Cole Publishing Company, 1980.

Schlesinger, L., R. Eccles and J. Gabarro. *Managerial Behavior in Organizations: Texts, Cases, and Readings.* New York: McGraw-Hill, 1983.

Shenson, H. and T. Anderson. *The Entrepreneurial Style and Success Indicator and Professional's Guide*. Abbotsford, B.C., Canada: Consulting Resource Group International, Inc., 1988.

Smith, M.C. and G.V. Glass. "Meta-analysis of Psychotherapy Outcome Studies." *American Psychologist*, 1977, 32, 752–761.

Smith, M.C., G.V. Glass and T.J. Miller. *The Benefits of Psychotherapy*. Baltimore: Johns Hopkins University Press, 1980.

Sproul, R. *Stronger Than Steel*, New York: Harper and Row, 1980.

Srivastva, S., D. Cooperrider and Associates. *Appreciative Management and Leadership: The Power of Positive Thought and Action in Organizations*. San Francisco: Jossey-Bass, 1990,

Stogdill, R.M. *Individual Behavior and Group Achievement*. New York: Oxford University Press, 1959.

Stogdill, Ralph M. *Handbook of Leadership*. New York: The Free Press, 1974.

Tead, O. "The Technique of Leadership." In *Human Nature and Management*, New York: McGraw-Hill, 1929.

Thomas, R. "From Affirmative Action to Affirming Diversity." *Harvard Business Review*. (March-April, 1990) Vol. 68, No. 2.

Tichy, N.M. *Managing Strategic Change: Organization Development Redefined*. New York: Wiley, 1983.

Tichy, N.M. and M.A. Devanna. *The Transformational Leader*. New York: Wiley, 1986.

Vroom V. and P. Yetton. *Leadership and Decision Making*. Pittsburgh: University of Pittsburgh Press, 1973.

Waitley, D. *Seeds of Greatness*. Old Tappan, New Jersey: Fleming H. Revell Company, 1983.

Waitley, D. *The Psychology of Winning*. New York: The Berkeley Publishing Company, 1979.

Watson, D. and R. Tharpe. *Self-directed Behavior*. 3rd. ed. Monterey, California: Brooks/Cole, 1981.

Westburg, E.M. "A Point of View: Studies in Leadership." *Journal of Abnormal Social Psychology*, 1931, 25, 418–423.

Index

About the Author

TERRY D. ANDERSON, Ph.D., is an experienced author, speaker, human resource development and management consultant, educator, trainer and counselor. He serves management in the corporate, government, education, health and social services sectors.

Dr. Anderson received a B.A. (Psychology), an M.A. (Education) from California State University, and a Ph.D. in Human Resource Development and Management through a joint program with faculty at University of Massachusetts School of Management and Columbia Pacific University, California. In
addition, he has a Professional Teaching Certificate, having received his teacher education from the University of Victoria, British Columbia.

He is the Chairman of the Board for Consulting Resource Group International, Inc. (1979), a full service publishing and human resource development and management consulting firm. For nearly two decades he has served as a full-time faculty member at University College of the Fraser Valley, and during the last decade as an adjunct faculty member at Trinity Western University and the University of British Columbia.

He has developed several major training curricula and conducted professional training sessions for staff trainers in the Correctional Services of Canada. He co-coordinated the development of a Life Skills Curriculum for prisoner development which won the 1985 President's Award for the most significant contribution to Life Skills in Canada from the Ontario Association for Life Skills Coaches. In 1987, his Style Shift Counseling Model for Counselor Education was published by MicroTraining Associates of Amherst, Mass., and in 1988 his co-authored work in the field of entrepreneurship research was nominated for the Innovations Award at the International Council for Small Business conference in Quebec City. His creative energy and success in speaking and conducting consulting and training sessions in business, government, social services and education sectors have resulted in repeated requests for his services.

Consulting Resource Group International, Inc. (1979), through its principals and alliance of associate companies provides speaking, training and consulting services to a wide range of clients. Clientele have been served in the business, government, education, health, human service and non-profit sectors. CRG seeks strategic alliance marketing partnerships with small-to-medium-sized consulting firms which have the development of individuals and leaders as their aim.

CRG provides the following services:

Organizational Culture Development
Transforming Leadership Programs
Customized Speaking Presentations
Custom Product and Program Design
Corporate Strategic Planning
Consultative Sales Skills Training

Management Team Development
Change Management Processes
Communication Skills Training
Career Planning and Pathing
Trainer Training
Beliefs, Purpose and Values
   Clarification

Publications from CRG

In addition to providing services CRG also publishes innovative software, learning tools and human resource development materials. These tools have been designed to be practical, self-directed learning systems, or they can be presented by qualified professionals. They are theoretically sophisticated, "user-friendly" and cost effective.

To receive detailed information on these publications, request the most recent edition of CRG's catalog.

Consulting Resource Group International, Inc.
FAX (604) 850-3003
(604) 852-0566